RUSSELL

RUSSELL

C.W. Kilmister
*Professor of Mathematics,
King's College, London*

ST. MARTIN'S PRESS   New York

Printed in Great Britain
First published in the United States of America in 1984

ISBN 0-312-69613-2

Library of Congress Cataloging in Publication Data

Kilmister, C. W. (Clive William)
    Russell

    Bibliography: p.
    Includes index.
    1. Russell, Bertrand, 1872–1970.   I. Title.
B1649.R94K43   1984   192   84-18050
ISBN 0-312-69613-2

To Peggy

Contents

Preface

Another book on Russell needs an apology or at least an explanation. We have come a long way since G. Bergmann could write in a review in 1957 ([1] p. 48) 'The silence that now virtually blankets Russell's name at Oxford, the failure or unwillingness to do justice to his epochal work, shock me profoundly.' This series allows me an opportunity which is, perhaps, more valuable in the case of Russell than any other philosopher, for the context of his thought is unusually helpful in understanding it. Most existing descriptions of Russell's philosophy have drawn attention to the numerous changes in his ideas as his thought developed. This has, it is true, given an agreeable, and truthful, impression of a man of immense integrity, willing to follow the dictates of his logic even when it went against all his previous convictions – just as, outside philosophy he was willing to follow the dictates of his conscience even when it went against all the social canons. But there is a corresponding disadvantage, for the sheer keeping track of the various changes makes a 'difficult philosopher' out of someone who, whatever the difficulty of the problems he tackled, strove always to be simple and direct in style.

My approach in this book is different. In the first place, I am writing primarily for the interested layman and the philosophy student who is not making a special study of Russell. For this reason I have tried to give a treatment of the relevant ideas of formal logic and mathematics *ab initio*. None the less, I hope that I also have something to say to the specialist in logic, who will omit the explanatory passages. I am thus aiming to provide in a small compass a perspective to a part of the early Russell which, as well as being available in his printed works, is shortly to be augmented by the publication of his collected papers.[2] I have concentrated on the essential unity of Russell's thought, a unity which I see as giving a key with which the reader may unlock for himself Russell's own lucid books. This unity is to be found in his earliest work, leading up to the co-operation with Whitehead on *Principia Mathematica*. This way of looking at Russell's development is therefore quite different from, but I hope a useful complement to, that of D. F. Pears, who sets out with the idea ([3]p. 11): 'Much of his time was spent on the foundations of logic and mathematics. That side of his work will only be described in a minimal way . . .' My idea, on the contrary, is that once this work is clearly set in its context, and understood, all the rest falls into place as applications to general philosophy of the ideas generated in the philosophy of mathematics – though, it must be admitted, to a general philosophy that has to be prepared to receive them.

The first version of this book benefited greatly from the criticism of my son, Andrew. The criticisms of that version by an American reader have been helpful in making what I believe to be a much better second version. But, of course, neither critic has any responsibility for the final form.

Notes

[1] E. D. Klemke (ed.) *Essays on Bertrand Russell*, University of Illinois, 1970.

[2] K. Blackwell (ed.), *The Collected Papers of Bertrand Russell*, Allen and Unwin, London. (28 volumes are to appear between 1983 and 2000. Volume 1, *Cambridge Essays 1888–99* appeared 1983. Edited versions of Russell's logical papers are promised in Vols. 3–6, combined with his philosophical writings for 1898–1913.)

[3] D. F. Pears, *Bertrand Russell & the British Tradition in Philosophy*, Collins, Fontana, London, 1967.

CHAPTER I

1872–1898 Towards truth and relations

Section 1: Family Background

1.1 There are several distinct answers to the question: why should one study Russell? Perhaps the one that leaps first to mind, because it is unique to him, is that he was a practical philosopher. He tried to discover by intellectual effort the truth about practical questions in the external world. When he felt that he had done this, whether it was over women's rights, moral judgments in the First World War, the question of nuclear arms after the Second World War, or equally the severe foundational problems in mathematics, he tried by his writings to convince others of the correct solutions. All of this can easily be read in his own words, for he was a master of clarity. But the question which repays further study is that of the source of his continuing quest for practical truth by intellectual effort: in other words, the basic ideas which one feels recur in different forms. A second reason for studying Russell and a more important one, is that his greatest work – which I would unhesitatingly argue to be his collaboration with Whitehead in *Principia Mathematica*[1] – established him at once as one of the outstanding philosophers of the twentieth century. Perhaps only G. E. Moore and Wittgenstein are comparable, though Ayer says, with justice ([2]pp. 35–36) that Russell has a slightly old-fashioned air, for he is in the main tradition of British Empiricism:

> . . . he makes the now unfashionable assumption that all our beliefs are in need of philosophical justification . . . We are to start with the ele-

1

ments which are the least susceptible to doubt and then see what can be
constructed out of them, or inferred from them.

Principia Mathematica is less easy to read than some of
Russell's books but it is of vital importance to the understanding of his outlook. And as he says himself in 1900,
about Leibniz ([3]p. vi):

> Where we are inquiring into the opinions of a truly eminent
> philosopher, it is probable that these opinions will form in the main, a
> closely connected system, and that by learning to understand them, we
> shall ourselves acquire knowledge of important philosophical truths.

Finally, he was an early friend and helper of Wittgenstein,
and by studying his reaction to Wittgenstein (misguided
though much of it undoubtedly was) we can, through
Russell's eyes, get another view of Wittgenstein's early
philosophy.

Accordingly I shall concentrate in this book on early Russell, because I am convinced that a good understanding of
that allows all the later books to speak for themselves. I aim,
in short, to provide a fairly complete context for the later
work. I see this context as falling into three parts, clearly
separated (and not of equal importance). The first part is the
intellectual and family background of the young Russell, a
background which formed the later man to a much greater
extent than with some thinkers. Included in this discussion
which forms Chapter I, are his early books, on the foundations of geometry, and on Leibniz.

The second part is the situation which had developed over
the difficulties in the foundations of mathematics. As I shall
argue, the importance of these difficulties for Russell
depends on aspects of the first part. The third more traditional part is the philosophical context in which Russell
found himself internationally (Frege and Peano) as well as in
twentieth century Cambridge (Whitehead, Moore and then
Wittgenstein) and the way it guided his conclusions from the
second part. The second part will be dealt with at some
length in Chapters 2 and 3 and the third, though it pervades
the book, recurs in a more concentrated form from Chapter
4 onwards.

There are two threads of argument that run through the whole of this book. The first one arises from my desire to show clearly the difference between Russell's plan to demonstrate the *truth* of mathematics, by basing it on logic, and other foundational exercises. These others, with the sole exception of L. E. J. Brouwer's intuitionism, concerned themselves with the consistency of mathematics. Russell came to see the need for truth in mathematics as part of his personal need for certain knowledge in any field. One could almost say that he selected mathematics for the establishment of this certain truth because it was the most hopeful area for it. This is the epistemological thread.

There is also an ontological thread which is closely connected. Russell chose to establish the real existence of mathematical entities by using the real existence of relations. These two threads arise from the very beginning. In this chapter I shall show how the work on the foundations of geometry was inspired by the first thread and contains the germ of the second in the way in which points are defined. Later the two threads join together in Russell's main contribution, which is that of finding a way in which Frege's programme for providing a secure foundation for mathematics can be rescued from the contradictions which threatened to submerge it. The way proposed is the Theory of Types, and although this in turn runs into trouble, it still constitutes the best hope for such a programme.

These preoccupations of Russell led him on to many problems in the philosophy of language, the theory of meaning and other regions of general philosophy. Many people come to a study of Russell after beginning from some such area, which is really an end-point rather than a beginning. Sometimes this leads to a misunderstanding of what Russell did, and of what he was trying to do. I hope that this book will serve to correct such misunderstandings as well as some others which are found more amongst mathematicians. Russell, and Frege before him, sought to place the ideas of mathematics in their proper context in the world of ideas. Most mathematicians have no such wish, and so accordingly fail to see what Russell was trying to do.

1.2 Bertrand A. W. Russell was born on May 18 1872 into the English Whig aristocracy, though it would be unfair so to pigeon-hole his parents for, as Robert Parker has said,[4] they 'vaguely resemble the heroic characters of a George Meredith novel.' They were friends of John Stuart Mill, who was Russell's godfather, but none of these facts is of particular importance in my argument, for Russell has told ([5] Chapter 1) how little he remembered of his parents. They both died by the time he was four and we may judge for ourselves how little influence came from Mill who died about the same time. He, it is true, published a study of logic[6] which ran to eight editions – the last a 'people's edition' – though it is fanciful to see in this success an analogy with Russell's later work. But the book is written from the standpoint that 'all Inference, consequently all proof, and all discoveries of truths not self-evident, consists of inductions, and the interpretation of inductions' ([6]p. 185), a position as far from any that Russell took up as any that may be imagined. The most that can be said is that Mill and Russell were both British Empiricists who based their positions on logic, but Russell was the only one with an adequate logical apparatus. Mill, like Hume before him, saw logic as providing the rationale of human thinking, rather than of correct inference. To this extent, Mill's logic was psychological.

Russell was brought up by his grandmother, the widow of Lord John Russell who was, from Russell's description a woman of intelligence, wide learning and strong character. 'She gave me a Bible with her favourite texts written on the fly-leaf. Among these was "Thou shalt not follow a multitude to do evil." Her emphasis on this text led me in later life to be not afraid of belonging to small minorities.'[7] There was also in the house his uncle Rollo,[8] who early aroused his scientific interests. At eleven Russell started Euclid, under his brother's guidance: 'This was one of the great events of my life, as dazzling as first love. I had not imagined there was anything so delicious in the world.'[5] But he was dismayed at the need to accept the axioms of geometry without good reason, and this doubt stayed with him, determining his work on the foundations of mathematics. At fifteen his doubts extended to the calculus. This was indeed in a fairly parlous state, although, as a mathematical technique, highly efficient. It was still necessary to give proofs in which hypothetical infinitesimal quantities were freely used. These were positive quantities behaving like ordinary number. The usefulness of infinitesimals was that, much of the time, they could be regarded as being zero, though not all the time. Their ontological status was quite mysterious. Unknown to the young Russell, the first substantially correct formulation was being given by Weierstrass in his lectures in Berlin at about this time. Meanwhile Russell read Clifford and Karl Pearson and the account went a long way to settling his doubts.[9]

1.3 His brother went to Oxford, but Russell's interest in mathematics made Cambridge preferable and he went up to Trinity with a minor scholarship in 1890, having already, in the examination, excited the interest of Whitehead. Russell was bracketed seventh in the mathematical tripos of 1893, having, he says, derived no benefit from lectures. His throw away comments on the Cambridge course are generous. More detail of what evidently caused him disappointment is provided in a passage by Grace Chisholm, a year senior to him, quoted by Grattan-Guiness, ([10]pp. 1,2):

> Mathematical science had reached the acme of perfection. Through the long future ages, no new ideas, no new methods, no new subjects were to appear. The edifice of mathematical science was complete, roof on and everything . . .
> At Cambridge the pursuit of pure learning was impossible. There was no mathematician – or more properly no mathematical thinker – in the place. The depressing character of the intellectual atmosphere was due to the examination. Everything pointed to examinations, everything was judged by examination standards, progress stopped at the Tripos.

As Grattan-Guiness says, this was unfair to Whitehead, of whom she knew little and who was important to Russell.

But it was with evident relief that Russell threw himself into the work for Part II of the Moral Sciences (that is, Philosophy) Tripos which he took in 1894. Also, as Ayer ([11]p. 5) adds, '. . . it was his desire to find some good reason to believe in the truths of mathematics that led him in his third year at Cambridge to make philosophy his principal study.' (Ayer here seems to confuse Russell's course with the more modern Cambridge system. Russell was in his fourth year, after the complete maths tripos.) Evidence for Ayer's view could be found in Russell's 1902 article on the Study of Mathematics in which he quotes Plato with approval in the *Laws*: ' "There is in mathematics," he says, "something which is *necessary* and cannot be set aside . . . and, if I mistake not, of divine necessity;" '. And Russell adds, with evident regret, 'but the mathematicians do not read Plato, while those who read him know no mathematics, and regard his opinion upon this question as merely a curious aberration.'

James Ward also became an influence on him at this time, and, a year or two later, gave him copies of Cantor's *Mannigfaltigkeitslehre* and Frege's *Begriffsschrift*. Russell notes[5] that they at last gave him what he wanted about the philosophy of mathematics, though he did not understand the Frege for years, until he had discovered for himself most of its contents.

Section 2: The Foundations of Geometry

1.4   The next year was taken up in preparing his fellowship dissertation, on the foundations of geometry: the fellowship was awarded in 1895 and a rewritten version of the dissertation was published in 1897.[12] Russell later thought the book much too Kantian, and certainly Kant's influence is very strong. As Ayer says ([11]p. 3): 'The strength of Russell's attachment to idealist doctrine is reflected in his Kantian *Essay on the Foundations of Geometry*.' Ayer also describes Kant as 'a philosopher for whom he (that is, Russell) later came to have little respect', but this seems to go further than I would about Russell's opinions. But from the point of view of establishing the early context for Russell's work the *Geometry* is very valuable. Much the same is to be said for the other early work surveyed in Section 3 of this chapter, the critical study of Leibniz.

It might seem rather natural for a mathematically-trained thinker – one, too, who was discontented with the Cambridge mathematical ethos – to turn as a philosopher to the foundations of some part of mathematics, such as geometry. But I wish to argue that there is considerably more in the choice than that. To do this I shall have first to look back, both at the general history of geometry, and at the history of ideas in the second half of the nineteenth century in England.

I shall begin in this section by sketching some of the relevant history of the development of early Greek geometry. In §1.5 I go on to consider the earliest example of a foundational difficulty in geometry, and the way round it, which is crystallised in the axiom-system of Euclid's *Elements*. Then in §1.6 and §1.7 I sketch the development of the non-Euclidean geometries, whose existence is made evident by a critical study of Euclid's axioms. Finally, in §1.8 and §1.9 I draw attention to the different attitudes to axiomatisation in the later part of the nineteenth century. This is particularly relevant, since Cambridge was the intellectual home of one attitude which is now quite unfashionable. All of this would automatically have been in the background to Russell's thought. I then resume the main discussion of Russell's *Essay* in §1.10, when I begin the task of analysing it in detail.

Geometrical ideas – facts – were known to both the Egyptians and Babylonians, but it is to the Greeks that we attribute the notion of proof. Given the Greek pre-eminence in geometry and the enquiring mind typified by Plato and Aristotle it comes as no surprise to find the first major difficulty in the foundations of mathematics arising in Greece. In fact two such difficulties arose and they were not entirely unconnected. The first one came with the School of Pythagoras, and so at the very beginning of Greek geometry. It is hard to be specific about dates. Pythagoras himself is said to have been born in 585 BC and to have been murdered (for political reasons) in 497 BC. But his School continued until 400 BC and its members tended (especially early on) to take no personal credit for any discoveries, which are accordingly attributed to Pythagoras.

Their most famous result is the theorem that the square on the hypotenuse of a right-angled triangle is the sum of the squares on the other two sides. Scholars differ about

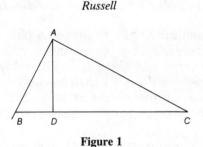

Figure 1

whether the Pythagoreans gave a formal proof of this: it seems as if a realisation of the importance of proof developed slowly, later in the life of the School. The legend has it that Pythagoras sacrificed an ox to celebrate its discovery: but discovery is not the same as proof. The Egyptians used special cases (especially the one in which the sides of the triangle are 3, 4 and $5 - 3^2 + 4^2 = 9 + 16 = 25 = 5^2$) in laying out boundaries of fields after the Nile had receded. But in some way or other Pythagoras or his students found the general result.

I must go into a little detail about how they could do this. Some historians believe that this discovery was by a similar triangle argument: if ABC is the triangle, right-angled at A, and AD is drawn perpendicular to BC, then triangle ABD is similar to triangle CBA, since both have angle B and a right angle. In the same way triangle ACD is similar to triangle BCA. If this were the Pythagoreans' method, then they would next have used the property of similar triangles that the corresponding sides are in a constant ratio, so that

$$\frac{AB}{BD} = \frac{CB}{BA}, \qquad \frac{AC}{CD} = \frac{BC}{CA},$$

and so (I shorten the proof, anachronistically, without obscuring any essential point),

$$AB^2 = BD.BC,$$
$$AC^2 = DC.BC,$$

and, adding, $AB^2 + AC^2 = (BD + DC)BC = BC^2$. But how did the Pythagoreans come to know the required property of similar triangles? By some such argument as this one: if ABC, DEF are two similar triangles, divide AB into m equal parts and *DE* into *n* equal parts, choosing *m*, *n* so that the parts are of the same size. Then draw parallels to *BC*, *EF* through the points of subdivision and so generate corresponding divisions of *AC*, *DF*. So it was essential for this that the subdivision was possible: that there were natural numbers m, n such that

$$\frac{AB}{m} = \frac{DE}{n},$$

or *AB/DE* = *m/n*. Nor was this likely to be a matter of any great worry to the early Pythagoreans. As Aristotle says, they considered numbers as the ultimate constituents of material objects. This is to be interpreted in a rather surprising physical sense, in which doctrine that 'all things are numbers' could be taken either literally or metaphorically, but in one form or another was basic to Pythagorean views even down to Aristotle's time. In the system of Ecphantus, for example, the world is analysed into atoms and the void and the atoms are identified as units.

So the natural numbers played for their discourse a somewhat similar role to that played by protons and electrons for a modern reader. But also, and inconsistently, they seem to have regarded numbers as not distinguished from the collections of geometrical dots by which they represented them. The discovery of the theorem was based, then, on a rather specific ontological presupposition, that ratios of natural numbers provided the measure of ratios of lengths.

1.5 This comfortable 'number-atomism' was rudely shattered by the discovery that, in the case of the isosceles right-angled triangle, the hypotenuse and one side were not lengths whose ratio could be expressed as *m/n*, with *m*, *n* natural numbers. The date of this discovery is not very precise. There is a tradition that the discovery was made in the fifth century BC by Hippasus of Metapontum, who was a member of the Pythagorean School. Since Plato probably heard of the result on his voyage to Cyrene (after 390 BC) it was already known then. Democritus (born about 460 BC) was involved in studies of irrationals, which suggests interest in the problem around 430 BC. These datings are therefore consistent. There is a rival view that the discovery was much earlier, and so accounts for Zeno's paradoxes as growing naturally out of the resultant crisis in mathematics. This will hardly hold water; for Zeno's argument, for example, that the sum

$$\tfrac{1}{2} + \tfrac{1}{4} + \tfrac{1}{8} + \tfrac{1}{16} \ldots$$

never reaches unity has nothing to do with incommensurability. Indeed, one might take the opposite view. Since Zeno, as well as Parmenides and Melissus, has nothing to say on incommensurable, the discovery could not then have become public.

According to Aristotle,[13] the proof was by *reductio ad absurdum* on these lines: suppose m, n are natural numbers with no common factor (for, if they had one, it could be cancelled in the ratio). Then the geometrical theorem implies $m^2 = n^2 + n^2 = 2n^2$, so that m^2 is an even number. Now the square of an odd number is odd,[14] so m must be even, say $m = 2r$, and so $2n^2 = 4r^2, n^2 = 2r^2$. Repeating the argument proves that n is even, and so m and n do have a common factor, namely 2, contrary to the initial hypothesis. So the ontological status of ratios of natural numbers and ratios of lengths were not the same.

There seem with hindsight to be two possible approaches to this, one changing the idea of number to fit geometry, one accepting that the fit was impossible, and changing geometry accordingly. The first is the modern view, which really developed properly amongst the late nineteenth century mathematicians. They constructed a system of *real numbers* that would be adequate to deal with any ratios of lengths that seemed likely to arise. But of course this really gives up the Pythagorean argument altogether, for the 'numbers' now are complex artefacts, quite unsuitable to serve as atoms. Moreover, though it is a convenient way for practising mathematicians, it confuses the whole issue, since it confronts and evades the ontological discrepancy between natural numbers and lengths by inventing new kinds of numbers whose own existence is in question.

The Greeks wisely followed the second alternative. They preserved the two ontologies and learnt how to deal with geometrical magnitudes without invoking numbers. This was codified by Euclid in the *Elements* (Books V–X) circa 300 BC. (It is conjectured that the relevant work is by Eudoxus.) But though the techniques changed, it remained the Greek view that geometry was about the real world, whether directly in dealing with the Platonic Forms which were the true reality or indirectly as dealing with abstractions which represented the real objects in some conventional sense.

There is more of importance in the *Elements* than the theory of proportion, however. Partly as the result of the growing Greek emphasis on proof, partly perhaps as a reaction to the shock of inconsistency, Euclid is careful to list at the beginning five postulates and five 'common notions' or axioms. The axioms are of a general mathematical character ('things that are equal to the same thing are also equal to each other' for example). They have to be taken in conjunction with definitions: 'A point is that which has not part. A curve is breadthless length. The extremities of a curve are points. A straight line is a curve which lies evenly with the points on itself . . .'

Following Aristotle the distinction here is between the general axioms which must be accepted as true, since it is the real world to which they are supposed to apply, and the postulates which are special to one subject (here, geometry) and which need not be self-evident, but which are to be accepted provisionally and justified by the agreement of their consequences with the real world. The five postulates are:

1. To draw a straight line from any point to any point.
2. To extend a straight line continuously in a straight line.
3. To describe a circle with any centre and radius.

(These first three elliptically worded postulates are to be interpreted as meaning that the constructions are possible.)

4. That all right angles are equal to one another.
5. That, if a straight line falling on two straight lines makes the interior angles on the same side less than two right angles, the two straight lines, if produced indefinitely, meet on that side on which are the angles less than the two right angles.

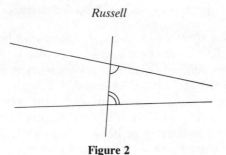

Figure 2

The use made of this by Euclid is to show that, through a point outside a line a unique parallel can be drawn to the line, a result which is exactly equivalent to the original postulate.

1.6   It is at once evident – and it was so from an early stage – that the fifth postulate is of a very different status from the other four. Thus Proclus (410–485 AD) says 'This ought to be struck from the postulates altogether. For it is a theorem . . .' He tried to establish that it was a theorem, but needed two further assumptions: that the distance between two intersecting lines increases without limit as we go away from the intersection, and that the distance between parallel lines does not increase without limit. But these further assumptions are no more self-evident than the fifth postulate. Other classical attempts to prove the postulate suffered the same fate of not gaining aceptance, by needing further assumptions, sometimes explicit like Proclus, more often, concealed.

It will be easier to see just what is at stake by considering an intuitive argument involving the idea of motion. Let l be any line, P a point outside it and m any line through P. As m rotates about P in the direction of the arrow, the point of intersection, Q, moves to the right along l. Then as the rotation continues, Q moves off to the right and reappears on the left, still moving to the right. Is there an intermediate position of the line m for which no point Q exists? And is this position unique? It is clear now, but was not to the Greeks, that these questions cannot be answered on the basis of Euclid's other postulates alone. For example, the geometry

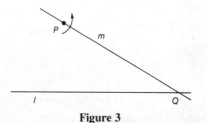

Figure 3

of the surface of a sphere can be set up. Great circles, that is, the curves, like the parallels of longitude on the surface of the earth, which are produced by intersecting the surface with a plane through the centre, are what play the part of lines. In such a geometry it is easy to verify that all Euclid's postulates, with *line* read as *great circle*, continue to hold, with two exceptions. Two great circles intersect in two diametrically opposite points, instead of in one point, and they always do intersect. The first of these exceptions can be removed by considering, not the surface of the sphere, but a new surface defined by considering any pair of diametrically opposite points to be a single point. This process is called *identifying* opposite points by mathematicians. We are then left with a surface on which the geometry satisfies all Euclid's postulates except the parallel postulate.

If then it were possible to show, in plane geometry, that parallels must exist, it would also be possible on this new surface, by using an identical argument, and this would be a contradiction.[15] The argument which I have given, which uses the geometry of a surface derived from a sphere, illustrates the necessity for a definite assumption that a parallel always exists in the plane. It does not give any information about whether the parallel, if it exists, is unique, or whether two different lines in opposite directions could both be parallel. It is possible to construct a surface whose geometry illustrates this possibility in the same way that the sphere illustrates the possibility of having no parallels. The technical details are difficult, and so I omit it. In that case it is possible for the right-hand point *Q* to disappear before the left-hand appears, in a situation like this:

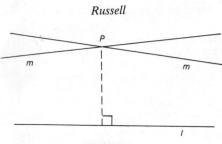

Figure 4

(the angle between the limiting lines, *m*, drawn in each direction evidently being dependent on the distance of *P* from the line), so that the parallel would not be unique.

Very many unsuccessful attempts were made to deduce the fifth postulate from the others. It is unnecessary to list all the history but early in the eighteenth century events took a significantly different turn in the hands of the Jesuit Gerolamo Saccheri. Saccheri's achievement was to see that a more powerful approach was the indirect one. Since it turned out to be possible to make a precise negation of the fifth postulate, one could assume this negation and hope, by this means, to be led to a contradiction. Then, by *reductio ad absurdum*, the postulate would be established.

Saccheri failed, though he believed that he had succeeded. But it is only a small step from his position to one in which the geometries resulting from the assumption of negations of the fifth postulate are considered as possible geometries in their own right rather than fields for development of contradictions. The beginnings of this are seen in Gauss, as early as 1795 and it was only a quarter of a century later that Lobatchevsky and Bolyai formulated quite explicitly non-Euclidean geometries, or as Russell calls them, *metageometries*. There remains a question of interpretation, however; and that is the important aspect for my argument.

In 1781 Kant could say[16] 'geometry is a science which determines the properties of space synthetically, and yet *a priori*', and in the following paragraph:

Space is nothing else than the form of all phenomena of the external sense . . . under which alone external intuition is possible. Now, because the receptivity or capacity of the subject to be affected by objects necessarily antecedes all intuitions of these objects, it is easily understood how the form of all phenomena can be given in the mind previous to all actual perceptions, therefore *a priori*, and how it, as a pure intuition, in which all objects must be determined, can contain principles of the relations of these objects prior to all experience.

So for Kant the certainty of applicability of Euclidean geometry in the world lay in the way in which our minds compel us to organise our experience. And this view persisted with those mathematicians who did not ignore him completely. They saw the non-Euclidean geometries only as consistent fictions. The development up to about 1830, which I have now sketched, is described by Russell as the first of three stages in the history of metageometry.

1.7   The second stage begins in the 1860s with Riemann and Helmholtz. Riemann was at Göttingen under Gauss and it was Gauss who suggested the foundations of geometry as a title for his *Habilitationsvortrag*.[17] Riemann set out to consider the presuppositions in the idea we have of space as a 'multiply extended magnitude' derived from a general idea of quantity. These presuppositions must come before we can set up particular axioms for physical space, for the magnitudes turn out to have the possibility of various metrical relations, only one of which will be that appropriate to the actual world. Part of his aim was to make clear that Euclid's axioms were empirical, not self-evident. And he did this in terms of an approach to geometry that regarded position, direction and distance as basic concepts. The importance of distance is fundamental. Riemann considered local properties exclusively; so (to take a very simple special case) the difference between the ordinary Euclidean geometry of the plane and the geometry on the surface of a sphere is removed from the realm of the surface (plane or sphere) on which it is drawn. Both geometrics could be drawn on a plane (or on many other surfaces); but of course to compensate for the distortion of the spherical figures a different definition of distance has to be employed in that case and so 'straight lines' will be different.

   The way is open for a thorough-going conventionalism, in which distance is an arbitrary device for organising experience and it is only an empirical matter to determine which

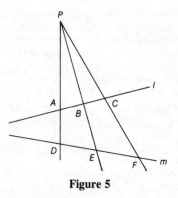

Figure 5

such chosen distance agrees with Euclid's choice. But though this would have been a possible consequence of Riemann's lecture, it was not taken up for half a century and instead the third stage began.

To explain this stage I have to go back in history a little to describe parallel developments that had been going on under the name of 'projective geometry'. This, originally considered as a part of Euclidean geometry, deals with the properties of figures that are unchanged under projection from a point. Evidently, taking *P* as the point of projection, lengths are not unchanged, for *AB* projects into *DE*. Indeed, not only lengths, but ratios of lengths are changed; *AB/BC* is different from *DE/EF* unless the two lines *l*, *m* are parallel. But Desargues (1591–1661) discovered the surprising fact

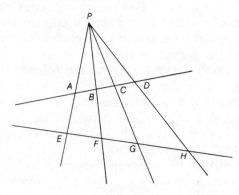

Figure 6

that, if four points are taken, then $(AB/BC)/(AD/DC)$, the ratio of two ratios (called the *cross-ratio*) is unchanged under projection. A partial result, but proved with quite a different spirit was in the *Mathematical Collection* of Pappus (end of third century AD). But, what is more important for my argument, eighteenth century projective geometry was able to establish results about points and lines involving no measurement at all. The simplest example is perhaps the following. A, B, C are three points on a fixed line l. Draw any line 1 through A, any line, 2, through B, cutting 1 in E, any line, 3, through A, cutting 2 in F. Draw CE to cut 3 in G. Draw BG to cut 1 in H. Draw HF to cut l in D. Then *whatever* lines 1, 2, 3 are drawn, the same point D is reached. That the results of projective geometry included some without any mention of distance at all suggests a logically prior system to Euclid's (and a completely different approach from Riemann's).

Two developments took place during the next two centuries. In the first place, the cross-ratio has been defined above in terms of distances, that is, quantities associated with two points. A way was found to avoid this, by beginning with some quantity associated with four points. This was achieved by von Staudt in 1847, though imperfectly. (A defect in von Staudt's presentation was corrected by Felix Klein in 1873.)

I must digress slightly here to give a little more of the flavour of projective geometry, because it seems at first a

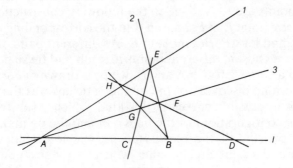

Figure 7

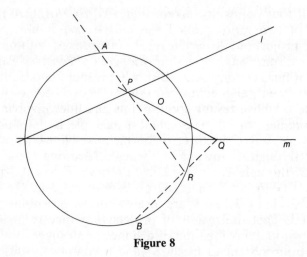

Figure 8

rather arid discipline. It begins with only non-metrical postulates such as

Two points are joined by a unique line.
Two lines meet in a unique point.

None the less, from these and similar postulates a fruitful
geometry can be built up on the basis of two lines. To give
one example, consider (*Fig.* 8) two lines *l*, *m* and a 1:1
correspondence between the points of *l* and those of *m*. This
correspondence is set up by a point *O* according to the rule:
a point *P* on *l* corresponds to a point *Q* on *m* if *PO* cuts *m* in
Q. Now choose any two points *A, B* not on either line. These
two points are to be fixed in the following construction. Join
A to *any* point *P* of *l* and join *B* to the corresponding point *Q*
of *m*, and let *AP, BQ* meet in *R*. As different pairs of points
P, Q are chosen, different points *R* result and these points all
lie on a curve through *A* and *B*, which is drawn in *Fig.* 8. The
astonishing discovery of the mathematicians was that all the
different possible curves of this kind, which result from different configurations of the lines *l, m* and the points *O, A, B*,
were exactly all the *conic sections*, the intersections of a
plane and a right circular cone, which had been studied from
a purely metrical point of view by the Greeks. There was

then no doubt that projective geometry was logically prior to Euclidean. But what was still unclear was the extent to which this logically prior geometry overlapped Euclidean.

The second development answers this question. The work of Laguerre in 1853 (on angles) and Cayley in 1859 (on distances) showed how to define Euclidean quantities in terms of cross-ratios of points of a line together with the fixed points of intersection of the line with a fixed curve (called the *absolute*) whose Euclidean distance away would therefore turn out to be infinite. And Klein showed, some ten years later, that a slight modification of Cayley's construction gave, instead, the non-Euclidean distance. So from this point of view neither Euclidean nor non-Euclidean geometry was in a logically privileged position. This new approach to the foundations of geometry was the third stage; it took over from Riemann's approach because it seemed evidently more powerful in its classificatory ability. Cayley went so far as to say 'Projective geometry is all geometry and reciprocally'.[18]

1.8   But it is clear that none of these developments necessarily affects our attitudes to the relationship between geometry and the physical world. If we regard Euclidean geometry as based on our experience of the physical world, projective geometry is simply based on a more refined analysis of experience. If our taste is more for an abstract system, inspired by but only loosely connected with the actual world, the same can be said of either Euclidean or projective geometries. However, the attitudes which began to develop after 1860 differed considerably on the two sides of the Channel, and because Russell came to this problem from an English, indeed from a specifically Cambridge, position I must now say a little more about the history of ideas in Cambridge in the nineteenth century.

1.9   A tradition arose there in the earlier part of the century which tended to see the philosophy of science (including mathematics) as fundamental to general metaphysics. An important exemplar of this is Whewell, the Master of Trinity and an idealist. He saw mankind as having true knowledge inherent in his mind in its capacity to recognise fundamental ideas, such as space. But Herschel, though an empiricist, reached a surprisingly similar conclusion from the stand-point that human minds have a structure that leads them, in interaction with experience, to reach true knowledge about it. And, for both, geometry was the clearest example of this, just as it had been the example of the synthetic *a priori* for Kant. So, of course, geometry was not seen as a formal system: it was the ordered development of the idea of space. This development had to be differentiated carefully from the development of an empirical science from a series of exper-iments and this was achieved through the notion of con-ceivability. In physics one could conceive of situations con-trary to theoretical prediction, but not in geometry.

The related situation in algebra throws some light on this. Joan Richards discusses 'why the English, despite their attention to the elements of abstract algebra, never pro-duced a system comparable to modern algebra.'[19] By the latter phrase she means the logically consistent development of an abstract axiom system: but such an approach has its own tensions. How is one to understand the connection bet-ween the results generated by the internally-guided development of the axiom-system and the subject-matter that the axioms are supposed to describe? As Richards says:

> One approach to this conflict is to emphasise mathematics as logical development and to ignore its relation to a particular subject-matter. Nineteenth century English mathematicians took another approach which was more in line with their interpretation of the nature of the human inttellectual endeavour.'

By 1840 Whewell is urging, against Dugald Stewart's opin-ion 'that the certainty of mathematical reasoning arises from its depending upon definitions', that 'the definitions which we employ in mathematics are not arbitrary or hypothetical, but necessary definitions.' And de Morgan (in London) writes to Whewell in 1853 of something 'which was at first incredible, then certainly true, then axiomatic . . .', which emphasises the way in which axiomatic had come to mean, in England, something evidently true but which cannot be seen to be provable from simpler facts.

Riemann's position was as different as it could be. Euclidean geometry was no longer necessary or universal; it was determined empirically. As Riemann says (in Clifford's translation) 'These matters of fact are – like all matters of fact – not necessary, but only of empirical certainty; they are hypotheses.'[20] Evidently the threat to mid-nineteenth century Cambridge was not only mathematical, but philosophical and even theological as well. The consistency of systems of non-Euclidean geometry was not an issue, but their application to space was. The initial reaction, of trying to continue to maintain the unique necessity of Euclidean geometry, was evidently doomed. But projective geometry containing both the Euclidean and non-Euclidean systems seemed to have more of a claim to absoluteness. Then the empirical area was narrowed down to the choice of definition of measurement. And the metaphysical doubts raised by Riemann's approach could be ignored: so that Cayley could tell the British Association in 1883 that the fundamental notion that needed clarifying in modern geometry was the one involved in his metrical definition in projective geometry, and could encourage metaphysicians to consider this problem. It was this that Russell turned to fourteen years later.

1.10 I have now sketched in the background to Russell's fellowship dissertation[12] and I turn to the book itself. As well as the published form, some of it was published in *Mind* and he gave lectures on most of it at Johns Hopkins and Bryn Mawr.[21] In the Introduction he expresses his main obligation to the writings of Felix Klein, and, amongst direct contacts, especially A. N. Whitehead. But the dedication is to McTaggart 'to whose discourse and friendship is owing the existence of this book' – McTaggart, 'the last English Hegelian', beautifully encapsulated by J. B. Priestley[22] who attended his metaphysics lectures: 'He was one of the great originals of Cambridge. Some odd disability gave him a crab-like walk, and one met him coming sideways round buildings, like a sheriff about to shoot it out with the bad man in a Western'.

Reading Russell's book is like listening to *Lohengrin* with the knowledge that the *Ring* is still to be composed (to use a

musical analogy). Already there is some of the clarity and
directness which has become Cambridge style but (largely)
begins with Russell and G. E. Moore, yet it is mixed and, to
be just, integrated with very Hegelian passages.

The four arguments about geometry that Russell seeks to
put forward in this essay are:

(i) that the philosopher must draw a sharp distinction between projective and metrical geometry and (ii) that the
'usual' (though not at that time clearly formulated) axioms
of projective geometry are deducible (by a transcendental
argument) from these principles:

    I We can distinguish different parts of space, but all
       parts are qualitatively similar, and are distinguished
       only by the immediate fact that they lie outside one
       another,
   II Space is continuous and infinitely divisible; the result
       of infinite division, the zero of extension, is called a
       point.
  III A finite-dimensionality axiom (the number of dimen-
       sions need not be three) so that the sequence of
       statements 'n points determine a flat of $(n - 1)$
       dimensions', for $n = 2, 3, 4$' . . ., stops somewhere.

By a transcendental argument is meant, somewhat on Kantian lines, a metaphysical discussion rather than one in the
formal system of geometry that is being formulated.

(iii) Kant believed that Euclidean geometry was synthetic
and *a priori*. The existence of non-Euclidean geometries is
seen by Russell as fatal to Kant's view. The reason for Kant's
confusion is that the sharp distinction between metrical and
non-metrical geometries has not been attended to. (iv) In
both cases there is not free creation of the human spirit, as
with 'pure mathematics' but something 'given' *in one way or
another* in the external world. The implication is that a modified Kantian position, with projective geometry playing the
role that Euclidean geometry played for Kant, will be possible.

I shall return to the general features of Russell's argument
after I have considered the details of the book. The Introduction is an exceedingly Kantian passage, though with a

difference. Russell explains that he is going to establish a logical relation between the subjective and the *a priori*. It is historically interesting to notice the growing influence of practical psychology. For:

> If Psychology declares that some things, which I have declared *a priori* are not subjective, then, failing an error in detail in my proofs, the connection of the *a priori* and subjective so far as these things are concerned, must be given up.

This introduction is followed by a history of the development of other geometries than Euclidean, both the non-Euclidean as explained in 1.6 above and the projective as in §1.7. These are shown as closely connected, of course, following Klein's *Über die sogenannte Nicht Euklidischen Geometry*[23] because there the projective is a more general framework into which the others may be fitted. Russell then poses the Kantian question: 'What must space be in order that we may be able to regard it as a magnitude at all?' This, in preference to Riemann's actual problem, 'What sort of magnitude is space?'

The advantage of this modified form of the question is that the way is then clear for Russell's principal position, which is stated here (and returned to in stating the axioms):

> We shall find them to be deducible, as before, from the homogeneity of space, or, more generally still, from the possibility of experiencing externality. They will therefore appear as *a priori*, as essential to the existence of any geometry and to the experience of an external world as such.

As an aside in this history (in a footnote) attention is drawn to the distinction between local and global properties:

> Nevertheless, the Geometries of different surfaces of equal curvature are liable to important differences. For example, the cylinder is a surface of zero curvature but since its lines of curvature in one direction are finite, its geometry coincides with that of the plane only for lengths smaller than the circumference of its generating circle . . . the identity extends only to the properties of figures not exceeding a certain size.

This distinction would have been congenial to Hegel, but, leaving Hegelians on one side, it was unusual and regrettably still is. Philosophers still argue in many fields that what is unchanged in small variations remains so in large.

1.11   In order to explain Russell's next distinction between his position and Riemann's, I must sketch in a little more background. Riemann chooses to describe his manifolds in terms of coordinates, that is, sets of numbers, the idea being based on Descartes' original notion of specifying the points of a plane by means of their distances x, y from two fixed perpendicular lines in the plane. Russell seems to emphasise this original construction of coordinates by arguing that, in the general Riemannian case:

> . . . it is logically impossible to set up a precise coordinate-system, in which the coordinates represent spatial magnitudes, without the axiom of Free Mobility and this axiom as we have just seen, holds on surfaces only when the measure of curvature is constant.

The 'axiom of free mobility' refers to Helmholtz's investigation of the possibility of the motion of rigid bodies. The surface of a sphere (for example) shares with the plane the property that a rigid triangle on it may be moved into any other position on it. But if the sphere were squashed into a more oval form, this would obviously not be fulfilled, for it is no longer the case that any point on the surface is as good as any other point. Russell is concerned here to establish the logical impossibility of coordinates in detail, not merely to rest his case on the historical fact that the coordinates of a point P were originally numbers defined metrically, that is, in terms of measurements of distances of P from a fixed point O along two mutually perpendicular directions. The proof of Russell's contention comes much later in the essay (§176). It rests on the idea that a projective coordinate-system can only *label* points, but a metrical one does much more 'defining each point quantitively'. By this is meant, I think, that notions of nearness of points are also prescribed by the coordinates. Such a definition is held to involve the straight line.

Whether or not there is an element of correctness in Russell's argument, he seems to go too far at the next stage in the discussion (p. 21) where he argues against a quantity being defined by Riemann as a measure of curvature of the surface. This is the kind of quantity we would need in order to say that as a result of this quantity having different values at different points of the squashed sphere we could not freely move a rigid triangle on it. His argument is that Riemann's definition is applicable only if free mobility is possible, and so the curvature has to be constant. He does not, of course, argue that variable curvature is impossible for a surface, but that it cannot be properly defined without reference to the third dimension of the space in which the surface is embedded. The point he is making is, of course, that correspondingly in three-dimensional geometry only constant curvatures are logically possible (since there no extra dimension is available). But this is a very curious argument, for its premiss is strikingly at variance with a famous result of Gauss, which even he called *Theorema Egregium* – a result out of the herd. Gauss carefully distinguished in surface geometry between properties that the surface had by virtue of its embedding in the three-dimensional space, and those which were independent of the embedding (so, we could imagine, would be discoverable, or measurable, by two-dimensional creatures living on the surface). And the Riemann measure of curvature is shown by Gauss's result to be a property of this second kind.

Russell's wrong emphasis is repeated when he comes to Beltrami's work in 1868 where straightest-possible curves, 'geodesics', are taken as lines on an arbitrary surface:

> If we were to define distance on the plane as that function of the co-ordinates which gives the corresponding distance on the surface, we should obtain what Klein calls "a plane with a hyperbolic system of measurement" in which Cayley's theory of distance would hold. It is evident, however, that the ordinary notion of distance has been presupposed in setting up the coordinate-system, so that we do not really get alternative geometries on one and the same plane.

There are two curious aspects of this statement. In the first place it seems to miss Cayley's point altogether for Cayley, whatever his other views, certainly showed that, by means of projective geometry and a fixed curve (or surface in three dimensions) one can define a distance. In what way have we used distance already? According to Russell in using straight lines: but it is logically possible to begin with those as undefined elements, which would remove all connection with distance. Secondly, the phrase seems to suggest a lack of appreciation of the value of the Cayley theory as providing an automatic consistency proof of the non-Euclidean systems relative to the Euclidean. For if a non-Euclidean system were to lead to a logical contradiction, this contradiction would show up equally in the Euclidean case, since this differed only in the choice of Absolute (see §1.7).

It should not be seen as too surprising that Russell did not see the advantage of a consistency proof approach here. This stems directly from his concern for truth rather than merely consistency, and so was exactly in the English and Cambridge tradition that I described in §1.9. The same considerations will arise later over the axioms for logic, and there the argument gets an extra twist, since the carrying out of any such consistency argument must be done by logic. This leads Russell to hold that it is absurd to use it in discussing the foundations of logic. The emphasis on truth was in line with Frege, whom Russell had not at this stage understood, who, in correspondence with Hilbert;[24] opposes Hilbert's 'if the arbitrarily given axioms do not contradict one another with all their consequences, then they are true and the things defined by the axioms exist.' with 'I call axioms propositions that are true but are not proved because our knowledge of them flows from a source very different from the logical source, a source which might be called intuition'.

To be fair to Russell about consistency proofs, he does say on p. 36 '. . . the correlation with Euclidean space is regarded as valuable . . . because this correlation proves, when truly interpreted, that the other spaces are self-subsistent.' But, on the next page, taking Cayley's definition of distance in terms of the Absolute (§1.7), he adds 'our straight line remains, all the while, an ordinary Euclidean straight line . . . though it may serve to illustrate other Geometries than Euclid's, it can only be dealt with correctly by Euclid' a fairly clear statement of his 'absolute truth' view.

1.12   Not that Russell is unaware of the important von Staudt-Felix Klein construction which defines cross-ratios in a manner quite independent of distance. The necessity for this was recognised by Cayley and Russell promises later (and performs) a transcription of the Klein construction:

> But 'projective coordinates – so our argument will contend – though perfectly adequate for all projective properties, and entirely free from any metrical presupposition, are inadequate to express metrical properties, just because they have no metrical presupposition.

This is a strange criticism. It is, of course, literally correct, and the Cayley-Klein theory would not deny it. Rather would it contend that it is the projective framework, together with a fixed Absolute, that provides the metrical properties. None the less there is a further point implied here which troubled Cayley, and which Russell takes up later. It lies in the peculiar nature of the Absolute for the Euclidean case. This gives rise to a further ontological question, almost as serious as the one that had faced the Pythagoreans. For although the geometers spoke and probably thought a lot of the time as if the Absolute in the plane were a closed oval curve which (from the definition) must lie at infinity, yet this picture is appropriate only in the case of two parallels to a line *l* from a point *P* outside it. Then the two parallels are the lines joining *P* to the intersections of *l* with the absolute. This curve has, in mathematical jargon, to be imaginary in the Euclidean case or, even more, in the Cayley representation of the geometry of the surface of a sphere.

The idea of imaginary points in geometry was about a century old. The algebraic idea is clear enough if we consider

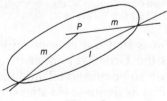

Figure 9

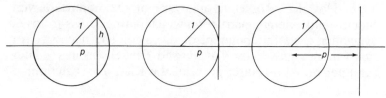

Figure 10

a line of perpendicular distance p from a circle of unit radius. In the first case we can ask for the (equal) height and depth of the points of intersection and, by Pythagoras' theorem, these are $1 - p^2$. If, now, $p = 1$ these become equal, and zero, in the second figure. What then of the case when p is greater than 1? The algebraic approach relies on giving a clear algebraic meaning to -1, usually called i; a quantity which is evidently not an ordinary real number. If this were accepted as done, then $\sqrt{1 - p^2} = i\sqrt{p^2 - 1}$ would be simply a multiple of i.

Geometers came, particularly in the nineteenth century, to speak freely of the line meeting the circle in two imaginery points. They chose to ignore the ontological change involved in suddenly endowing the plane with an infinite number of new points. Cayley and Klein initially felt no more compunction than had the Pythagoreans in using numbers as the measures of lengths in the fact that, for Euclidean geometry, the Absolute had to be chosen as a very bizarre, half imaginary curve.

This is the context of Cayley's challenge in his Presidential Address to the British Association (1883) on *Geometrical use and meaning of imaginary quantities*:

> Say even the conclusion were that the notion belongs to mere technical mathematics, . . . still it seems to me that (as a subject of philosophical discussion), the notion ought not to be thus ignored; it should at least be shown that there is a right to ignore it.

Russell's argument is that the correct rejoinder here is on the same lines as the Greek rejoinder in the Pythagorean case: the ontology is to be preserved, and the apparent extra objects to be treated as fictions. He starts by conceding, for convenience, that the use of imaginaries in algebra may be justified; he then argues: not in geometry. More precisely, let a point have imaginary *Cartesian* coordinates. Russell argues that the trouble has arisen simply by turning the truism 'If three coordinates determine a point at all they do so uniquely' into 'To every set of coordinates a point must correspond' for which there is 'no vestige of evidence'. That is the negative side of his argument. The positive is to say 'all space is covered by the range of these three variable quantities'. So any convenience arising from the intermediate use of imaginaries is merely that coming from any auxiliary devices:

> The metaphysician, who should invent anything so preposterous as the circular points (that is, some particular imaginary points widely used in this context), would be hooted from the field. But the mathematician may steal the horse with impunity.

Another way of expressing the need for the Absolute follows:

> Quantities, as used in projective Geometry, do not stand for spatial magnitudes, but are convenient symbols for purely qualitative spatial relations. But Distance in the ordinary sense is, in short, that quantitative relation between two points on a line, by which their difference from other points can be defined. The projective definition, however, being unable to distinguish a collection of less than four points from any other on the same line, makes distance depend on two other points besides those whose relation it defines.

The historical section then concludes with a discussion, which is important for assessing Russell's later views, about the relative weight to be given to mathematics and to philosophy in the foundations of geometry:

> The same gradual development out of philosophy might, I believe, be traced in the infancy of most branches of mathematics; when philosophical motives cease to operate, this is, in general, a sign that the stage of uncertainty as to premisses is past, so that the future belongs entirely to mathematical technique. When this stable stage has been attained it is time for Philosophy to borrow of Science, accepting its final premisses as those imposed by a real necessity of fact or logic.

1.13   The rest of the *Essay* may be considered rather more shortly. A critical second chapter quotes a succinct statement of Russell's (Kantian) position:

> Metageometry has destroyed the legitimacy of the argument from Geometry to space: we can no longer affirm, on purely geometrical grounds, the apodeictic certainty of Euclid.

But, Russell holds,

> The actual space we know . . . is admittedly Euclidean, and is proved, without any reference to Geometry, to be *a priori*; *hence* Euclid has apodeictic certainty, and non-Euclid stands condemned.

Russell's views on axioms again comes out clearly in his discussion of Riemann:

> In formulating the axioms of metrical Geometry, our question should be: What axioms, that is, what adjectives of space, must be presupposed, in order that quantitative comparison of the parts of space may be possible at all?

Are there any limitations on the Euclidean nature of space? Riemann showed what must seem, in the light of modern physics, to be astonishing foresight in saying that empirical length measurements may be impossible for very *small* distances, where rigid body and light ray lose their validity, but Russell says 'From this conclusion I must entirely dissent'. He looks for deviation only at very great distances. Here again, Russell's point of view arises from his emphasis on free mobility.

Geometrical axioms are, then, the result of the analysis of the concept of space, and not at all in keeping with Erdmann's assertion

> that the question as to the nature of geometrical axioms is completely analogous to the corresponding question of the foundations of pure mathematics. This is, I think, a radical error: for the function of the axioms seems to be, to establish that qualitative basis on which, as we saw, all quantitative comparison must rest. But in pure mathematics, this qualitative basis is irrelevant, for we deal there with pure quantity . . . . . . Geometry, as Grassmann insists, ought not to be classed with pure mathematics, for it deals with a matter which is given to the intellect, not created by it.

Amongst the French Poincaré is mentioned as a conventionalist. He is quoted as maintaining:

> that the question, whether Euclid or Metageometry should be accepted, is one of convenience and convention, not of truth; axioms are definitions in disguise, and the choice between definitions is arbitrary.

But though Poincaré is nowadays often cited as the arch-conventionalist, this is a view which does less than justice to the subtle character of Poincaré's philosophical thought. And, despite his earlier statement, Russell rightly refers this particular version of conventionalism back to Lotze.

1.14   Chapter 3, after a curious (and mistaken) argument that projective properties are common to all spaces, goes on to consider axioms, and it is of the greatest importance to my argument to note that Russell proposes to do this in terms of *relations*. This is the real importance of his *Geometry*. The thought here is that the basic notions of geometry are relations such as 'between', 'to the left of', 'collinear'. These notions are built into sentences by supplying terms P, Q, R:

> P lies between Q and R,
> Q is to the left of P,
> P, Q. R are collinear.

The terms P, Q, R, which the formal system requires to be introduced, are defined as points. It will be interesting to note this later as the germ of the idea which plays a vital role in Russell's 1905 paper *On Denoting*. I shall then argue this to be the key to his subsequent thought.

Russell concedes in a foot-note that the introduction of points in this way may be (he says, is) introducing metrical ideas, because without them there is nothing to give a point precedence over a straight line. Then 'the straight line is defined as the relation between two points and the plane as the relation between three'. He follows this with a philosophical proof that four collinear points A, B, C, D are needed and are sufficient to determine an invariant number, $(ABCD)$, since the relation defined by two points *is* the line. Given two points, there is only the one relation that a third should be collinear with them. With four, von Staudt's quadrilateral construction enables more to be found.

The details of this construction are unimportant for my present argument, but it may perhaps help to see how it is carried out. In the figure A, B, C, D are the four points. One then derives new points in turn, which I denote by numbers $1, 2, 3, \ldots$, in this way:

$$AC, BD \text{ meet in } 1.$$

Write this as

$$1 = (AC,BD)$$
$$2 = (AB,CD)$$
$$3 = (DA,CB)$$
$$4 = (12,BC)$$
$$5 = (41,AD)$$
$$\cdots\cdots\cdots\cdots$$

and since the first three stages of construction may be repeated again starting with a new set of four points, say *1,2,B,C*, and so on, a 'net' of points if formed, covering 'the whole plane'.

There follows a puzzling and rather confused passage about Grassman. Russell praises Grassmann, not only for his suggestion that geometry is really a branch of applied mathematics, but also for his contention that it should be possible to construct a branch of pure mathematics, 'which

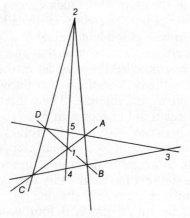

Figure 11

should yet deal, as Geometry does, with extension – extension as conceived however, not as empirically perceived in sensation or intuition.'

It is not at all clear how Russell sees this as being consistent with his own neo-Kantian position, in which Kant's mistaken emphasis on Euclidean geometry is replaced by one on projective geometry. Moreover he does not face the question of whether there are to be two complete sets of geometrical facts, one for perception, one for conception. But Russell follows this distinction of Grassmann in trying to construct an '*a priori* and purely conceptual form of externality'.

An important development now shows Russell groping his way towards a calculus of relations:

> From what has been said of homogeneity and relativity, follows one of the strangest properties of a form of externality. This property is, that the relation of externality between any two things is infinitely divisible, and may be regarded, consequently, as made up of an infinite number of the would-be elements of our form, or again as the sum of two elements of externality. To speak of dividing or adding relations may well sound absurd . . .

Finally, the argument is summarised, with an appropriately Hegelian gloss:

> With this our deduction of projective Geometry from the *a priori* conceptual properties of a form of externality is completed. That such a form, when regarded as an independent thing, is self-contradictory, has been abundantly evident throughout the discussion. But the science of the form has been founded on the opposite way of regarding it: we have held it throughout to be a mere complex of relations, and have deduced its properties exclusively from this view of it . . . projective Geometry is wholly *a priori*; . . . it deals with an object whose properties are logically deduced from its definition, not empirically discovered from data; . . . its definition, again, is founded on the possibility of experiencing diversity in relation, or multiplicity in unity; and . . . our whole science, therefore, is logically implied in, and deducible from, the possibility of such experience.

Finally, in this chapter is a quotation from James' *Psychology*:

> *The line is the relation* . . . The relation of position between the top and bottom points of a vertical line is that line, and nothing else.

In summarising the conclusions of Russell's essay, I wish to distinguish two that look backwards and two, more important, that look forwards. The first two are (i) the evidently strong influences of Kant and German idealism, which pervade the whole structure of the book and (ii) the distinction, directly derived from the British nineteenth century tradition, between geometry as dealing with subject matter given to the intellect and pure mathematics dealing with matter created by the intellect. The second two, to which I shall return later are (iii) that mathematics is about the actual world, so that its axioms need to be true and consistency proofs are of little value and (iv) the importance of relations.

It is useful at this stage to contrast Russell's position on (ii) and (iii) with that which he took up in 1914 in his Herbert Spencer lecture in Oxford ([25]p. 109). Here he considers 'the problem of space as presented in Kant's *Transcendental Aesthetic*,' which Russell sees as primarily the epistemological one, of how we come to *a priori* knowledge of geometry. He sees the confusion in this problem as caused by the conjunction of three related problems. First there is the logical problem, produced by the existence of non-Euclidean geometry. Space, as an object of *study*, is no longer unique. The answer to the problem is exact and perfect. The geometer considers geometry as the study of a certain class of relations determing a class of spaces. Since he is working abstractly and logically, he is no longer committed to one particular space. Instead, that consideration is pushed on to the next problem, the physical one: to find in the physical world a realisation of a particular one of the geometer's spaces. The difficulty of this problem, according to Russell, lies in the requirement of accommodating the roughness and vagueness of the physical world with the clarity and exactness of mathematics. The crux of this physical problem is the idea of a point, which Russell sees solved by Whitehead's definition of a point as a class of objects (that is, those intervals of the line which would normally be said to contain the point). The most obscure and difficult problem, the epistemological one remains. True, as Russell says, the problem has been clarified. The knowledge of pure geometry may be *a priori* but it is purely logical; that of geometry in the physical world is synthetic but not *a priori*. So as far as geometry is concerned, Kant is answered: *a priori* synthetic knowledge is not possible.

Section 3: Leibniz

1.15   The other work of Russell's youth, the *Critical Study of the Philosophy of Leibniz*[3] is at first sight a very different sort of book from the *Geometry*, leaning much more in the direction of philosophy and away from mathematics. But there are underlying connections; in both there is the development and use of *relations*. As Russell says ([5]p. 134)

> I was at this time (that is, 1898) beginning to emerge from the bath of German idealism in which I had been plunged by McTaggart and Stout. I was very much assisted in this process by Moore . . . I was glad to think that relations are real.

The precise sense of this last sentence needs considerable clarification, for it has to be seen in the context of Russell's idea of the nature of a proposition. A general idea of it can be obtained by means of an example. Consider 'P is to the left of Q'. The position that Russell was now accepting was the one which, as well as allowing reality to P and Q (as points on a line, for example) would also allow that 'to the left of' was a part of the philosophical furniture of the world. It did not see this relation as merely subsisting by virtue of the relative positions of P and Q. Russell had already in the *Geometry* come near to this in beginning with relations and defining points as their terms.

There is no doubting the immense effect of this change of heart for Russell's development. Morris Weitz goes, perhaps, further than I would, claiming he does, that ([26]p. 59):

> Russell's motivation in his rejection of Absolute Idealism was his desire to establish the irreducibility of relations and a Platonic theory of propositions, which could render them independent of mental activity. He needed these doctrines in order to satisfy his desire to establish the foundations of mathematics.

None the less, this question of the nature of propositions and relations provides a vital clue to Russell's thinking at this time, and I devote the rest of this section to it and return to his Leibniz in §1.16. English-speaking philosophers have, until recently, commonly distinguished propositions from sentences. They have been clear that sentences were linguistic entities; but exactly what propositions were was less obvious. The distinction, moreover, begins to look a little suspicious when it is translated into German, in which *Satz* serves very well for both. To understand this doctrine, I shall have to begin by contrasting it with the more modern view that sentences are the unambiguous constituents with which we have to deal. An honourable exception to the Anglo-Saxon trend is Quine[27] who puts the argument for the modern view as:

> If there were propositions, they would induce a certain relation of synonymy or equivalence between sentences themselves . . . Now my objection is going to be that the appropriate equivalence relation makes no objective sense at the level of sentences.

The point that Quine is making here is that the introduction of the idea of a proposition is seen as desirable because, for instance, the situation in which an Englishman says 'It is raining' is seen as the same as when a German says 'es regnet'. For anyone who sees this as the *raison d'être* for propositions it is natural to see the proposition as the class of all equivalent sentences. Yet what sort of equivalence can this be? The only obvious candidate is logical equivalence, but this leads to the absurd view that all the theorems of a mathematical theory are but one proposition, since they are all logically equivalent to the axioms. Quine believes, then, that the concept of proposition plays no useful part, in the sense that any correct argument which appears to use it can be expressed in terms of sentences instead. Under the influence of this view many modern textbooks of formal logic speak of the sentential calculus instead of the propositional calculus. But although Russell sometimes speaks as if he held the same view,[28] this is confusing, for it is not held in the straightforward way in which Quine expresses it, and not held at all in most of Russell's writings. That concludes my brief remarks on the modern view, and I now look at the older views that formed Russell's opinions.

An earlier English view that bears some resemblance to Quine's is that of Mill,[6] who says:

> A proposition is a portion of discourse in which a predicate is affirmed or denied of a substance. A predicate and a subject are all that is necessarily required to make up a proposition; but as we cannot conclude from merely seeing two names put together, that they are a predicate and a subject, that is, that one of them is intended to be affirmed or denied of the other, it is necessary that there should be some mode or form of indicating . . .

This passage of Mill is very modern in the way in which it speaks of the proposition as a purely linguistic object, but it is much more a piece of its time in seeing all such propositions as capable of analysis into subject-predicate form. This contention, which stems from Aristotle, plays an important part in Leibniz's system in the derivation of the concept of substance, as we shall see below (§1.16). But Mill, although treating the proposition as merely linguistic, goes on to draw a distinction between *judgement* (or *belief*) and what is believed. And about this he says:

> Philosophers, however, from Descartes downwards, and especially from the era of Leibniz and Locke, have by no means observed this distinction; and would have treated with great disrespect any attempt to analyse the import of Propositions, unless founded on an analysis of the act of Judgement. A proposition, they would have said, is but the expression in words of a Judgement. The thing expressed, not the verbal expression, is the important matter.

I have drawn attention to this passage because this shift of the meaning of such words as proposition and judgment needs to be borne in mind in reading the nineteenth century writers who, directly or indirectly, influenced Russell. For Keynes,[29] for example, in 1884, a proposition is a judgment, and yet a name is employed as a constituent of a proposition, and for Joseph[30] (in 1916 but in a book that had been delayed by the War) a judgment, which is said to be equivalent to a proposition, makes an assertion. By 1921 Johnson[31] is claiming that propositions are not judgments, because propositions are true or false. Neither can they be the verbal expression of judgments, since appropriate terms for verbal expressions are, for example, obscure, or ungrammatical, not true or false. So for Johnson there are the three notions of sentence, proposition and judgment.

The question of being true or false is the second *raison d'être* for inventing propositions. On any straightforward correspondence theory of truth 'it is raining' is a true sentence only if spoken at a time when it is raining. The proposition is thought of as an all-embracing entity for which the truth or falsehood can be stated as part of the properties of the entity, internally, as it were, not of its correspondence with the world. This is very much Russell's view and I think we can point fairly definitely to its direct origin in his thought in Bradley.[32] We know that Russell was reading Bradley as early as 1894 and again in 1897.[33] It seems clear that Bradley's

> ... consider the nature of judgement, for which we find thought in its completed form. In judgement an idea is predicated of a reality. Now, in the first place what is predicated is not a mental image ... When I say 'this horse is a Mammal' it is surely absurd to suppose that I am harnessing my mental state to the beast between the shafts.

and again

> Just as in 'this horse is a Mammal' the predicate was not a fact, so most assuredly the subject is an actual existence ... No one ever *means* to assert about anything but reality.

form sources for Russell's view of a proposition as a complex whose component parts are the actual objects about which assertions are made. (See §3.3 in Chapter 3 for more on this in relation to Frege.) The reader is warned that this close agreement with Bradley over propositions does not imply any similar agreement over relations. In terms of Russell's view of propositions, strange as it seems to modern readers, the question of the reality of relations becomes more transparent. The sentence that I considered before, 'P is to the left of Q' corresponds to a certain proposition which certainly has the points as component parts. The view that Russell was putting forward on his emergence from German idealism, then, is that the proposition has a third component part, the relation.

1.16 The *Geometry* had sought to tie up some loose ends by answering rather detailed questions provoked by the curious tradition in the philosophy of science and mathematics that I have described in §1.9. Russell felt able to tackle these questions by his use of relations. None the less, the *Geometry* is the end-product of a misguided line of argument, but the *Leibniz* came about purely by a happy chance. McTaggart was to be away for a term and Trinity asked Russell to give a substitute for McTaggart's usual course on Leibniz. The book resulted, shortly afterwards.

It is no more a modern view of Leibniz than the *Foundations of Geometry* is of geometry, but for a more specific reason. Whereas the *Geometry* came at the end of a long and basically misguided tradition, the *Leibniz* came just before Leibniz's unpublished papers began to appear. He was a rather curious case – Russell always thought him 'not admirable' as a human being –

> His best thought was not such as would win him popularity, and he left his records of it unpublished in his desk. What he published was designed to win the approbation of princes and princesses ([34]p. 570)

These 'best thoughts' began to be published only in 1901–3, by Louis Couturat.[35] Russell expresses himself pleased ([5]p. 134) to find the unpublished papers confirmed his own interpretation of Leibniz. He had gained his insight into what lay behind Leibniz's *Monadology* by studying the *Discourse de Metaphysique* and the letters to Arnauld.[36] From these Russell argues that the whole Leibniz system is based, rather like geometry, on a few simple premises. The fact that his system does genuinely follow from them is the evidence of his excellence. But what is the status of these premises? Russell contends that, if it were not for the conclusions drawn from them, 'many, if not most' philosophers would have accepted Leibniz's premises. But, nevertheless, since, according to Russell, it will be found that they actually lead to contradictions, the conclusion is, inevitably, that one or more is false.

Russell sees Leibniz as the principal example of a philosopher who uses logic as a basis for metaphysics. I shall argue that this feature of Leibniz, whether or not it is important in understanding him, is of the greatest importance for a study of Russell. He achieved this understanding of Leibniz in a flash of insight. This profoundly influenced Russell's attitude to logic as a way of understanding the world, and mathematics in particular. He says himself ([26]p. 12) that he realised in 1898 that 'mathematics could be *quite* true and not merely a stage in dialectic. Something of this point of view appeared in my *Philosophy of Leibniz*.' This emphasis on the *truth* of mathematics was to stay with him.

The crucial use of logic for Leibniz is in the derivation of the concept of *substance*, which is as important for him as it was for Descartes and Spinoza. I shall explain this more fully. Leibniz sees every proposition as ultimately reducible to one attributing a predicate to a subject, with one single exception, that is, when the predicate is that of existence. Setting that case aside, the subject is simply *defined* as the bundle of its predicates and so, as a result, it is always a necessary fact that a predicate holds for a subject.

Thus 'the cricket ball is red', 'the cricket ball is round', 'the cricket ball has a seam', 'the cricket ball weighs so many ounces' . . . are a bundle of subject-predicate propositions, and the notion of 'cricket ball' could be *defined* as 'a red, round, seamed object weighing . . . etc.' As a result of this analysis, Leibniz postulates the *identity of indiscernibles*, that is, the principle that if A, B have all their predicates in common, then they are identical, A = B. Of course, this can be correct only if, amongst the predicates, the position of the objects A, B at a certain time is specified. This turns out to be a difficulty for Leibniz since he needs his theory of identity in order to set up his theory of space, and Russell later draws attention to this difficulty. None the less, he is strongly influenced both by the idea of the subject as its bundle of predicates, and by the identity of indiscernibles and this agrees with the enthusiasm Russell was later to show for Wittgenstein's *Tractatus*, where the analysis into atomic facts is very much in the same spirit.

It follows from the analysis of the subject as a bundle of its predicates that every true judgment about a subject is necessary, except for judgments of existence; Leibniz considers these to be contingent. Leibniz tends to identify analytic with necessary and synthetic with contingent. Indeed, that all true propositions are analytic is Leibniz's form of the principle of sufficient reason. Thus Leibniz asserts that there is an external world, on the basis of sense-perception; but 'it is logic that says what such a world must be like, if it exists.' In what follows I shall, like Russell, use the words 'analytic' and 'synthetic' although Leibniz uses 'necessary' and 'contingent' since Leibniz's usage begs some questions.

Since true judgments have this secure logical status, they form an adequate basis for distinctions about substance. Some words, such as the names of colours, can function as both subjects and as predicates, in different sentences. Others, such as proper names, can never occur as predicates. This second class of words is held by Leibniz to denote substances. But, of course, this definition of substance relies on the subject being the bundle of its predicates. This raises in turn the problem of personal identity, of persistence through time. Leibniz is forced, in order to save ordinary discourse, to conceive some attributes which exist in different parts of time as attributes of the same subject. The sameness cannot be provided by internal experience, but must be given *a priori*. So a substance cannot be identical with the sum of its states; the aggregate of states requires a substance around which to collect.

The logical structure of this difficulty is strongly reminiscient of the corresponding one over classes to which Russell was later to turn his attention. A class is, in one sense, simply the aggregate of its members; but to say that is to do less than justice to the possibility of considering the class as a single entity.

1.16   The previous paragraph gives a bare but adequate outline of Leibniz's metaphysics, for it is only with Russell's views on the metaphysics that I will really be concerned. In connection with the metaphysics, Russell raises seven fundamental questions, with which I shall deal in turn ([3]p. 11). It is in the answering of these questions that Russell's philosophical development becomes clear. It will transpire that the first four questions are answered in a straightforward way, and the description of Russell's answers will occupy §1.16. I turn to the remaining three in §1.17.

(1) Are all propositions reducible to the subject-predicate form?

With regard to question (1), Russell's position is that the question must be answered in the negative. Amongst other contradictions to the subject-predicate analysis, propositions which express or employ mathematical ideas, such as assertions of numbers (for example, 'There are three men') are not of this form. However, Leibniz's contention is that all propositions can be reduced to subject-predicate form, not that they are already of that form. As Parkinson points out,[37] Leibniz had already tried to answer Russell's criticism by rendering 'there are three men' as 'a is m, b is m, c is m and a, b, c are disparate'. I would argue against this account that the final clause 'a, b, c are disparate' is not of a subject-predicate form and so Leibniz has failed to save his analysis. However, Russell chooses instead to argue that 'the number only results from the singleness of the proposition, and would be absent if three propositions . . . were juxtaposed'.

A more serious criticism of Leibniz's position, however, is Russell's second example, of relations between subjects, such as relations of position, of relative magnitude, and so on. In order to maintain the subject-predicate theory, Leibniz is, says Russell, 'forced to the Kantian theory that relations, though veritable, are the work of the mind'. Thus Leibniz writes

> No accidents can be at the same time in two or more subjects . . . Paternity in David is one thing and sonship in Solomon is another thing. But the common relation is something merely mental, whose foundation is the modification of the several terms.'

But clearly Leibniz's analysis cannot cope with 'A is taller than B.' Russell was probably more familiar (from his undergraduate training) with the analogous view of F. H. Bradley.[32] Bradley put forward Leibniz's position as his own first position about the non-reality of relations but he later retreated to a second view in which the relation between A and B is seen as a property of the pair (A, B).

As W. J. Winslade says ([38]p. 89), 'Contrary to Bradley, Russell argued that the reality of relations established that pluralism rather than monism is a correct theory about the structure of the world.' Russell objected to Bradley's second view that it could cope only with symmetric relations (for which A has a certain relation to B if and only if B has it to A). At first sight this seems a blunder on Russell's part; if the unordered pair or class (A, B) is intended, Russell's objection would hold, but not if (A, B) is differentiated from (B, A). My real objection to Bradley's second view is that, by changing the universe of discourse, he has merely made a notational change. It is not that there is anything technically wrong in Bradley's analysis. This would be very unlikely since it has become a standard method of procedure amongst mathematicians, without any disaster ensuing. But there is probably a deeper reason for Russell's objections to Bradley. Russell considered propositions to have constituents which were the actual objects and this has two consequences: firstly, it is very natural to interpret the bracket as simply grouping the two components A and B and it is unnatural to see it as doing so in a definite order. It is true that the technically-minded could reply to this by defining an ordered pair [A, B] by some such rule as

$$[A, B] = ((A, B), B),$$

but this hardly meets the objection. But secondly, and more seriously, the proposition ARB has three constituents and each of these should appear.

In short, then, Leibniz's position is too much in conflict with Russell's new-found freedom to regard relations as real. Moreover, Russell contends, a complete discussion would show 'that judgments of subject and predicate are themselves relational'.([3]p. 15)

(2) Are there any analytic propositions, and if so, are these fundamental and alone necessary?

(3) What is the true principle of Leibniz's distinction between necessary and contingent propositions?

In turning to these questions, Russell explains how Leibniz regarded as analytic all the truths of Logic, Arithmetic and

Geometry, but all existential statements as contingent. Leibniz's view is determined by his realisation that the laws of motion – indeed, all causal laws – are synthetic, and therefore contingent. As I explained, (§1.15), the analytic nature of all *a priori* truths derives from the subject-predicate reduction, in which the subject is defined as a bundle of predicates. So definition is possible only for complex ideas (and is then simply the analysis of these ideas into their simple constituents.) A vicious circle is avoided only by admitting some undefinable simple ideas, and this situation was fully understood by Leibniz. But difficulty arises as soon as these simple constituents are found to be incompatible; for the round square is not a subject, but its non-existence ought, for Leibniz, to be a contingent matter. So the answer to both questions (2) and (3) is that, within Leibniz's system, there is no true principle to distinguish necessary and contingent propositions. What is most interesting here is that Russell confronts the problem of empty reference. The essence of his theory of descriptions of 1905, with which I shall deal in Chapter 3, is to solve this problem completely by a correct analysis of 'denoting phrases', which are statements attributing a predicate to an object. Most of this, then, derives from Russell's study of Leibniz, though not all. The remaining ingredient, as will be clear in Chapter 3, is the idea of quantifying a variable.

1.17

(4) What is the meaning of the principle of sufficient reason, and in what sense do contingent propositions depend upon it?

(5) What is the relation of this principle to the Law of Contradiction?

I need not dwell on Russell's discussion of the fourth question, for it is essentially contained in the analysis of the subject as a bundle of predicates.

I turn now to Russell's argument on the remaining three questions, which turn out to be rather deeper. Question (5) refers to the Law of Contradiction, but in fact Russell mainly concentrates on causation. This is not such a *non sequitur* as it may seem. Russell, following Leibniz, uses the Law of Contradiction as a shorthand way of referring to logical argument in general. This arises as follows: we can distinguish primitive from derived analytical propositions. The primitive are those stating that some predicate holds for a subject when it is a matter of direct intuition that it does so. The derived ones are then derived by testing whether or not they give rise to a contradiction.

Now Leibniz, accepting that statements of existence were contingent inferred also that causal connections between existent things at different times were contingent. Hence, his argument proceeded, the actual world is not necessary and, in particular, causes do not produce their effects necessarily. So he saw, as clearly as Hume and Kant were to do, that causal connections must be synthetic. But whereas Hume deduced from this that causation is not a real connection and Kant that synthetic propositions may none the less be necessary, Leibniz preferred to allow that a connection may be invariable without being necessary. The relationship between questions (4) and (5) is therefore rather complicated; all individual causal laws are contingent but the law of Causality – which states, in effect, that there must be causal laws – is analytic and necessary.

(6) Does the activity of substance unduly presuppose time?

(7) Is there any validity in Leibniz's deduction of the Identity of Indiscernibles?

The remaining two questions involve the ideas of time, the continuum and indiscernibles. I prefer to treat these together; they are the deepest of the questions that Russell raises against Leibniz. I begin with the Identity of Indiscernibles, which Leibniz derives from his definition of substance in terms of a subject defined by its bundle of predicates. Russell says that Leibniz must be in error in confounding a substance with the sum of its predicates 'since there would be no ground for opposing subjects to predicates, if subjects were nothing but collections of predicates.' This must be a straightforward error on Russell's part in not seeing at this stage in his development, the important difference between an entity (here, a predicate) and a class, that is a collection of the same entities. By 1900 Russell had this quite clear (see §2.6). Evidently, Leibniz's difficulty is not caused by a direct logical error as Russell assumes, but by the question of the continuing existence of entities over time. The answer to this question comes by considering complex entities, such as people; a law of continuity is required in order to associate a person with himself a year ago.[39] In fact, says Russell, one can include both the identity of indiscernibles and the law of continuity in the one law that substances form a series in which every position is filled once (continuity) and only once (identity of indiscernibles).

There are, however, two further difficulties; one is whether the bundle of predicates includes space and time locations. For Leibniz, Russell points out, relies on his readers admitting that two things could not be at the same spatio-temporal point, although, since he also used the Identity of Indiscernibles to prove the non-reality of space and time, he could not logically so rely. Leibniz's treatment of time is ambiguous, and the ambiguity has something in common with McTaggart's[40] paradoxes about time.

McTaggart distinguished two time-series, the A-series of past, present, future and the B-series of earlier and later. B-series propositions are eternally true or false, but A-series ones have more than one truth-value; one wants to say that this feature of A-series statements does not conflict with the Principle of Contradiction 'because the different truth-values are at different times' but this way out is not available if the object of the discussion is to explain time. On the other hand reduction of all tense statements to B-series ones (supposing it to be logically possible) fails to capture the essential feature of time, its transitory character.

Since a substance is a subject persisting in time, time is real for Leibniz; yet he tries, by means of the doctrine that the states of a substance are eternally its predicates, to eliminate dependence on time. In the McTaggart language, the time in which subjects persist is an A-series; but Leibniz tries to reduce it to a B-series. As Russell says ([3]p. 52–53)

Thus time is necessarily presupposed in Leibniz's treatment of substance. That is is denied in the conclusion, is not a triumph, but a contradiction. A precisely similar result will appear as regards space, when we come to the grounds for the plurality of substances.

The second difficulty concerns the precise meaning of continuity here and 'the labyrinth of the continuum'. Here Russell observed Leibniz face to face with the same difficulties that had been urged against the Greek mathematicians by Zeno, but which we have only secondhand through Aristotle and others. I will say something more about Zeno's arguments in Chapter 2 in connection with Cantor, but for the present I will just draw attention to two notions. One is the notion of the difference between the potential infinite and the actual infinite. I can say that the natural numbers are potentially infinite, meaning by this simply that any collection of them can always be augmented by more; to say that the collection of all natural numbers is actually infinite, however, involves first, giving a clear sense to that collection and, second, giving a clear sense to the number of members of the collection. Mathematicians abstained from using the actual infinite for the long period – more than two thousand years – from Zeno to Cantor.

The second, related, notion is Aristotle's distinction between the infinite by addition and the infinite by division. I can thing of a line as 'made up' of the points into which it could be divided by sufficiently small subdivision. But if I try to think of it as made up by adding points, I am in a difficulty. The following argument is a modern one, not Aristotle's, but I use it because it is clearer. Suppose that the line PQ, of unit length, is made up by adding points, say A_1, A_2, A_3, . . ., (of course, an infinite sum is involved here – though it could be a potential infinity.) Imagine a way of covering the line PQ with small segments in this way: take A_1 as the centre of a segment of length $\frac{1}{4}$. Then take A_2 as the centre of a segment of length $\frac{1}{8}$. Then A_3 as centre of one of length $\frac{1}{16}$, and so on. Every point is now at the centre of some segment. The segments may overlap and some may protrude outside the confines of the line PQ. None the less, even with those disabilities, the covering of the line has been carried out very efficiently because the total length of the segments is

$\frac{1}{4} + \frac{1}{8} + \frac{1}{16} + \ldots = \frac{1}{2}$, although the whole line is of length 1. That is, my original assumption that the whole line can be made up of points by addition has led to a contradiction and so must be rejected. Aristotle's distinction has therefore to be accepted.

Russell picks out two salient features from Leibniz's discussions:

> Every one who has ever heard of Leibniz knows that he believed in the actual infinite . . .
> But this is by no means the whole truth on the matter. To begin with, Leibniz denied infinite *number*, and supported his denial by very solid arguments. In the second place, he was familiar with the distinction, afterwards used by Hegel, between the true and false infinite . . . an inifinite aggregate is not truly a whole, and therefore not truly infinite.

This Hegelian gloss conceals Russell's preoccupation already with the problem of the class as a single object.

1.18   There is one other feature of Leibniz to which Russell attached the greatest importance; this was his notion of a *Characteristica Universalis*:

> He seems to have thought that the symbolic method, in which formal rules obviate the necessity of thinking, could produce everywhere the same fruitful results as it has produced in the sciences of number and quantity . . .
> What he desired was evidently akin to the modern science of Symbolic Logic, which is definitely a branch of Mathematics, and was developed by Boole under the impression that he was dealing with the *Laws of Thought*.

Russell later came to see this as a most important contribution of Leibniz, the lack of effectiveness of which was determined only by the inadequate logical machinery available to him, so that *Principia Mathematica* was in the same tradition.

But at this stage Russell took logic as able to deal only with problems which had been reduced to a suitable form. The real philosophical problems came in the reduction to that form, not after it, so he concludes:

> An idea which can be defined, or a proposition which can be proved, is

of only subordinate philosophical interest. The emphasis should be laid on the indefinable and indemonstrable, and here no method is available save intuition. The Universal Characteristic, therefore, though in Mathematics it was an idea of the highest importance, showed, in philosophy, a radical misconception, encouraged by the syllogism, and based upon the belief in the analytic nature of necessary truths.

What then, finally, is to be learnt from Russell's *Leibniz*? The most important ingredient of Russell's later thought is, I would argue, the idea of basing a metaphysics on logic. The *Characteristica Universalis* must be seen as less important at this stage in Russell's development, as his own statement makes clear; but none the less the idea must surely have gone into his consciousness and, as I said about the idea of empty reference, lain fallow for a time. The evidence for this is that, firstly, he later wrote with great approval of Leibniz's idea and, secondly, this same idea bore fruit in the basic idea of *Principia Mathematica*. But scarcely less important than the notion of logic as fundamental in metaphysics is the growing realisation, compared with the position in the *Geometry*, of the importance of relations and the logic of relations.

Synopsis

In this chapter I have explored Russell's two early books, on geometry and Leibniz respectively. The direct effect of these on his later work is limited, but their indirect influence on his development is considerable.

The *Geometry* seeks to repair the damage that the discovery of non-Euclidean geometry did to Kant's view of the certainty of Euclidean geometry, a certainty derived from its *a priori* synthetic character. Russell's argument is that the non-Euclidean geometries of constant curvature, which are the only ones he accepts, are derivable as special cases of projective geometry and he undertakes to establish a position for that which Kant would perhaps have recognised as synthetic *a priori*. At any rate, Russell's view of geometry, which he was later to extend to the whole of mathematics, was that *the* foundational problem was to establish its truth.

Questions of consistency were subsidiary. It is the valid existence of mathematical entities in the real world which is at issue. Russell's argument for geometry rests on his ontological commitment to relations as real; points can then acquire a real status as the terms of relations.

The *Leibniz* is a first exercise in deriving a logically complete system from a small number of assumptions. The reality of relations again plays a part, particularly in assessing Leibniz's definition of the subject as the bundle of its predicates, a position to which Russell was to return in the 1927 second edition of *Principia Mathematica* (see Chapter 4). What is more disappointing about Russell's assessment of Leibniz, however, is the lack of importance that he attached to the use of logic as a *Characteristica Universalis*, although something very like that position was to be his own within ten years in *Principia Mathematica*.

Notes

Section 1

1 A. N. Whitehead and B. Russell, *Principia Mathematica*, Cambridge, 1913. A second edition 1927.
2 A. J. Ayer, *Russell*, Collins/Fontana, London, 1972.
3 B. Russell, *A critical exposition of the philosophy of Leibniz*, Cambridge, 1900.
4 Robert Allerton Parker, *A family of Friends*, Museum Press, London, 1960.
5 B. Russell, *The Autobiography of Bertrand Russell*, Volume 1, Allen & Unwin, London, 1967.
6 J. S. Mill, *A system of logic*, Longmans, London, Eighth (Peoples') Edition, 1884.
7 In [5]p. 33
     She was one of the principal people concerned in the foundation of Girton College, and her portrait hangs in Girton Hall, but her policies were abandoned at her death. 'So long as I live,' she used to say, 'there shall be no chapel at Girton.' The present chapel began to be built the day she died.
8 As a meterorologist he investigated the effects of the Krakatoa earthquake of 1883, which caused unusual sunsets over much of the world, including England.
9 B. Russell, *My Philosophical Development*, Allen & Unwin, London, 1959 or in K. Pearson, *The Common Sense of the Exact Sciences*,

newly edited with an introduction by J. R. Newman, preface by B. Russell, Knopf 1946, Dover reprint 1955.

[10] I. Grattan-Guiness, *Dear Russell – Dear Jourdain*, Duckworth, London, 1977.

[11] A. J. Ayer, *Russell and Moore: the analytical heritage*, Macmillan, London, 1971.

[12] B. Russell, *An Essay on the Foundations of Geometry* Cambridge, 1897.

[13] Aristole, *Metaphysics* I.v.

[14] For an odd number differs by one from an even one, so has the form *2k + 1* and the square of this is *4k² + 4k + 1 = 4k(k + 1) + 1*, so differs by one from an even number, and so is odd.

[15] The angle-sum of a triangle on the surface of a sphere depends on the area and is greater than two right-angles. Curiously, Aristotle (*Posterior Analytics* I.v) says that, from the assumption that the angle-sum of a triangle exceeds two right angles, one can deduce that parallels meet. But apart from that oblique reference, the Greeks made no use of the spherical geometry to settle the problem of the fifth postulate.

[16] I. Kant, *Critique of Pure Reason*, Part I Section I §3.

[17] That is, the lecture which he would give to the faculty to qualify to be a *Privatdozent*; and so to have the privilege of teaching, though without any salary. The lecture was delivered in 1854 and published fourteen years later under the title *Über die Hypothesen, welche der Geometrie zu Grunder liegen*.

[18] A. Cayley, Sixth Memoir on Quantics, *Phil. Trans. 149*, 61–91, 1859 (in *Collected Mathematical Papers II*, 561–606).

[19] J. L. Richards, *Historia Mathematica 7*, 345, 1980.

[20] B. Riemann *Über die Hypothesen, welche der Geometrie zu Grunde liegen*, in *Abh. d. König. Ges. der Wiss. zu Göttingen 13*, 132–152, 1867, translated W. K. Clifford, On the hypotheses which lie at the bases of geometry *Nature 8*, 14–17 and 36–37 (1873).

[21] In the Autumn of 1896 on a three month trip to meet the relations of his wife Alys; [5](p. 132).

[22] J. B. Priestley, *Man and Time*, Aldus Books, London, 1964.

[23] F. Klein, *Über die sogenannte Nicht-Euklidische Geometrie, Math. Ann. 4*, 573–625, 1871 and *6*, 112–145, 1873.

[24] G. Gabriel & others (ed.), *Philosophical and Mathematical Correspondence of G. Frege*, (trans. H. Kaal), Blackwell, Oxford, 1980.

[25] B. Russell, *Mysticism and Logic*, Pelican, London, 1953.

[26] P. Schilpp (ed.), *The Philosophy of Bertrand Russell*, Library of Living Philosophers, Cambridge, 1946.

[27] W. V. Quine, *Philosophy of Logic*, 1970.

[28] A very full analysis of Russell's different usages is to be found in the paper, 'Propositions and Sentences' by Alan R. White in G. W. Roberts (ed), *Bertrand Russell Memorial Volume*, G. Allen & Unwin, (Muirhead Library of Philosophy) London, 1979.

[29] J. N. Keynes, *Formal Logic*, 1884.

[30] H. N. B. Joseph, *An Introduction to Logic*, Oxford, 1916.

[31] W. E. Johnson, *Logic*, Cambridge, 1921–4.

[32] F. H. Bradley, *Appearance and Reality*, Oxford, 1893.

[33] K. Blackwell (ed.), *The Collected Papers of Bertrand Russell*, Allen & Unwin, London. Vol. 1 *Cambridge Essays 1888–99* Appendix 2.

[34] B. Russell, *History of Western Philosophy*, Allen & Unwin, London, 1946, second edition 1961.

[35] Louis Couturat, a professor in Caen, who in 1897 began an acquaintance with Russell by writing to congratulate him on the *Foundations of Geometry* and remained a friend until Couturat's death in 1914.

[36] The letters to Arnauld had been published in the nineteenth century but Russell was the first to attach importance to them.

[37] G. H. R. Parkinson, *Logic and Reality in Leibniz's Metaphysics*, Oxford, 1965.

[38] E. D. Klemke (ed.), *Essays on Bertrand Russell*, University of Illinois, 1970.

[39] The problem put so movingly by von Hoffmannstahl, in Act I of *Der Rosenkavalier*:- *Marschallin* (looking into her hand-mirror): *Wie kann das wirklich sein, dass ich die kleine Resi war, und dass ich auch einmal die alte Frau sein werd*.

[40] J. M. E. McTaggart, *The nature of existence*, (Vol. 2) Cambridge, 1927.

CHAPTER II

1896–1902 The problems arise

Section 1: The Logic of Relations

2.1   In this chapter I shall deal with the years of Russell's life from 1896 to 1905. It is convenient to break up the narrative in this way but there was no sharp break in Russell's activity. The year 1900, as I shall explain, marked the point at which the undercurrent of ideas about relations that I have described in Chapter I burst out into the foreground. This enabled Russell to connect two of his preoccupations, Cantor's theory for infinite classes and Frege's logical foundations of arithmetic. These two profound influences on Russell's thought could be joined, characteristically for Russell, by a suitable notation. This was the logical notation introduced by Peano, which Russell extended to relations. During 1896 to 1905 Russell came to understand that relations were the key to the philosophy of mathematics, but then he found, in common with Cantor, that paradoxes arose. How these came to be recognised is the subject of Section 2. Even without a solution of the paradoxes, Russell was able to finish *The Philosophy of Mathematics* and this, together with his other work in 1903–5, is described in Section 3. My contention is that this apparently restricted work, overtly involved only in the foundations of mathematics, is critically important for two closely related reasons; because the problems which arise in formalising mathematics are in fact general philosophical problems whose importance is obscured in the rest of philosophy by its comparitive obscurity and lack of organised development, and because, as one might expect from that, their consideration led Russell to his later philosophical positions.

Early in 1896 Russell gave a course of lectures at the newly-founded London School of Economics (then in John Street, Adelphi) on German Social Democracy. He had spent some time in Berlin, studying this at first hand; but the time was not only of political importance, for as he says, ([1]p. 11):

> These travels were useful in curing me of a certain Cambridge provincialism; in particular, I came to know the work of Weierstrass, whom my Cambridge teachers had never mentioned.

(This fact might now seem incredible even to Cambridge mathematicians.) But, he notes in his *Autobiography*, he was also at the time 'reading Georg Cantor, and copying the gist of him into a notebook.' He supposed the arguments to be wrong, but studied them in detail none the less. This proves to be a very important aspect of the context for the next few years of his life, so it is necessary to go into some detail about Cantor's book and this occupies §2.1 to §2.3.

Many of Cantor's contemporaries in mathematics considered his set theory outrageous; with hind-sight, it is referred to by twentieth century mathematicians as 'naïve set theory'. But both of these views do violence to the way in which it grew up and to its subtlety, and so I begin with its origins.

The starting point for Cantor was a very specific problem in mathematical analysis, with its roots deep in practical applications of mathematics. As far back as 1807, Fourier had tackled a number of problems in the conduction of heat in solid bodies by expressing the temperature, at a certain point of the solid at a certain time, as an 'infinite sum' of terms involving trigonometric functions (sines and cosines). By an 'infinite sum' it is not implied that *all* terms of the series of terms have to be added; the phrase is rather a mathematician's typical obscurantism for the true situation, that the terms eventually became small, and that a sufficient approximation to the temperature can always be obtained by adding up enough terms.

Mathematicians had been accustomed for many years to the use of infinite series as a means of approximation, but we are evidently in the close proximity here to one of the paradoxes of Zeno. He had argued that motion was impossible because, before the arrow can get from A to B it must first reach the point C half-way along. Before it can reach C it must first reach the point D half-way from A to C; and so on. This way of putting it involves the idea of time, but a closely related paradox can be expressed without the notion of time by looking at the flight of the arrow from the point of view of its approach to the target B. If the arrow were to reach C, its distance from B would then be $\frac{1}{2}$AB. But, according to Zeno's argument, it would earlier have had to reach D and if it had done this, its distance from C would then be $\frac{1}{4}$AB and so its distance from B would be $(\frac{1}{2} + \frac{1}{4})$AB. Continuing the argument as before, the arrow would earlier have had to reach a point E distant $(\frac{1}{2} + \frac{1}{4} + \frac{1}{8})$AB from B and so on.

The mathematicians chose simply to ignore Zeno's point that the sum of any number of terms of the series $\frac{1}{2} + \frac{1}{4} + \frac{1}{8} + \ldots$ was always less than 1, replacing it by the equally true but irrelevant point that the sum could become as near to 1 as desired by taking a sufficient number of terms. In Aristotle's terms, the available number of terms was potentially infinite, so the sum could, potentially, be as near to 1 as desired: but Zeno's point was that the arrow reaches its target only after an actually infinite number of terms has been added up.

For the purposes of calculating temperature distribution in solids as accurately as desired, however, the mathematicians' approach is perfectly adequate, and Zeno's difficulty can be ignored. But there is a further difference between the series which occurs in Zeno's argument and the series used by Fourier, and indeed sixty years earlier by Euler. This difference lies in the nature of the approximation. The earlier kind of approximation, as in the mathematicians' mistaken answer to Zeno, may be exemplified by the so-called geometric series,

$$x + x^2 + x^3 + \ldots,$$

which became the Zeno series in the special case when $x = \frac{1}{2}$.

Since the result of multiplying this series by x is

$$x^2 + x^3 + x^4 + \ldots,$$

it follows by subtraction that $(1 - x)$ times the sum is simply
x, so that the sum is $x/(1 - x)$:

$$\frac{x}{1 - x} = x + x^2 + x^3 + \cdots.$$

Here the idea is, again, that sufficient terms on the right give
the left-hand side, but the number of terms required
increases with x. Obviously one term is enough when x = 0,
and for x = 0.1 it will be found that 3 are sufficient to give
the first 3 significant figures (0.111) correctly. For x = 0.2
four are required, but for x = 0.5 nine terms are only just
enough. Conversely for a given number of terms the approximation is the better the nearer one is to just one point,
x = 0.

The behaviour of the Fourier series, on the other hand,
provides an approximation which is best possible (in a certain technical sense) not at one point of the body but all over
a fixed range. As a result of this, however, two fairly disastrous things can happen. It might be (in a mathematically
idealised case, if not in reality) that the temperature had a
sudden jump upwards at one point, returning to its original
value immediately past the point. This will not, of course,
affect the series, since that is, as it were, trying to fit the
temperature over the whole range and an isolated point is
not a substantial enough part of the range to have its voice
heard in this. The second thing that may happen merely
mirrors exactly what might also happen in the geometrical
progression case where, if x = 1 or if x is even larger the
series fails to have a 'sum to infinity' and so cannot represent
the left-hand side; in the technical jargon, the series does not
converge.

Cantor as a young man was introduced to the problem of
whether there is a unique Fourier series for a particular
temperature distribution, and this is easily seen to turn upon
the number of 'points of exception', that is, values of x at
which either of the two disasters occurs. Within three years
he was able to show that there could even be an infinite

number of such exceptional points, so long as they were
distributed in an appropriate way. He needed to express this
more clearly, and felt the lack of any technique for talking
about infinite 'sets' (collections) of real numbers. He set
about supplying this, and within ten years he had embarked
on such a descriptive theory, from which his later work followed in a direct way.

2.2 I have taken pains to stress the bread-and-butter
mathematical beginnings of Cantor's work because this is
often neglected. I am concerned to contest the idea that any
of the difficulties of Cantor's later work could be avoided
simply by ignoring it; this will not do since the work is a
(more-or-less) inevitable development of problems clearly
set, not just in mathematics but even in its applications in
physics.

But it was not, of course, this aspect which Russell was
studying in 1896, but what had grown out of it. Cantor found
it necessary to re-introduce into mathematics the idea of
actual infinity. Aristotle, who found this concept in earlier
Greek mathematics, distinguished it carefully from the
potential infinity which is implied, for instance, in the 'sum to
infinity' of the geometrical progression or in Euclid's proof
of the existence of an infinity of prime numbers, a fact which
Euclid actually states and proves in the form that there is no
largest prime. (The proof proceeds by supposing that there
is, and then showing how to construct a larger one.) But
some of Zeno's paradoxes involve the use of actual infinity,
and form a highly successful attack on it. So much so, that we
have no record of whether or not there was any highly organised Greek mathematics using actual infinity; by Euclid's
time it had been banished, though Aristotle still felt the need
to oppose it, and it remained banished until Cantor.

The key to Cantor's advance was his discovery that there
were two different methods of counting, corresponding to
the cardinal and ordinal numbers, and that although both of
these methods could be generalised to infinite collections
and although, for finite collections, they gave the same answer, for infinite collections the two generalisations were different. Counting by cardinal numbers relies on two con-

cepts: the first is that of a 1:1 correspondence between two collections, so that the members of each collection are each assigned a unique mate in the other. Two collections which can be paired off, that is, put in such a 1:1 correspondence, are then said to have the same cardinal number. But this method only provides a means of saying when the cardinal numbers are the same; it does not say what the cardinal number is, and Cantor provides a second concept to do this, a 'principle of abstraction'. Such a principle postulates that, for example, the cardinal number *three* is simply the property that all triads have in common.

This is the point seized on by Russell as an important defect. As he says in a later essay[2] 'logical constructions are to be preferred to inferred entities'. For Cantor is only inferring (without any formal proof) that there is such a common property with the required arithmetic properties of a number. The need is to construct (from the real furniture of the world) such an object. What real furniture is going to be of any use in this construction? A moment's thought will suggest that all is going to depend on relations; so that Russell's approach is going to rest crucially on his new-found belief in their reality.

Counting by ordinals, on the other hand, relies on the ordering of the natural numbers 0, 1, 2 . . . (that 3 is greater than 2 or 1 and so on). Two collections of natural numbers are called similar if there is not only a 1:1 correspondence between them, but if also this correspondence preserves the ordering. Similar collections then have the same ordinal number; and evidently in the finite case when the elements can be ordered arbitrarily, this is no more than having the same cardinal number. But if one takes as a set S the set (0, 1, 2, 3, . . .) of the natural numbers, with the usual ordering, and as a set T the set of all (positive as well as negative) integers {. . ., −3, −2, −1, 0, 1, 2, 3, . . .}, then S and T can be proved to have the same cardinal number in the sense of Cantor's definition. To prove this we can set up a correspondence in this way: 0 in S can be paired with 0 in T and 1 in S with 1 in T. Now −1 in T must not be forgotten, so it is paired with 2 in S. Then 3 in S can be paired with 2 in T, and since −2 in T must not be forgotten, it can be paired with 4 in S. This can obviously be continued. But S and T must have different ordinals, since T has no smallest element, but S has. (This is a very oversimplified description of Cantor's theory).

2.3   How then was Cantor able to set up this theory? He was an extreme Platonist, and this inspired him to begin with the assumption that every union of distinct objects into an aggregate forms a *set* or *class*. (Nowadays, *set* is universally used by mathematicians for a corresponding, but more refined, concept; and *class* means something different again. But Russell used *class* for something rather like the modern *set* and I shall follow him in this since it seems likely to lead to least confusion.)

Russell was not yet at the stage where he would have found Cantor's Platonism uncongenial. Cantor also had a pronounced anti-Kantian streak, which may also have found favour with the changing Russell. It is, perhaps, less conspicuous in his *Mannigfaltigskeitlehre* but in his first letter to Russell, much later in 1911, he describes himself as 'quite an adversary of Old Kant, who, in my eyes has done much harm and mischief to philosophy, even to mankind.'

By *object* Cantor would include numbers, points, lines, functions, relations. We suppose then, that all mathematical objects with some property, φ, in common form a class, the class (of objects) defined by that property; one says that they *belong* to the class or are *members* of it. Notation becomes important here, for part of the power of Cantor's approach was his ability to carry out quite complex constructions, and constructions become very hard to follow in words. I shall therefore introduce a suitable notation: but instead of following Cantor, I shall prefer, for the most part, the one used later by Russell in *Principia Mathematica*, since I shall have to use it later in discussing that book.

The statement that x has the property φ is written φx, and the class of x's with that property is denoted (by Russell) by $\hat{x}\varphi x$. So the 'belonging relation', that y belongs to the class S of objects having φ, y ε S, is defined by

$$y\varepsilon\ \hat{x}\varphi x \quad \text{if and only if} \quad \varphi y.$$

Since classes are, for the thorough-going Platonist, mathematical objects like the others, they can in turn belong to other classes.

This step constitutes, for Cantor, a kind of ontological population explosion. Once two objects appear in a theory, so also does the class of both objects, as well as the classes consisting of each object separately. And these five objects are not all, for of course they belong in turn to larger classes ... But the explosion is a little more dramatic even than that, for if every property defines a class, then some such property as being a round square defines the class of all round squares, and this class, we know, has no members (is called the null class). So the null class exists for the Platonist even before the other objects; it is often denoted by ϕ or Λ.

Its definition can take many forms, but one version would be

$$\Lambda = \hat{x}(x \neq x),$$

using the symbol $\neq$ for 'not equal to'. Here I am, of course, just dodging for the moment the introduction of the logical negation, $\sim$. If I have that at my disposal, I could write

$$\Lambda = \hat{x}(\phi x \,\&\sim \phi x).$$

Just as the null class exists, so also does the class $\{\Lambda\}$ whose only member is the null class. That is,

$$\{\Lambda\} = \hat{x}(x = \Lambda)$$

Equally so for such classes as $\{\Lambda, \{\Lambda\}\}$ and $\{\{\Lambda\}\}$; so that an indefinite number of classes is generated from no original objects at all.

Cantor restricts this ontological explosion a little by a restriction (which I already assumed implicitly in the previous paragraph) that classes are to be considered *in extension* only; that is to say, two classes are to be considered the same when they have the same elements, so that the class defined by the property of being the first three prime numbers (that is, $\{2, 3, 5\}$) is to be considered as identical with the class defined by the (intensionally different) property of being a non-square natural number less than six, that is,

$$\hat{x}(x \text{ is prime } \& \ x < 7) = \hat{x}(x \text{ is not square } \& \ x < 6).$$

The distinction between a property understood in extension and in intension is essentially the same as Mill's distinction between denotation and connotation. This historical antecedent is not the important aspect here. What is important is that mathematical results are exclusively concerned with extensionality. It is the more surprising to hear from Russell, in a letter to Jourdain[3] about his work on relations,

> Oddly enough, I was largely guided by the belief that relations must be taken in *intension*, which I have since abandoned, though I have not abandoned the notations which it led me to adopt.

More of this later (§2.16).

It is now easy to define the *intersection*, $S \cap T$, of two classes S, T as the collection of elements possessing both the properties defining S, T, respectively, and the *union* $S \cup T$ as the collection of elements possessing at least one of the two. Any intersection, T, of S with some other class is called a *sub-class* of S, $T \subseteq S$; and, finally, for any class S, P(S) is defined as the class of all sub-classes of S. So, if $S = \hat{x}\phi x$, $T = \hat{x}\psi x$, then

$$S \cap T = \hat{x}(\phi x \ \& \ \psi x),$$
$$S \cup T = \hat{x}(\phi x \ v \ \psi x),$$
$$T \subset S \text{ means that, if ever } \psi x, \text{ then } \phi x,$$
$$P(S) \ = \hat{x}(x \subset \hat{y}\phi y) = \hat{x}(\text{If } z \ \varepsilon \ x, \text{ then } z \ \varepsilon \ S).$$

If S has two members, then, remembering the null class, which is evidently a sub-class of every class, and including in the count the whole class as an (improper) sub-class of itself, P(S) will have $4 = 2^2$ members, and this is true for finite classes in general: if S has n members, P(S) has 2^n. Now $2^n > n$; and Cantor was able to show by 1892 that a similar result was true of the cardinal numbers of infinite classes, when the ordering relation was defined in the correct way.

In what way? Two classes S and T have the same cardinal if there is a 1:1 relation between them, and this gives the clue: he defined $T < S$ to mean that there is a 1:1 relation between T and a subclass of S but not between S and a subclass of T. As far as cardinality is concerned, one could put it (slightly inaccurately) this way: that S contains a copy of T but T cannot contain a copy of S. The intuition behind this definition of Cantor's is, of course, that we are to look for smaller classes than S amongst the subclasses of S. Not *all* subclasses are smaller by this definition; the class of even natural numbers $\{0, 2, 4, 6, \ldots\}$ is a subclass of the class of all natural numbers $\{0, 1, 2, 3, \ldots\}$ but evidently these two classes have the same cardinal number. A suitable 1:1 relationship to prove this is to match each even number with its half: $0 \to 0$, $2 \to 1$, $4 \to 2$, ... This summary of Cantor's theory, inadequate as it is, must serve for my purpose and I return to Russell.

2.4   I have already drawn attention in Chapter 1 to Russell's emergence from German idealism about this time, to his relief at being able to consider relations as real, and to the effect of this on his *Leibniz* volume. The importance of this should not misunderstood. It is doubtful to what extent the English Hegelians really embraced Hegel and German Idealism, a movement aptly described by Lichtheim[4] as one in which

> the educated strata ... entrenched themselves in the unconquerable regions of philosophy, literature and art ... Thus the German Renaissance, originally the offspring of Northern Germany's traditional Protestant culture, issued in an idealist philosophy which from a secret doctrine of the elect evolved by stages into an openly proclaimed cult of the elite.

Certainly Russell's chapter on Hegel in *History of Western Philosophy* does not justice to Hegel's derivation of idealism as a prerequisite for knowledge of the world to be possible. Russell came later to the view that Hegelianism was a more or less wholly bad influence on his philosophy, from which he was lucky to escape early (though not so quickly as G. E. Moore, who assisted Russell's return to more traditional English themes). But it can be argued that Hegel had one lasting influence which, if not absolutely valuable, determined much of Russell's most important thought in 1900–1914, and that is a propensity to see contradictions and paradoxes.

Another strand at this time is evidenced by Grattan-

Guiness,[3] who records that, after the *Foundations of Geometry*, Russell started sequels on physics and arithmetic, with the intention of spreading the certainty gained in geometry outwards to the other sciences. In fact, Russell[3] says that, after reading Cantor in 1896:

> I then worked for some time at the principles of Dynamics; I went to the Cavendish Laboratory, and I studied Clerk Maxwell. Gradually I found that most of what is philosophically important in the principles of dynamics belongs to problems in logic and arithmetic. This opinion was encouraged by my adoption of Moore's view on philosophy.

An important influence here was Moore's 1899 *Mind* article on 'The Nature of Judgement', but the influence of this will be noted more in Chapter 3. Russell's work, however, did not go well. But 1900 was to be a turning-point. Whitehead and Russell decided to attend an International Congress of Philosophy in Paris, and there met Peano.

It is a significant fact that both of the important influences on Russell's mathematical philosophy, Frege and Peano, were propounding a definite symbolism; like anyone trained in mathematics, a correct symbolism was seen by Russell as immensely valuable – perhaps, in the later volumes of *Principia Mathematica* as unduly so. To say this is not to say that the natures of the two influences were comparable. Peano's notation was one for stating propositions in symbolic logic unambiguously more or less as is done now; Peano himself did not use it for proof. And his intention was to provide a clear vehicle to express mathematics, with the idea that clarity would dissolve away difficulties. The Frege *Begriffsschrift* on the other hand was a notation for logic – more correctly, for writing concepts – of a highly idiosyncratic kind, which was of no use to Russell; but Frege brought to bear, as we shall see, a very definite metaphysics which was largely adopted by Russell.

It is possible however to overestimate Frege's direct influence on Russell. As he says:[5]

> I was led to buy Frege's *Grundgesetze* by an unfavourable review by Peano ... accusing Frege of unnecessary subtlety. The introduction struck me as admirable, but I could not understand Frege's use of

Greek, German and Latin letters, and I put him away for nearly two years, by which time I had discovered for myself most of what he had to say, and was therefore able to understand him.

The two years mentioned here would be from late 1900 to 1902. It is not, of course, of much value to be able to assign priorities: but what Russell says here will prove relevant to the question of his interpretation or misinterpretation of Frege's distinction between *Sinn* and *Bedeutung*. Indirect influence through Peano and Schröder there may well have been.

To return to 1900, Russell observed Peano's grasp of foundations and, as he says,[3]

I was struck by the argumentative superiority of Peano and his disciples to all their adversaries, and became convinced that Peano's methods must lead to clearer thinking.

So when he returned to England he began to study the Peano technique. What he found intoxicated him:

Suddenly, in the space of a few weeks, I discovered what appeared to be definitive answers to the problems which had baffled me for years.[5]

What had Russell found that so excited him? Essentially it was a notation. Peano was concerned to set down the assumptions of arithmetic in a symbolic style of his own. The principal symbols that he introduced were these:

Signs for connecting propositions:

p ∩ q   for *p and q*, p ∨ q for *p or q*, −p for *not p*
p C q   for *p is a consequence of q*, and its inversion
q Ɔ p   for *from q one deduces p*.

Signs for classes:

a ε b   for *a is a member of the class b*
ab   for the class consisting of members of both a and b
a ∪ b   for the class consisting of members of a or b
a Ɔ b   for *class a is contained in class b*

Most of the concepts denoted by Peano's signs are still

important. Most commonly we would now replace

$$p \cap q, p \cup q, -p, p \mathrel{C} q \quad \text{or} \quad q \mathrel{\supset} p, ab,$$

by

$$p \mathbin{\&} q, p \vee q, \mathord{\sim} p, q \supset p, a \cap b.$$

Peano was concerned to express the assumptions of arithmetic in a formal language, to avoid ambiguity. He did not seek to carry out proofs in the language. By September, however, Russell was applying the lessons learned from Leibniz by extending Peano's techniques to relations, and he realised that he was making substantial advances. As he says in a letter to Jourdain:[4]

> I had already discovered that relations with assigned formal properties (transitiveness etc.) are the essential thing in mathematics, and Moore's philosophy led me to make relations explicit, instead of using only ε and $\subset$.

(Note the delicate interplay between philosophy and notation, characteristic of Russell at his best.) 'This hangs together with my attack on the subject-predicate logic in my book on Leibniz.'

He wrote out a paper which he sent to Peano's journal in the same month.[6] Its appearance marked Russell's position as a first-rate philosophical mind; on the basis of this and his *Mathematical Logic as based on the theory of types*,[7] eight years later, he was elected to the Royal Society.

Before I go into the details of the Peano paper, I shall try to illustrate the sudden clarification that Russell achieved at this time by referring to his more popular essay of 1901, *Mathematics and the Metaphysicians*, which is to be found reprinted in *Mysticism and Logic*.[2] He begins this essay with the provocative assertion that pure mathematics was discovered in the nineteenth century by George Boole. It consists of assertions of the form that if p is true of anything, then q is also true of it. Although individual branches of the subject have usually started with axioms, there are no axioms or indefinables in pure mathematics as a whole, except those of general logic, a subject which has developed greatly since 1850 as a result of symbolic methods. One great value of this advance (which is attributed largely to Peano) is that 'self-evident' propositions need proof, and sometimes turn out to be false.

Consider, continues Russell, Zeno's paradox of the arrow, which at every instant is in a state of rest, so that motion is impossible. Zeno has been reinstated by Weierstrass:

> . . . we live in an unchanging world, and . . . the arrow in its flight is truly at rest. Zeno's only error lay in inferring (if he did infer) that, because there is no such thing as a state of change, therefore the world is in the same state at any one time as at any other.

Weierstrass showed that the calculus did not need the tricky concept of the infinitesimal, which leads to all sorts of odd consequences' in such discussions as of motion. To this negative approach has now been added the positive doctrine of a completed infinity by Cantor, based on the one-to-one definition of cardinal number. Because it is possible for a subclass of an infinite class to have the same cardinal as the whole class, another of Zeno's paradoxes is explained.

> We can now understand why Zeno believed that Achilles cannot overtake the tortoise . . . all the people who disagreed with Zeno had no right to do so, because they all accepted premises from which his conclusion followed . . . if Achilles were to catch up with the tortoise, the places where the tortoise would have been would be only part of the places where Achilles would have been. Here, we must suppose, Zeno appealed to the axiom that the whole is greater than the part . . .

Russell goes on to praise Cantor's grasp of the idea of continuity, by means of his understanding of order, and so, he goes on to argue, relations are the essentials of pure mathematics. Finally, geometry is no more about space, according to the treatment of Peano and his disciples, than arithmetic is about numbers of people; Euclid is dethroned, mathematics is made exact through logic, and that is seen as a fatal blow to Kant and the tradition of the synthetic *a priori*.

So much for the joyful reaction of the excited Russell at his sudden discovery of so many new techniques and corresponding ideas. As October began, he started to embody these ideas in *The Principles of Mathematics*[8] and the later part of this was in its final (published) form by the end of December, though the first half needed rewriting for publication in 1902. The aim was the highly Leibnizian one, to show that all mathematics follows from symbolic logic and also to discover the principles of such logic. It is, then, evident that the paper Russell sent to Peano will repay careful study. There is, however, a difficulty; it is for the most part written in Peano's notation. I think that the importance of notation in this field should not be underestimated, and so, when I come to consider *Principia Mathematica* I shall make no apology for insisting on at least a slight acquaintance with the ideography. But in the present paper the notation differs in a number of significant ways from the later one, a consequence of Russell's imperfect understanding – the improvement came only with Frege – of the exact concepts to be introduced, and so it seems preferable to try to explain the philosophical basis of the paper in words, as far as possible. To do this without the tortuous sentences with which Russell, very un-Russell-like, explains one or two of the key steps in the paper will require the introduction of various subsidiary concepts and neologisms to name them.

2.5   Russell's paper[6] is called *The Logic of Relations*. The title sounds like that of a philosophical paper but in fact the paper is one of his mathematical ones. Peano's journal was essentially a mathematical journal. The point is important, for the style and emphasis tends to be quite different in journals of these two types. Russell was well able to mould his style to the place of publication. I could caricature the difference, yet with a good deal of truth, by saying that philosophical journals have a high proportion of their pages filled with explanation of what needs doing and how it should be done. By contrast the editors of mathematical journals regard such explanation as waste, and concentrate on the doing. So I must seek the ideas that lie behind the paper to a greater extent than usual with Russell.

His interest in relations is because[3] 'relations with assigned formal properties ... are the essential thing in mathematics,'. By *mathematics* Russell means *arithmetic*. Much the same view could be held of the rest of mathematics but this was an extension that Russell did not exploit till later. About arithmetic the general line of thought in the paper is very much Peano's, though apparently much generalised. Peano (and Dedekind before him) tried to characterise the natural numbers of five properties (now widely known as *Peano's axioms*) one form of which is:

1. 0 is a natural number.
2. Every natural number x has a unique successor x'.
3. x, y are equal if x' and y' are too.
4. Every natural number is either 0 or the successor of some other natural number.

(The axiom of induction):

5. If 0 has some property, and whenever x has the property, so has x', then all natural numbers have the property.

Such a grouping together of disparate axioms was natural enough to a mathematician. The thinking of Peano and Dedekind was that the natural numbers were simply the series that begins with zero and proceeds by steps from any natural number to its successor. Figure 12 will illustrate this thinking:

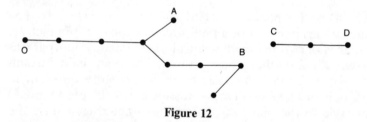

Figure 12

Axiom 1 provides the starting point on the left-hand side. Then axiom 2 forbids an extra branch growing out (as A) and also a termination of the Series (as D). Axiom 3 prevents an incoming branch (as at B) and axiom 4 prevents any breaks (like C). So axiom 1 provides an *absolute* ontological commitment to the existence of one number, zero. Axioms 2 and 3 extend this to a further *conditional* ontological commitment that, given one natural number, another, new, one is also implied. Axiom 4, on the other hand is a restriction on the ontology. It states that no other natural numbers are available than are generated by the actions implied in axioms 1, 2, 3.

I turn now to the axiom of induction, 5. Although, like the others, this is a statement of a property of the natural numbers, it is more instructive to see if from another point of view. It is the basis of a logical scheme of proof, the mathematician's 'proof by induction', which has been characterised by Poincaré as the essential *mathematical* proof. In this scheme of proof it is to be supposed that 0 is *proved* to have some property, φ, of the natural numbers, and that it is also proved that, whenver x has the property φ, so has its successor x′. Then axiom 5 justifies the assertion that these two steps together constitute a proof that all natural numbers have the property φ. So two steps are sufficient to justify an infinite number of conclusions: a 'short cut in logic' indeed, as Wittgenstein puts it.

To sum up, Russell's task can be seen with hindsight to fall into three parts:

(i) Since relations are to be used to furnish the ontological realism of the natural numbers, it will first be necessary to establish a satisfactory theory of relations.

(ii) Particular attention must then be given to two particular relations. First, the relation R that holds between a number x and its successor x′, so that xRx′ is always true. Second, the relation ε that holds between any member x of a set S and the set itself, x ε S.

(iii) All this then has to be applied to establish the existence of zero, and so, as a consequence, of the natural numbers. Moreover the concept of the natural numbers needs further analysis, since both cardinal and ordinal numbers are involved.

I deal with (i) and (ii) in section §2.6 and take up (iii) in §2.7.

2.6 Russell's paper begins in Section I of the first part by distinguishing his work from that with the same name by Peirce and Schröder. They lacked a clear distinction between the concept of class *membership* and the relation between two classes which holds when one is a *subclass* of the other (that is when any member of the first is also a member of the second). In the notation introduced earlier, let

$$S = \hat{x}(x = a), \quad T = \hat{x}(x = a \text{ or } x = b),$$

so that a ε S, a ε T, b ε T, and S ⊂ T. Since z ε S is equivalent to z = a, Schröder's mistake in this case is to confuse the correct S ⊂ T, and the incorrect S ε T (a wrong rendering of a ε T).

As Frege had already noticed in 1892 in *On Concept and Object*,

> Schröder must . . . be criticised for not distinguishing two fundamentally different relations: the relation of an object to a concept it falls under, and the subordination of one concept to another.

This distinction between class inclusion and class membership is closely related to that between the members of a class and the class itself; that is, a difference of type (to use more modern language). Russell, in his *Leibniz* was not altogether clear about this fundamental distinction for he argued against an object being defined as a bundle of predicates because there would then be no need for objects. In a finite class, for example, the pair-class T above, T = {a, b}, the members of T are a, b. The classes (properly) included in T are the two one-element classes S = {a}, and {b}, and these, as I have said, have to be carefully distinguished from a, b.

With the distinction clear, Russell then explains how Peano's notation is going to provide, in his paper, an enormous simplification of the logic of relations. A relation R for Russell always means a two-termed relation; for example, xRy might mean, in arithmetic, that the number x is less than the number y, or in geometry, that the point x lies on the line y, or, in general discussion that x is the father of y. He never considers in any detail three-termed (or higher) relations such as Rxyz, which might mean, in arithmetic for example, that the number y lies between the numbers x and z, or that the number z is the sum of the numbers x and y. I should draw attention here, perhaps, to a slight variation of notation. If a relation R holds between x and y, Russell and many others after him follow the notation for specific relations (a = b, a < b) in mathematics and insert the symbol R between the symbols x, y. For three-termed or higher relations this is obviously misleading so one writes Rxyz.

I have already drawn attention to the two principal uses of relations in the paper, the successor relation and the belonging relation ε. Much of the paper can be interpreted as a generalisation from the idea of the successor relation R. But of course the idea behind the paper is to *construct* the natural number series, so that although such an interpretation can be of help in visualising the theory, it must not be used in generating it. Instead, the whole cast of thinking in the paper can be grasped better if we simply think of xRy as the proposition which states that, starting from x, we can get to y in one R-step (or, we may say, simply, in one step, if no confusion results). Here no special interpretation is to be given to x, y. If one thinks of them as points (which is suggested by the picturesque language of 'steps') these are only points of a diagram. The class of possible starting points (x) is called the *domain* of R, and the class of possible finishing points (y) is the *converse domain*. Indeed, the *converse relation*, Ř, to R is simply defined by defining xŘy as the proposition that we can step *back* from y to x in one R-step (so that xŘy holds if and only if yRx).

From one or more relations, R, S say, others may be defined by operations formed by analogy with those in the theory of classes. For example R ∪ S denotes the relation which holds between x and y if it is possible to get from x to y in one step, which may be an R-step or an S-step, as desired. And R ∩ S denotes the relation which holds between x and y if it is possible to get from x to y in one step, whether or not this is required to be an R-step or an S-step. In the same way ~R denotes the relation which holds between x and y exactly when one *cannot* step from x to y by an R-step.

Two other operations need more attention however. The first of these is denoted by R ⊃ S, and is described by Russell as 'R is contained in S'. It is the relation which holds between R and S if, whenever there is an R-step from x to y, there is also an S-step. Both the notation and the name are a little strange; but both come from an alternative way of looking at relations, which should be briefly explained now. Instead of thinking of xRy as describing a step from x to y, one can think of it as describing a property of the *pair* of elements (x, y), so thinking of it in terms of a property of the elements of the class of pairs {(x, y)} rather than as relations between x,y. For example, let x,y . . . denote natural numbers less than 4, and let R be <, so that the true propositions are $1 < 2$, $1 < 3$, $2 < 3$ and any other propositions of the form $a < b$ (such as $3 < 1$) are false. The alternative view is then to replace the set {1, 2, 3} by the set of pairs:

$$\{(1, 1)\ (1, 2)\ (1, 3)\ (2, 1)\ (2, 2)\ (2, 3)\ (3, 1)\ (3, 2)\ (3, 3)\}$$

and to say that a pair (x, y) has the property R^*, R^* (x, y), corresponding to the original relation R, if and only if xRy.

Thus, in the general case, the pairs (x, y) which have the R-property (that there is indeed a single R-step from x to y), if $R \supset S$, must also have the S-property, so that the R-pairs belong to a sub-class of the class of S-pairs; and it becomes natural to speak of R as contained in S.

The second operation, introduced in Section 2 of Part I, is one which generates a new relation from R and S, but, unlike the earlier ones, this one has no analogue in the calculus of classes; it is called the *relative product* and is to be found in Frege (1879) (or earlier in J. H. Lambert (1782), De Morgan (1860), as well as in Peirce (1882)), and is denoted in this paper by RS (a notation which was changed to R|S in *Principia Mathematica*). It is defined to be the relation which holds between x and y in two steps, the first an R-step from x to a 'stepping-stone' z, and the second an S-step from z to y. As a consequence, the converse of RS is the product of the converses in reverse order ŠŘ. When R and S are the same, the notation R^2 is used for RR. A relation R is called *transitive* if R^2 is contained in R (so that any x, y connected *via* a stepping-stone are also connected by a single step).

The relation of class membership (x ε y, meaning that x is a member of the class y) is discussed at length in Russell's Section 3. The details are unimportant for my description.

The notation in the next, much more important, Section 4 borrows from Schröder. Russell says, in a letter to Jourdain,[4] 'I read Schröder on relation in September 1900, and found his methods hopeless'. The section introduces two further relations. The first is the *identity* relation, which Schröder writes 1'. It is more convenient here to use I and to write xIy if and only if x and y are the same. The more important negation of this relation, $\sim I = J$ (say) (denoted by 0' by Schröder) is *diversity*. As Russell says, the condition that a relation R 'yields a series' is that it is both transitive and contained in diversity. Here the guiding thought is obviously the series of natural numbers; the relation R is not to be the successor relation for this is not transitive. But it *is* to be interpreted as a relation derived from the successor relation by successive applications. For example, in a more modern notation, I could write $x R y$ if and only if either $y = x'$ or else $y = z'$ and $x R z$. Thus $0 R y$ is true if and only if either $y = 1$ or $y = z'$ and $0 R z$. Here z could be 1, so that y could be 2. But then, since $0 R 2$, z could be 2, so that a new y could be 3, and so on. From Russell's point of view what is achieved by this reexpression of the generation of the natural number series from zero by the successor relation is the following: the natural number series is simply the class of objects reached by one R-step from zero. The relation R is what was later called the *ancestral* of the successor relation, which was seen as important by Frege and was later dealt with at length by Russell (see §4.9). Given the reality of R, the question of the ontology of arithmetic is thrown back on the existence of zero and is to this question that Russell turns in Section 5. But referring back to Peano's axioms for a moment, it will be clear that 'transitive and contained in diversity' amounts to axioms 2 and 3.

2.7 The identity relation is used in Section 5 to define 'many-one' relations; these are relations in which a given starting point leads in one step to a unique finish so that, if $x R y$, $x R z$ both hold, then $y I z$. Their converses are the one-many relations, where any final point can be reached from only one start: and those relations which are in both of these classes are the one-one relations. Finally, Section 6 of the first part uses all these concepts to encapsulate a form of definition by abstraction by proving, firstly that if S is many-one, then $S\check{S}$ is transitive and symmetric (that is, is its own converse), but secondly, and more important, that any transitive, symmetric relation can be written as $S\check{S}$ in terms of some many-one relation S.

Russell lays great stress on this result, and so I had better examine why. One of the main uses of it will prove to be in his definition of cardinal numbers, by means of which he proposes to make good what he sees as the defect of Cantor's approach. Here Russell is leaning on Frege. As he says in a letter to Jourdain in 1902 ([3]p. 17) after arguing that a passage in Cantor does not serve as a definition of numbers,

> This definition however (as I have learnt since giving my lectures) is quite explicitly set forth by Frege . . . He is a very able man; I have been corresponding with him for some time about my paradox.

The lectures were in 1902. In his opening letter to Frege, June 1902, Russell seems to claim a longer acquaintance with Frege's work. This may possibly have been politeness, or else that, intially, he had failed to understand it.

Russell's argument against Cantor proceeds in this way: one can indeed say that two classes (finite ot infinite) have the *same* cardinal number if there is a one-one relation between them. Thus the class of natural numbers has the same cardinal as the class of even natural numbers in virtue of the relation described in §2.3. But, in either the finite or infinite case, this gives only the definition of the *same* cardinal number and does not define this cardinal number. To do this, T is to be taken in the proposition as the relation between two classes of their having the same cardinal number (this is evidently transitive and symmetric). Then R may be written in terms of S, and S then relates the two classes to a single element, that is, to their common cardinal number, for the proposition proved by Russell, that R can be written SŠ, means that two classes u, v, related by R, satisfy uRv. But this is uSŠv and the definition of this is that there exists a stepping-stone z with the property uSz and zŠv, that is, uSz and vSz. The stepping-stone z is then the common cardinal number.

It should be noted that it is not asserted, nor is it true, that only one such relation S exists. There is a class of such relations and correspondingly a class of objects z. This is an embarrassing situation but Russell is able to relieve it by using a fact that becomes obvious in the course of his proof. This fact is that it is always possible to choose as the object z a particular class, to wit, the cardinal number of x can be defined as the class of all classes y that satisfy xRy.

This then, is Russell's answer to the ontological defect of Cantor's 'inferring' a cardinal number from a 1:1 correspondence between two classes of the same cardinal number. It could be written, slightly ungrammatically, and using the non-Russellian notation $|y|$ for the cardinal number of a class y, as

$$|y| = \hat{x}(xRy \ \& \ R \ \varepsilon \ (1 \rightarrow 1)),$$

so cutting out the intermediate stage with S (since S is, in any case, not unique). This formula defines the cardinal number $|y|$ of the class y as a class. It states that this is the class of all x's which stand in a 1:1 relation to y, as indeed it should. Of course, a cardinal number is here defined as a class of classes, which has a certain lack of intuitive directness.

I have now described in some detail the whole of the first part of Russell's paper. It will not be necessary to go into such detail about the remaining parts.

Part 2 is concerned with cardinal numbers and begins by defining the relation, sim, of similarity (1:1 relation) between classes, in terms of the existence of a relation S as described above. Then the ordering relation 'greater than' is defined between cardinals of classes by requiring

(a) non-similarity of the two classes,

together with

(b) the similarity of the lesser class with a sub-class of the greater.

This exactly follows Cantor's definition which I described in §2.3. 0 is defined as the cardinal of the null class and 1 of the unit class (defined by introducing the phrase 'the unique x such that . . .'). Russell has said that the single fact that the Peano school has recognised the need for this quantifier was a turning-point in his realisation of their superiority.

Addition of cardinals is defined in terms of the union of classes; but it is necessary to make sure that the two classes have no common members, since one cannot rely on any dodge of 'counting them twice'. So the rule has to be a little more complex, and to require the choice of two non-intersecting classes u, v respectively similar to the assumed classes m, n. Then the cardinal of u ∪ v can be defined as the required sum of m and n.

I must deal in a little more detail with Part 3, for this is the part of the paper that makes the link with Peano's axioms for arithmetic. Part 3 begins with a definition of the *ordinal number ω*. This ordinal number is a class (just as a cardinal number is a class) but it is a class with an ordering on it. The idea is that ω is to be (or, rather, to be similar to) the class of all natural numbers {0, 1, 2, 3, . . .} with their usual ordering. The definition is fairly complex. Russell gives a verbal definition as well, but it is one that produces even more mystery; I shall essay a different verbal explanation.

Since the theory is intended to be that of progressions, such as the natural numbers (0, 1, 2, 3, . . .), it is framed in terms of definitions of a particular relation R which is intended to correspond to the successor relation. The whole obscurity is related to Russell's care to avoid misunderstanding about possible question-begging. He seeks to do this by not mentioning the intended interpretation. By the time he came to write the *Principles* he had decided that it was better to risk the misunderstanding for the sake of clarity ([8]p. 127).

I shall say, firstly, that a class u is *reduced* by one of the 1:1 relations R whose domain includes u if the class v of elements reached by one R-step from any element of u is a strict sub-class of u (meaning by *strict* that it is not the whole of u). Thus R can be thought of as dividing u into an inside, v, and an outside, u − v. Secondly, I shall describe a class, s, as *closed under* R if, for any initial element of s, one R-step carries me only to another element of s. (So, if u is reduced to v by R, it is closed under R but not vice versa and v is closed under R). Finally ω is defined as the class of those classes u that have a reducing relation R together with the further property, which I shall call the final proviso, that any class s, which overlaps the outside of u and is closed under R, includes the whole of u. Such classes, u, are called *progressions*.

It is instructive to disentangle the meaning of these definitions in the intended interpretation. The class u is then the class of natural numbers, u = {0, 1, 2, 3, . . .} and the relation R is the successor relation. The inside of u is v = {1, 2, 3,

...}, so the outside is {0}. The final proviso then refers to any class s which includes zero and is closed under the successor relation. The proviso states that s includes the whole of u. This final proviso captures both axiom 4 and axiom 5 of Peano. For the statement of it that I have just made is essentially axiom 4. And axiom 5 follows in the same way by applying the proviso to x̂φx, the class of objects with the property φ.

But what is worrying at first sight is that the axioms seem to be much more general than Peano's. It is not only that numbers are never mentioned and it is all expressed (in my terms) by terms like inside and outside. Might not the outside of u be a class of more than one element, even perhaps an infinite class? Russell moves immediately to disarm such criticism by proving that all progressions are similar. By this is meant the following: suppose that one progression is generated by a relation R, and two typical elements x,y of the progression satisfy xRy. Then any other progression, generated by a relation Q, is connected to the first in terms of a 1:1 similarity relation P. This means that there are unique elements u, v of the second progression such that xPu and yPv and that, as a consequence of xRy it follows that uQv.

The rest of the paper need not concern us in detail. Russell goes on to set up the (ordinal) arithmetic of progressions. Then he shows that the theory he has set up applies most naturally to infinite numbers of the kind that Cantor had considered but can be readily extended to include finite ones. And finally there is a long section setting up the foundations of mathematical analysis – here and later we shall find two reinforcing effects: once Russell had a development underway he was very loth to let it go before he had carried it on a long way. But also, at the time he was writing, there was much less adequate discussion of the foundations of mathematics in the treatises on the subject than there would be now. These two effects combine to produce final sections here and elsewhere in Russell's writings which would nowadays (and this is a measure of his success) be thought to belong to mathematics proper.

Just what has Russell done in this paper and how has he done it? Technically, all he has achieved is this: he has altered the emphasis in Peano's axioms. The first four axioms tend to be grouped together, as in some way more fundamental: then the fifth comes along – almost like the parallel postulate of Euclid – to delimit a special case. Russell saw that, since, in any case, arithmetic was impossible without the induction axiom, one might as well derive the maximum benefit from it by weakening the others and using it instead. For example, there is no need to postulate a unique non-successor. For in the final proviso for ω, there can be only one member of the outside of u, since if there were two, say α, β I could select one, α for instance, and take for s the class consisting of α and all its successors α_1, α_2, α_3, $\ldots$ where $\alpha R\alpha_1$, $\alpha_1 R\alpha_2$ (or $\alpha\, R^2\alpha_2$), etc. Then s overlaps the outside of u and is closed under R, so by the final proviso contains the whole of u and so, in particular, contains β. But this is a contradiction, since β is in the outside of u. Once it is clear that the outside has one member, all is apparent. In a way, then, the technical trick here is the way in which s is said to *overlap* the outside of u.

But it would be wrong to see the technical trick as the important aspect. The *Logic of Relations* could have been written only by someone convinced of the reality of relations. As Winslade says,[9]

> Among those who classify relations as real are Aristotle, Aquinas, McTaggart and Wittgenstein; among those who classify relations as mental are Ockham, Locke, Leibniz and Bradley. Russell clearly should be listed with those who think that at least some relations are real features of the world, not products of the mind.

He goes on to distinguish six of Russell's ontological commitments concerning the nature of relations: '1. Relations are real features of the world. 2. Relations cannot be reduced to properties.' (So, for example, 'A is greater than B' cannot be captured as two-subject-predicate propositions attributing certain magnitudes to A and B). '3. Relations have a sense', (so aRb must be distinguished from bRa). '4. Relations and pluralism are interdependent. 5. Relations are constituents of relational facts. 6. Relations are unparticularised universals.'

Since progressions (ordinal numbers) and cardinal numbers (of classes) are defined by relations, these are equally real. So a sure foundation for arithmetic was being given in terms of the real furniture of the world-relations and what can be constructed from them.

Ayer[10] has emphasised that Russell

makes the now unfashionable assumption that every belief we hold stands in need of philosophical justification ... we cannot have reason to believe that the propositions in question are true unless we have reason to believe that certain types of entity exist ... The central part which this ontological question plays in Russell's treatment of philosophy has not, I think, been at all widely recognised.

And Quine[9] remarks in 1970 that '... the problem of ontological realism has never ceased to occupy, and, I dare say, to vex him.'

The paper is a natural successor to the book on Leibniz, and must have seemed at the time a natural precursor to further constructions of the whole of mathematics – geometry, and perhaps physics (as Russell had tried to do before). Moreover, it is an optimistic work with a panache engendered by the conviction that all the outstanding problems in the foundations of mathematics were now solved:

The only part played by Cantor's work was that I tested my logic of relations by its applicability to Cantor. But geometry was also much in my mind. ([3]p. 134).

This then was the situation immediately before contradictions appeared in the foundations of this impressive edifice.

Section 2: The Discovery of Contradictions

2.8 The presence of severe contradictions in the foundations of mathematics came to light at the beginning of this century but it is curiously difficult to put an exact date on it. Russell has said:[3]

In June 1901 I came upon the Contradiction about classes which are not members of themselves, which occupied the bulk of my time and thought for the next five or six years.'

In other places he has put Spring or May 1901 as alternative dates. Jourdain has stated[3] that Russell told him he discovered Cantor's paradox of the largest cardinal in January 1901 and his own in June. The confusion arises because it was only a gradual process by which the discoverers of contradictions became aware of their full seriousness for mathematics. I shall concentrate first on the technical details of the paradoxes now associated with the names of Cantor, Burali-Forti and Russell, though, I shall argue, Russell's part in this was paramount (and, of course, the result of his earlier Hegelianism).

Historians tend to relate these paradoxes to earlier situations in mathematics, especially to Zeno. Historically there are resemblances. But there is an important philosophical difference. As Murray Code has said: [11]

> The perennially pertinent message conveyed by Zeno is that the nature of physical continuity is not well understood: yet mathematical treatments presuppose a clear understanding of continuity.

By contrast, the twentieth century paradoxes appear more internalised, striking at the foundations of mathematics, not at its applicability. From what has been said it should be clear that the widely held view that the paradoxes brought about the formalisation of mathematics is less than a half-truth. Formalisation had been in the air for the last thirty years of the old century. (My attention was drawn to this point by Michael Moss.)

I begin by stating the contradictions in a simple form which will serve to identify them, though it will turn out not to be wholly accurate. Cantor's paradox arises from the definition of cardinal number by means of a class. On the one hand Cantor had proved that the class $P(S)$ of all subclasses of a particular class S has a larger cardinal than S. But, on the other, the class of *all* classes, C, must have the largest possible cardinal. If C is chosen as S a contradiction results, since $P(C)$ is greater than C, although C was largest. The Burali-Forti paradox is on similar lines, but refers to ordinal numbers instead of cardinal. Russell, as I shall explain, came to his paradox in the process of a painstaking analysis of the Burali-Forti situation.

This paradox concerns the possibility of self-membership for classes; the class C, above, of all classes, is, since it is a class, a member of C. This fact by itself sounds suspiciously paradoxical; but Russell's paradox proceeds by considering, not such classes, but those that do *not* have this curious property of self-membership. If R is the class of all classes not belonging to themselves, the paradox arises by asking whether or not R belongs to itself. (For if it does not, then it satisfies its own defining property, and so does belong to itself. But if it belongs to itself, it fails to satisfy its defining property and so does not belong to itself.) The Russell paradox looks simpler than the other two because it makes no mention of cardinal or ordinal numbers. But in fact there is a close connection. One aspect of this is seen in the way that Cantor's and Burali-Forti's contradictions rely on the assumption that two unequal cardinals are related one way round or the other by the ordering relation, so one is prevented from supposing that there might be particular cardinals between which such a relation did not hold. In the same way Russell's paradox rests on excluding the possibility that class membership might be an inappropriate criterion to apply to the class of all classes.

One should not fall into the error of supposing that these paradoxes are not serious enough to worry about. Russell himself[5] says:

> At first I supposed that I should be able to overcome the contradiction quite easily, and that probably there was some trivial error in the reasoning. Gradually, however, it became clear that this was not the case, . . . Trivial or not, the matter was a challenge. Throughout the latter half of 1901 I supposed the solution would be easy, but by the end of that time I had concluded that it was a big job.

2.9 I have followed the usual convention in calling these contradictions in the foundations of mathematics. I should substantiate this further by showing the extent to which the foundations of mathematics are grounded on the theory of classes. It is not possible to point to only one particular use, because the idea of class naturally arises differently for different starting points. But one example is the justification one gives for the use of negative numbers ('two minuses make a plus' as children used to be taught by rote, since a plausible justification of this rule for multiplication was not available) and this justification goes back to Hamilton (1837),[12] though I present it here in a more modern form.

Suppose that the natural numbers including zero, are taken for granted; it does not matter for this purpose whether as given in the intuition or as justified in some other way. Since I wish to argue that the use of classes is more or less unavoidable, I do not at this point, postulate the existence in any Platonic sense of the class ω of natural numbers. For such an introduction is easily avoidable by simply refusing to consider such a totality. The natural numbers then allow the solution of such equations as $x + 2 = 3$, which has the unique solution $x = 1$, but they do not allow the solution of $x + 3 = 2$. Historically the approach of mathematicians (in this problem as in others) was gradually to go ahead uncritically and to write $x = -1$ for the solution – though such a development took a long time to mature.

None the less the needs of banking, or even more of primitive accountancy, buttressed the pure interest of mathematicians in making *some* sense of the equations $(-1) + 3 = 2$, so that $3 = 2 - (-1)$, though it took late twentieth century computer requirements to wean the bankers from their preference for using red ink in place of the mathematicians' minus sign. Perhaps the matter need never have been taken any further, except for the possible curiosity of philosophers in due course, but for the fact that the mathematicians' interest in a system of numbers has one significant difference from the bankers: that is, that a system of numbers allows multiplication as well as addition. And although the bankers are aware of the effect of doubling debts, so as to be able to testify to the indubiety of $2 \times (-3) = -6$, this interpretation fails to justify $(-2) \times (-3) = 6$ (if indeed it *should* equal 6).

To clarify this situation the mathematicians, over the centuries, had to decide what they wanted from a system of numbers; and this turned out to be that, for any numbers a, b, c, . . ., they would always want to use the properties:

$$a + b = b + a, \qquad a \times b = b \times a,$$
$$a + (b + c) = (a + b) + c, \qquad a \times (b \times c) = (a \times b) \times c,$$
$$a \times (b + c) = a \times b + a \times c$$

together with the special results

$$a + 0 = a, \qquad a \times 1 = a.$$

These properties, true for the natural numbers, gradually emerged as the *sine qua non* for any system of numbers, and it was necessary to make sure that, when the natural numbers were extended by adjoining $-1, -2, -3, \ldots$, the new system (the integers) still satisfied these conditions.

Now one way of doing this which has, in Russell's phrase, the advantage of theft over honest toil, is simply to proclaim that the integers do satisfy these conditions, together with

$$a + (-a) = 0, \; a \times (-b) = -a \times b$$

and so on. But this fails to answer the severe ontological problem, a problem not merely of the sort devised by philosophers but a genuine doubt held by early mathematicians as to whether 'negative numbers' truly existed. (Such ontological doubts, as I noted above, were viewed very sympathetically by Russell.) So strongly did this doubt take root that a 'construction' of the negative numbers from the natural numbers, which answers the ontological doubt completely (relative to the assumed existence of the natural numbers), is still to be found in sufficiently careful mathematics texts, and it is this construction in which classes play an unavoidable role.

The construction, which goes back to Hamilton, begins with a simple trick: instead of the natural numbers a, b, c, ... we consider *pairs* of natural numbers (a, b), (a, c), (b, c), ... The idea *behind* this trick is that (a, b) will correspond to the integer $a - b$, if it exists, but this idea must not, of course, be made use of in the development. At this stage an appeal has been made to the real existence of pairs, that is, certain *finite* classes have been introduced. However, I ignore this fact in the present argument, partly because finite classes present few of the difficulties of infinite ones, and partly because a more serious question about introducing classes arises at the next stage.

Instead, we define the operations of addition and multiplication between pairs by the rules

$$(a, b) + (c, d) = (a + c, b + d),$$
$$(a, b) \times (c, d) = (a \times c + b \times d, a \times d + b \times c),$$

in which, it should be noticed, only known operations between natural numbers occur on the right-hand side. It is then easy to verify that the operations between pairs satisfy all the conditions above for a number-system, taking (0, 0) as the zero and (1, 0) as the unity. Then also (b, a) = −(a, b), and the new system of numbers contains a copy of the old, natural, numbers in the form of numbers like (a, 0).

So far all is straightforward, but the next step in the argument renders use of classes essential. For the new system does *not* answer the ontological question 'Does −1 exist?' by pointing to a unique pair, (0, 1) say, and saying 'Yes, for −1 is (0, 1)'. It cannot do this, for this would ignore (1, 2), (2, 3), (3, 4), . . . all equally good representations of −1. In order to answer the ontological question, it is necessary to say that −1 is, not a pair of natural numbers, but the class of all pairs (a, a + 1). The theory of classes play an essential part here.

I have emphasised the details of this introduction of classes because it is the first, and most basic, one in mathematics. But the same device is used again, in extending the class of integers again to get the class of rational numbers (that is, those like $\frac{1}{2}, \frac{2}{3}, \frac{1}{4}, \frac{2}{5}, \ldots$ which are *ratios* of natural numbers). In this case the same ontological problem, of the existence of such ratios, is answered by a suitable definition of the operations between pairs (a, b), a definition invented by a discreet use, following Hamilton again, of the idea that (a, b) will 'correspond to a/b', but again the actual definition of rationals will require the consideration of classes of pairs. Precisely the same trick was used in the passage from real to complex numbers; and one involving an even deeper use of classes is needed to bridge the gap between the rationals amongst which, as I mentioned in Chapter I, the Pythagoreans found that two had no square root, and the real numbers in which it did. These examples will serve to substantiate my point that paradoxes in the theory of classes will automatically be paradoxes in the foundations of mathematics.

2.10   The history of the discovery of the paradoxes is a complex one. In part this complexity derives from the tortuous logical situation in which they arise. I shall try to illuminate this by looking at some conclusions that come from a naïve approach to the theory of classes. In my description of the paradoxes in §2.8 it is clear that the important features of them are the notions of sub-classes, of all classes and of self-membership. Accordingly I shall investigate these notions. In this I lean heavily on a paper by Grattan-Guinness[13] which comments on the history in the same way.

I begin with some notation. Let S denote the class of all classes, T the class of all classes of classes and U the class of classes of classes of classes. The process of definition could obviously be continued, but these three classes are sufficient for my purpose. Evidently, since every class of classes of classes is automatically a class of classes, but not vice versa, it is the case that:

$$U \subset T \subset S.$$

However, since S is a class it belongs to S, since T is a class of classes it belongs to T and so on. So each of S, T, U have the rather peculiar property of self-membership:

$$S \, \varepsilon \, S, \ T \, \varepsilon \, T, \ U \, \varepsilon \, U.$$

Nor is this all; for T is a class of classes of classes, so that T ε U, and U is a class of classes (of classes) so that U ε T. For two classes to be such that each is a member of the other is again highly peculiar. Moreover the same analysis serves to show that S ε T, and putting this beside T $\subset$ S yields another strange situation; T is a part of one of its own members.

From the method of formation it will be clear also that every subclass of S is a class of classes and that all the sub-classes of S taken together must constitute T. That is,

$$P(S) = T, \ P(T) = U.$$

So T $\subset$ S becomes P(S) $\subset$ S, a result which looks decidedly odd beside Cantor's theorem that the cardinal of P(S) is greater than that of S. Indeed, once one comes to cardinals it is more than a mere appearance of oddness; a logical paradox results. For P(S) $\subset$ S shows that there is a one:one relation between P(S) and a sub-class of S whilst the precise content of Cantor's theorem is that, although there is a one:one relation between S and a sub-class of P(S), there *cannot* be one between P(S) and a subclass of S, which is a contradiction. So this is essentially the Cantor paradox of the greatest cardinal; and the greatest ordinal arises in somewhat the same way. Cantor had both of these paradoxes as early as 1896, but did not consider them important enough to publish. It seems as if he was prepared to believe that the 'greatest' ordinal, β could satisfy $\beta > \beta$. In 1897 Burali-Forti published a paper,[14] often wrongly credited with containing his paradox, which questioned the so-called trichotomy law for ordinals. This is the statement that, for any two ordinals α, β exactly one of the three statements

$$\alpha < \beta, \; \alpha = \beta, \; \alpha > \beta$$

holds. This paper has often been misunderstood. I base the following more correct analysis of it on that of Moore and Garciadiego.[15] Like Russell, Burali-Forti had been inspired by both Peano and Cantor but in 1894 he[16] exhibits a misunderstanding of Cantor's concept of 'well-ordered'. It is unnecessary for my argument to have any clear idea of the meaning of well-ordered, but I mention Cantor's definition in order that Burali-Forti's position can be clarified. Cantor had defined a set as well-ordered when it has a first element, any element which has any successors has an immediate one, and a (finite or infinite) set with any successors has an immediate one, but Burali-Forti omitted this last proviso. He investigated trichotomy for cardinals, and deduced it from two other postulates (which would not now be thought simpler). Then in his 1897 paper[14] he made an attempt to refute trichotomy for ordinals, not with the idea of sabotaging the whole Cantor edifice, but merely of showing an essential limitation in the theory of order-types. He concluded (correctly) that he had misread Cantor's definition. He made no mention of a paradox and the suggestion that has been made that his paradox aroused immediate interest is belied by the fact that no mention was made of it in print for five years, till in fact, Russell's in 1903.[8]

Coming now to Russell himself, I have already drawn attention to his interest in paradoxes. More specifically, as early as 1896 in an unpublished essay in his Hegelian period,

On some difficulties of Continuous Quantity (referred to in[15]), he says

> philosophical antinomies, in this sphere, find their counterpart in mathematical fallacies. These fallacies seem . . . to pervade the calculus, and even the more elaborate machinery of Cantor's collections (*Mengen*).

By 1899 a draft outline of Part II of the *Principles of Mathematics* contains:

> Antinomy of infinite number. This arises most simply from applying the idea of a totality to numbers. There is, and is not, a number of numbers.

By this time, or at any rate by late 1900, Russell proved the result which in the notation above reads T ⊂ S; and so concluded, since this was P(S) ⊂ S, that he had a counter example to Cantor's theorem. He sought for a mistake in Cantor's proof and thought (incorrectly) that he had found it.

He thought that Cantor had assumed the existence of classes contained in u that were not members of u. Such an assumption, had Cantor made it, would obviously be true for most classes u but, because T is a class of classes of classes, so also is any class contained in T. It must therefore be a member of T. That is, the assumption would be false if u = T. Cantor had not made this assumption.

2.11   At this point the story seems to divide. One development, with which I deal in this section, was that Russell looked closely at the way in which Cantor had proved his theorem. This was by trying to set up a one:one relation between a class α and P(α) and showing that the particular aggregate β of members of α which do not belong to their images under the attempted complete one:one relation is a member of P(α) which does not correspond to any member of α. This shows that the relation is not complete after all. That is, Cantor considered an alleged relation R, between members x of α and members X of P(α) and assumes that such a complete one:one relation is possible. Then those x for which xRX but not x ε X constitute a class of x's, that is, a sub-class of α, and so a member of P(α). But if this member of P(α), call it V, is such that vRV, then ask the question whether or not v ε V? If it were the case that v did not belong to V, then we have 'vRV but not v ε V', so that v satisfies the defining condition for V, that is v ε V, which is a contradiction. But if, on the other hand it were the case that v ε V, then that means that vRV but not v ε V, and again we have a contradiction.

This argument, of course, bears a suspicious resemblance to the later one producing Russell's paradox. At this time, however, (1900) Russell imitated Cantor's proof in the particular case α = S so that P(α) = T, by defining the one:one relation *R* by the rule:

$$\text{xRx} \quad \text{for} \quad \text{x in T,}$$
$$\text{xR\{x\}} \quad \text{for} \quad \text{x in S but not in T.}$$

The second part of the rule is not used in the following argument.

He then considered the particular V which is the aggregate of those x's for which x ε S and xRX, but not x ε X. This aggregate belongs, of course, to T, so that VRV and this is in contradiction to Cantor's proof above that no v exists for which vRV. So, if Cantor's theorem is indeed true, we have that it is both the case and not the case that V ε V. It seems here as if we have Russell's paradox deduced in a form derived from Cantor's theorem already in 1900, rather than 1901 as Russell himself states.

But this is not quite so. For V is not the class of *all* classes that do not belong to themselves, but the class of all classes of classes with that property. It was, apparently, between spring and June 1901 that Russell saw that he could move up by one stage, though at the same time severing the connexion with Cantor's theorem. Nor was his loss of interest in criticising Cantor (he wrote to Couturat in October 1901 that Cantor was irrefutable) the only major change in his ideas initiated at this point. One of the reasons surmised for the paradoxes was that of an unsuspected ontological limitation – that is, that certain aggregates, in fact the 'very large' ones, were not mathematical objects in the sense in which the 'smaller' ones, were. By 'very large' is meant that the class, like that of all classes, is not further enlargeable. Russell lost what interest he ever had in such 'limitation of size' theories. For the corresponding definition of the Russell paradox aggregate as the class of those x's such that x ε S, but not that x ε x is not 'very large' in the sense that the class of all classes is. As Russell says in a letter to Jourdain in June 1904 ([3]p. 35).

> It is a mistake to suppose that the 'inconsistent classes', or, as I prefer 'irreducible functions' [here Russell means by *function* a property, that is, predicate] are the very large ones. They are only half way up. For the negation of a reducible function is reducible.

(The point of the last sentence being that it implies the same for irreducible ones). Russell goes on to point out that to say a predicate φ is irreducible is to say that no class u exists such that x having the property φ, (φx), holds if and only if x ε u. Thus, he argues, given any u, either φx is true for an x outside u, or φx is false for an x in u. 'Thus it is just as much the terms not satisfying φx as the terms satisfying it, that make it irreducible'.

2.12   I now turn to the other branch of the story which starts, again, at Russell's criticism of Cantor's proof. Russell wrote to Couturat about his belief that Cantor had presupposed classes contained in u and not individuals of u and Couturat in return drew Russell's attention to the Burali-Forti paper.[14] So Russell began to consider Burali-Forti's arguments and the difficulties over ordinals in parallel with Cantor's and the cardinals. And, as he says, by June 1901 he had constructed Russell's paradox. Yet, having done so, he did nothing towards publishing it for a year. It is evident that he did not believe it a very important matter until he had written to Frege about it and recieved his reply (which Russell mentioned in a letter to Alys in 1902); but then he realised that the defect he was studying in Cantor and Frege was present also in his *Principles of Mathematics*. None the less he refused to allow it to prevent him from finishing the book and so in 1903 Burali-Forti's paradox was definitively stated in it, by Russell. (Though even then Russell saw it less as endangering the whole system but rather as coming from

Burali-Forti's assumption that, because any segment of the ordinals (that is, class of ordinals less than a given ordinal) can be well-ordered, the class of all ordinals can be). As he says in 1901 ([5]p. 147):

> I therefore decided to finish *The Principles of Mathematics*, leaving the solution in abeyance. In the autumn Alys and I went back to Cambridge, as I had been invited to give two terms' lectures on mathematical logic. These lectures contained the outline of *Principia Mathematica*, but without any method of dealing with the contradictions.

The two terms' lectures were attended by Philip Jourdain; a correspondence developed between them, the immensely valuable surviving letters of which have been edited by I. Grattan-Guiness.[3] I have already had occasion to refer to these frequently.

Section 3: The Principles of Mathematics

2.13   It will be clear from the last section that the *Principles of Mathematics* is a transitional work, that served to codify, for Russell, his progress in his programme up to 1901–2, and to point the way for future work. As Ayer says '. . . it contains a vein of Platonic Realism which Russell was later to reject.'[17] I do not feel it is appropriate to deal with its contents in full; much of them appear with only minor improvements, in *Principia Mathematica*, with which I shall deal in detail. But neither is it right to ignore it completely, so, in this section. I shall pick out some salient points in it. Alan Dorward has aptly said:[18]

> Russell's most creative work . . . is to be found in the two books, *The Principles of Mathematics* (1903) and *Principia Mathematica* (1910–13) . . . The titles of these books might lead the reader to suppose that they deal with mathematics in the ordinary sense of the word, but this is not so. It might be truer to say that both books deal with the foundations of logic.

The preface describes the book as having two main objects:

(i)   proof that pure mathematics deals exclusively with concepts definable in terms of a very small number of

fundamental logical concepts, and that all its propositions are deducible from a very small number of fundamental logical principles.

(ii) the explanation of the fundamental concepts which
mathematics accepts as undefinable. This is a purely
philosophical task.

It then goes on to say that the book has been largely anticipated by Frege, but, since Russell was unaware of this till
printing had begun, he has devoted an appendix to Frege. It
is interesting to compare the final sentence in the preface:

> The subjects treated are so difficult that I feel little confidence in my
> present opinions, and regard any conclusions which may be advocated
> as essentially hypotheses.

with some of the preface to the second edition, of 1937:

> Such interest as the book now possesses is historical . . . The fundamen-
> tal thesis on the following pages, that mathematics and logic are identi-
> cal, is (however) one which I have never seen any reason to modify.

Ayer has correctly remarked[17] that

> Russell says comparatively little about the status which he attributes to
> the propositions of logic themselves. In his earlier works, he rejects the
> received view that the propositions of logic are analytic, mainly on the
> ground that this would make them trivial, and prefers to characterise
> them in terms of their complete generality.

In this later preface Russell also outlines the reasons that
have been adduced against the logicist view. Firstly, mainly
as a result of the paradoxes, there are the unsolved difficulties in logic; a criticism associated with the name of Hilbert
and the formalists by Russell. Secondly, if the logical basis *is*
accepted, then it leads to Cantor's and other paradoxes, and
Russell sees this as the essence of the criticism of Brouwer
and the intuitionists. His answer to the first is curt: 'The
formalists have forgotten that numbers are needed not only
for doing sums, but for counting.' He shows more respect to
the intuitionists:

> Disastrous consequences, however, cannot be regarded as proving that

a doctrine is false: and the finitist doctrine, if it is to be disproved, can only be met by a complete theory of knowledge. I do not believe it to be true, but I think no short and easy refutation of it is possible.

Later in this preface to the second edition Russell neatly sums up the defects in the book; as well as certain technical (logical) defects, the rather crude theory of types intended to dodge the paradoxes and the belief in existence theorems,

> I shared with Frege a belief in the Platonic reality of numbers, which, in my imagination, peopled the timeless realm of Being. It was a comforting faith, which I later abandoned with regret.

Next he lists his statement that 'every word occurring in a sentence must have *some* meaning', a view of language he later came to see as mistaken. As Quine has justly said 'In *Principles of Mathematics*, (1903), Russell's ontology was unrestrained. Every word referred to something'. Russell later retreats, instead, to the much weaker position that every word contributes to the meaning of the sentence. A first step away from Platonism was the theory of descriptions; a second was the abolition of classes (except as logical fictions) in *Principia Mathematica*, with corresponding implications for cardinals.

Finally, in this preface, some remarks on how Russell saw the problem of logic by 1937:

> It seems clear that there must be some way of defining logic otherwise than in relation to a particular logical language. The fundamental characteristic of logic, obviously, is that which is indicated when we say that logical propositions are true in virtue of their form . . . this phrase, inadequate as it is, points, I think, to the problem which must be solved if an adequate definition of logic is to be found.

2.14   The book itself falls into seven main parts: 1. The Indefinables of mathematics. 2. Number. 3. Quantity 4. Order. 5. Infinity and Continuity. 6. Space. 7. Matter and Motion. These are followed by two appendices, A on Frege (as promised in the preface) B on the theory of types.

Part 1 begins by explaining that Pure Mathematics is

> the class of all propositions of the form 'p implies q', where p and q are propositions containing one or more variables, the same in the two

propositions, and neither p nor q contains any constants, except logical constants . . . In addition to these, mathematics *uses* a notion which is not a constituent of the propositions which it considers, the notion of truth.

Two remarks may be made at once about this definition. In the first place the definition as a class of propositions replaces what an earlier writer might have expressed in the form 'Pure Mathematics treats of propositions of the form . . .' This latter form makes a statement about what mathematics does; but Russell states what it is. And this is done by the same trick which, in the theory of relations, improved upon Cantor's treatment of cardinals. Secondly, Russell nails his flag securely to what is really (at this date) a Fregean masthead in introducing the notion of truth.

One is reminded of the acrimonious correspondence[19] between Frege and Hilbert about the truths of axioms. Hilbert seemed to Frege to take up two mutually inconsistent positions, described at the end of §1.11 of Chapter 1. I can sum up the earlier description by saying that the logical status of axioms (unproved) is for Frege a consequence of an epistemological state of affairs, but, for Hilbert, the matter is entirely a logical one, and the only requirement imposed on an axiom beyond not being proved is that it should not lead to inconsistency. Russell clearly retained, as we shall see, Frege's requirement about truth (possible in some variant form) for the rest of his life and certainly up to *Principia Mathematica*. He himself puts this controversy in a historical perspective shortly afterwards in Part 1:

> Although it was generally agreed that mathematics is in some sense true, philosophers disputed as to what mathematical propositions really meant.

Another aspect of Russell's thought at this time, which will prove important for my later discussion, is his view on variables. He says:

> Mathematical propositions are not only characterised by the fact that they contain implications, but also by the fact that they contain *variables*. The notion of the variable is one of the most difficult with which Logic has to deal, and in the present work a satisfactory theory as to its nature, in spite of much discussion, will hardly be found.

2.15 Chapters IV and V of part 1 make a first attempt at the linguistic analysis which is the predecessor of what is presented more formally in *On Denoting* (see Chapter 3). Russell begins by distinguishing amongst the terms in his discussion into *things* and *concepts*: things are indicated by proper names, but predicates (which correspond, of course, to concepts) differ from other terms particularly from the connection with what Russell calls *denoting*.

> One predicate always gives rise to a host of cognate notions: thus in addition to *human* and *humanity*, which only differ grammatically, we have *man, some man, an man, every man, all men*, all of which appear to be genuinely distinct one from another.

Evidently, then, the notion of denoting is seen by Russell at this stage as a logical one; indeed, the section in which this passage occurs is said by him to be dealing with grammar (philosophical grammar). He then passes on to the question of meaning:

> To have meaning, it seems to me, is a notion confusedly compounded of logical and psychological elements. *Words* all have meaning, in the simple sense that they stand for something other than themselves. But a proposition . . . does not itself contain words; it contains the entities indicated by words.

The first part of this quotation is a reference back to some idealist doctrines of Bradley. The last sentence harks back again to Russell's idiosyncratic view of the proposition. It is not very clear exactly how Russell, at this stage in his development, distinguished between words and things. But this sentence shows a fairly anti-formalist position, which, maintained later, explains his affinity with Wittgenstein. The passage continues:

> Thus meaning, in the sense in which words have meaning, is irrelevant to logic. But such concepts as *a man* have meaning in another sense; they are, so to speak, symbolic in their logical nature, because they have the property which I call *denoting*. That is to say, when *a man* occurs in a proposition (e.g. 'I met a man in the street') the proposition is not about the concept *a man*, but about something quite different, some actual biped denoted by the concept.

A concept denotes, he goes on to say,

> when, if it occurs in a proposition, the proposition is not about the concept but about a term connected in a certain peculiar way with the concept.

His example is 'I met a man', which is not about the concept 'a man' but about a thing, 'an actual man with a tailor and a bank account or a public house and a drunken wife.'

How does denoting arise? Usually through six words which, as well as in everyday life, occur ubiquitously in mathematics: all, every, any, a, some, the. Evidently a phrase with one of these in always denotes, and conversely a denoting phrase consists of a class concept preceded by one of these words (or a synonym of them). Russell sees one of the useful consequences of the idea of denoting as explaining why it is useful to assert identity, as in the sentence 'Edward VII is the King', where one part of the sentence consists of the term and the other of a denoting concept. I shall discuss Russell's views about denoting in more detail in the next chapter.

Part 2 of the *Principles*, in dealing with number, proceeds much on the lines of the paper on relations, and I do not deal with it here except to draw attention to one short passage. Having described Cantor's description of cardinal numbers, it proceeds:

> This is the definition of numbers by abstraction . . . (it) suffers from an absolutely fatal formal defect; it does not show that only one object satisfies the definition.

And, concludes Russell, the best way to remedy this is 'to define as the number of a class the class of all classes similar to the given class'. Peano's objection, that this is impossible, since 'these objects have different properties' gets short shrift: 'He does not tell us what these properties are, and for my part I am unable to discover them'.

The later parts of the book are of less interest now, and I shall content myself with drawing attention to one or two short passages, whose chief interest is the light they throw on the stage of development of Russell's ideas by 1905. In Part

3, on quantity, the chapter on zero contains the rather Kantian remark that it is to deal with 'not the numerical zero, nor yet with the infinitesimal, but with the pure zero of magnitude', noting besides that, although zero is a definite magnitude, no quantity whose magnitude is zero can exist.

It is hard to be sure just what is at issue here but it seems as if the difference is merely between the natural number, zero, (of which all other natural numbers are successors), the integer zero (class of pairs equivalent to $(0, 0)$) coming, as it were 'midway along' the line of integers ..., -3, -2, -1, 0, 1, 2, 3, ..., the rational number zero, and the real number zero (to be defined as a class of rationals). If so, the distinctions will be much clearer in Russell's Part 5 (see below) and could be left till then. For in Part 5, in the chapter on real numbers,

> real numbers are really not numbers at all but something quite different ... A real number, so I shall contend, is nothing but a certain class of rational numbers. Thus the class of rationals less than $\frac{1}{2}$ is a real number, associated with, but obviously different from, the rational number $\frac{1}{2}$.

He is here referring to what is now commonplace in mathematics, Dedekind's construction of the real numbers in terms of classes of rationals. The construction itself is very straightforward: I consider the special example of the Pythagorean dilemma over $\sqrt{2}$. Dedekind calls $\sqrt{2}$ a *cut* (Schnitt) in the rationals; that is, a division into a collection L of all those rationals whose square is less than 2 and a collection R of all those whose square is greater than 2. The real numbers *are* the cuts. If instead of $\sqrt{2}$ I consider $\sqrt{4}$ I have to modify this definition slightly by giving a prescription which allows the possibility of a rational (viz. 2) whose square is actually equal to 4; I simply decide always to put it into one of the two classes, say, into L.

Finally I draw attention to two remarks that serve to show the development of Russell's views. In Chapter XLI of this Part the sentence 'For I hold the paradoxical opinion that what can be mathematically demonstrated is true' is defiantly Fregean. Then in Part 6 Russell says,

> Geometry may be considered as a pure *a priori* science, or as the study

of actual space . . . But it is not in the latter sense that I wish to discuss it
. . . Geometry is the study of series of two or more dimensions.

This evidently shows a shift from the position taken up in the
Foundations of Geometry.

2.16　It remains to say a few words about Russell's appendix on Frege. Some attention has been devoted to this in the
past and to its showing to what extent Russell failed to
understand Frege. He was not, of course, alone in this; but
the contention is a little beside the point for it pays insuffi-
cient attention to Russell's own remarks in the preface. For
what we have in this appendix is very much an immediate
reaction, and an exposition of an allied doctrine to his own
'which appears to be far less well-known than it deserves.'
　It will be best to begin with a few words on Frege's importance as it is seen now. I shall have space only for a summary
treatment which will do less than justice to Frege's thought,
but I will be returning to some points of detail later, in
Chapter 3, as they become relevant. Frege's first great work,
the *Begriffsschrift* of 1879, provided (in an eccentric notation) the first formulations of the theory of quantification by
all or *there exists*, of the theory of identity, and of second
order logic, together with a development of the theory of
relations. This last included a discussion of the ancestral of a
given relation. (The ancestral of a relation R is that relation
which stands in the same relation to R as 'ancestor of' stands
to 'father of'. The problem, whose solution by Frege was
regarded very highly by Russell, is to give a precise definition of the ancestral of R without, of course, any informal
'and so on' phrases.) In 1884 this work was followed by
Frege's first construction of arithmetic from logic, in his
Foundations, and this is worked out in much more detail in
the *Basic Laws of Arithmetic* in 1893 and 1903. To sum up,
then, he denied Kant's view that arithmetic was synthetic *a
priori*, though he accepted Kant's analysis for geometry. For
him, numbers are objects, mathematical concepts are derivable from logical concepts, and likewise with axioms. He was
violently opposed to Mill's view that arithmetic was an
empirical science based on induction, but equally to such

views as those of Locke and Husserl, that the meaning of mathematical terms are the ideas we associate with them.

But, in addition to these important contributions to the philosophy of mathematics, Frege made at least three basic contributions to the philosophy of language. The most important of these is his distinction between *Sinn* and *Bedeutung* (here rendered as sense and reference). Connected with *every* sign, argues Frege, besides what it designates, (its reference) there is also its sense, which contains its 'mode of presentation' (Here sign denotes anything functioning as a proper name, so naming a definite object, but not a concept or a relation.)

Frege's ontology can be seen as the intersection of two distinctions, one between sense and reference, one between functions and objects. One of these grows from the other. The sense/reference distinction is employed to explain the puzzles of sentences under substituion. The relative usefulness of two such sentences as

Venus is the Morning Star

and

Venus is Venus

is tied up in their different senses. Their references are the same. But what are these references? Frege argues that all true propositions have the same reference, and so he is forced to conclude that this reference is the 'truth-value' of the proposition, the True (an object). But there is another language problem which perplexed Frege. How is our finite ability able to deal with the infinite number of expressions in our language? His answer to this is to analyse sentences into separate parts, and to see these parts as 'incomplete' or 'unsaturated', like function symbols in mathematics or logic. A numerical function is the thing expressed by a numerical formula with one or more 'indefinitely indicating' letters. As an example consider the square function $f(x) = x^2$. Then $f(x)$ is not itself a number, but it becomes a number when x, the variable, is replaced by a number (so, $f(1)$, $f(2)$, . . . are numbers). In the particular example of the square function,

$$f(1) = 1, f(2) = 4, f(3) = 9, \ldots$$

And a function φ of a propositional (or a numerical) variable q (or x) assigns a corresponding proposition φq or φx with just the same proviso. Frege prefers to avoid the use of the indicating letter, so would write ( )^2 instead of x^2. Thus for him a function is anything with an empty place, and an object is anything which is not a function.

I turn now to Russell's appendix. His first remark is about Frege's distinction between sense and reference (but rendered by Russell here as *meaning* and *indication*). This, he says, is 'roughly, though not exactly . . . my distinction between a concept as such and what the concept denotes'. It has been argued that this is a basic misunderstanding of Frege by Russell; but, if so, it is one in which he persisted.

He next turns to the Fregean categories of *Begriff* and *Gegenstand*, and to functions. For Russell, *Begriff* is near to *assertion* and *Gegenstand* is *thing*. On the other hand, this interpretation has to be reconciled also with Russell's remark that *Begriff* means nearly the same as *propositional function* (which is another name, of course, for a predicate). Here we enter quite a quicksand, for important and deep distinctions are being mixed up with rather minor questions of notation. Both Frege and Russell would be agreed that allied concepts in logic and mathematics were subsumed under the one name of *function*. In mathematics a function f of a numerical variable x assigns to each number x a corresponding number f(x). The notion of a variable, as Russell says, is fraught with difficulties. I defer discussion of these till Chapter 3.

Frege gives a definition of function which now reads oddly because it starts from the wrong end. It begins with the variable expression f(x), for the possible values of the function, and *removes* x, so as to have left the function f. (This is related to the common but wrong usage of mathematicians who always speak of, for instance, the logarithm function as log x, not simply log.) Russell considers Frege's definition inadequate because of a difficulty which arises if one applies it to the identity function (whose value is given by f(x) = x). For, he claims, if we remove x, we are left with f =, 'we find there is nothing left at all'.

Now it is clear that there is something basically inadequate about Frege's definition, but Russell's argument is not addressed to it. For Russell's argument simply depends on the curious historical fact that it has not been the case that mathematicians ever found the need to invent a notation for the identity function. So that Frege's rule, which applied to f(x) = log x correctly tells one that f = log, appears to give the curious result quoted by Russell. But if, for example, one defines the identity function, I, by Ix = x, one can then write f(x) = Ix, and this allows Frege's rules to be applied, to give f = I.

Coming now to classes, Russell at once admits that

> Frege's theory of classes is very difficult, and I am not sure that I have thoroughly understood it. He gives the name *Wertverlauf* to an entity which appears to be the same as what I call the class as one.

The distinction, to which Russell is referring when he speaks of the 'class as one' is one which arose over a now forgotten confusion, going back to Peirce and Schröder's failure to distinguish clearly between class membership, and being a subclass. Frege argues, correctly, that one cannot identify a class u with the class of which it is the only member, at least when u has more than one member. For if we *could* write u = {u}, then x ε u if and only if x ε {u} that is, if and only if x = u, so that there is a unique x, and u has only one member, contrary to assumption. This argument fails to prove, what is still true, that the identification still cannot be carried through even if u has only one member.

But Russell considers this an argument against the doctrine of classes being understood only in extension. As Gödel says,[1]

> Russell adduces two reasons against the extensional view of classes, namely the existence of (1) the null class, which cannot very well be a collection, and (2) the unit classes, which would have to be identified with their single elements. But it seems to me that these arguments could, if anything, at most prove that the null class and the unit classes (as distinct from their only elements) are fictions . . . not that all classes are fictions.

However Russell says

> In §74, I contended that the argument was met by the distinction bet-

ween the class as one and the class as many, but this contention now seems to me mistaken.

But, of course, there is no need to try to meet the argument. It is correct, and the fact that the extension of {u} is simply the single class u, whereas the extension of u is the (possible multiplicity) of the members of u means that the extensional theory of classes is left undamaged.

2.17 Where, then, do we stand in 1902, when Russell sent *The Principles of Mathematics* to the printer? His knowledge of relations was now extensive and he rightly saw them as a key to numbers, to the foundations of arithmetic, and hence to all of mathematics. But the theory of classes was much less clear; Cantor's theory was plagued by paradoxes, and the same was true of Frege's (for his correspondence with Frege began with Russell drawing the attention of Frege to the devastating consequence of Russell's paradox on Frege's *Grundgesetze*). Russell was still mildly Platonist about mathematics; as for Frege, mathematical objects were logical objects for Russell and their existence was, as it were, a genuine existence in some logical realm. So the class of all classes which were not members of themselves was perhaps no class at all; that is, the answer might lie in there being denoting phrases, like 'the round square', which corresponded to nothing. If the problem of empty reference could be solved, perhaps some progress would have been made towards the solution of the paradoxes?

In 1903 he made a first attempt at a solution, beginning with Frege's idea (following a suggestion made by him in a letter to Russell at the end of 1902[19]) that two non-equivalent functions might yet determine the same class but he came to the conclusion that this was inadequate. In May 1903[3]

I thought I had solved the whole thing by denying classes altogether; I still kept propositional functions and made φ do duty for $\hat{z}\varphi z$. I treated φ as an entity.

The first indication of this theory was perhaps his letter to Frege[19] of May 24:

I received your letter this morning and I am replying to it at once for I believe that I discovered that classes are entirely superflous.

Frege, however, was less impressed (despite his great interest in finding a way round the paradox) for, in November of the following year

> I cannot regard your attempts to make classes entirely dispensable as successful, the reason being that you use function letters in isolation . . .

(which was wholly at variance with Frege's idea of functions as incomplete symbols).

But by then, perhaps unsurprisingly, Russell had given up this approach because he had found that he could, just as easily as before, express Russell's paradox.

> Then in April 1904 I began working at the Contradiction again, and continued at it, with few intermissions, till January 1905. I was throughout much occupied by the question of Denoting, which I thought was probably relevant, as it proved to be.

In his autobiography,[5] Russell goes into more detail:

> Every morning I would sit down before a blank sheet of paper. Throughout the day, with a brief interval for lunch, I would stare at the blank sheet. Often when evening came it was still empty . . . the two summers of 1903 and 1904 remain in my mind as a period of complete intellectual deadlock.

In the next chapter I shall discuss the *On Denoting* paper, which was one crucial step towards Russell's reconciliation with the paradoxes. As Grattan-Guinnes says,[20]

> . . . the nature of the influence of his theory of descriptions on his logical system has never been properly understood, for its full impact occurs only in work which he decided not to publish.

I shall in fact try to argue an even stronger position: that the theory of descriptions is in fact the key that unlocks all of Russell's later philosophy if it is understood in terms of the difficulties that led to its formation. The other step for dealing with the paradoxes was the theory of types, and that will be dealt with later in Chapter 3.

Synopsis

In this chapter the main lines of Russell's development have become clear. He has begun to weld together Cantor's impressive but obscure theory of finite and infinite classes with Frege's painstaking analysis of arithmetic. The technique that Russell has for this is provided by Peano's notation and its further development. The experience with *Geometry* and *Leibniz* gave Russell the insight that Peano's notation would allow a thorough-going development of the foundations of mathematics in terms of relations. He carried this through to a considerable extent for arithmetic, in *The Logic of Relations*. Then the very superiority of his techniques allowed him to see clearly that contradictions were inevitable. Cantor had found contradictions already, without such a formal apparatus, but for that reason, did not take them so seriously.

The formal and precise way in which the contradictions occur for Russell meant that they could not be ignored. Moreover they were present everywhere, even in the careful development of Frege. None the less Russell decided to go ahead with the *Principles of Mathematics* even although the book was bound to be more of a detailed programme for the future establishment of mathematics, when the contradictions had been finally surmounted. In this book he set down clearly the logically later stages in constructing arithmetic, and mathematics, leaving undetermined how to carry out the very early stages, where the contradictions must be dealt with. Already in the *Principles* there is an outline of the theory of descriptions, which Russell is later to see as the clue to solving the contradictions.

Notes

[1] P. Schilpp (ed.), *The Philosophy of Bertrand Russell*, Library of Living Philosophers, Cambridge, 1946. K. Weierstrass (1815–1897) taught Cantor (not to mention Max Planck and H. A. Schwartz). He accomplished a thorough-going reconstruction of mathematical analysis, including the theory of real numbers, and his important contributions had begun already in the forties.

[2] B. Russell, *Mysticism and Logic*, (p. 148) Pelican, London, 1953.

[3] I. Grattan-Guinness, *Dear Russell . . . Dear Jourdain*, Duckworth, 1977.

[4] G. Lichtheim, *Marxism*, Routledge and Kegan Paul, London, 1961 (Second edition 1964) (p. 4).

[5] B. Russell, *The Autobiography of Bertrand Russell*, Vol. 1, Allen & Unwin, 1967.

[6] B. Russell, *Rivista di Matematica* VII, 115, 1900, a translation of which, as *Logic of Relations* appears in B. Russell, *Logic and Knowledge*, (ed. R. C. Marsh), Allen & Unwin, London, 1956.

[7] B. Russell, *Amer. Jour. Math 30*, 222–262, 1908, also to be found in *Logic and Knowledge* (ref. 6), or in J. van Heijenoort, *From Frege to Gödel*, Harvard, Cambridge (Mass.) 1967.

[8] B. Russell, *The Principles of Mathematics*, Cambridge, 1903 (a second edition, Allen & Unwin, London 1937).

[9] E. D. Klemke (ed.), *Essays on Bertrand Russell*, Illinois 1970.

[10] A. J. Ayer, *Russell and Moore: the Analytical Heritage*, Macmillan, London, 1971.

[11] M. Code. Personal communication.

[12] W. R. Hamilton, *Trans. Royal Irish Acad. 17*, 293 (1837).

[13] I. Grattan-Guinness, *Int. Jour. Math. Educ. Sci. Technol. 12*, 9–18, 1981.

[14] C. Burali-Forti, *Rend. del Circolo Mat. di Palermo 11*, 154–164 and 260, 1897. Both of these are translated in J. van Heijenoort, *From Frege to Gödel*, Harvard, Cambridge, (Mass) 1967.

[15] G. H. Moore and A. Garciadiego *Hist. Math. 8*, 319–350, 1981.

[16] C. Burali-Forti, *Rend. del Circolo Mat. di Palermo 8*, 169–179, 1894.

[17] A. J. Ayer, *Russell*, Collins/Fontana, London, 1972.

[18] A. Dorward, *Bertrand Russell*, British Council, London, 1951.

[19] G. Frege, *Philosophical and Mathematical Correspondence*, B. McGuinness (ed.) Blackwell. 1979.

[20] I. Grattan-Guinness, *Hist. Math. 2*, 498–493, 1975.

CHAPTER III

1901–1910 A solution suggested

Section 1: On Denoting

3.1 I have omitted some personal details of Russell's life, since the beginning of Chapter I. It is not possible to understand aspects of such a complex character in isolation. None the less it seemed best to consider the technical details of his early development first. I propose now to touch on those aspects of his personal life which may be of importance to his thought.

He was married for the first time in 1894 and this marriage was for a time very happy. His wife, Alys, came from a strict Philadelphia Quaker background and they were married in London at the Friends Meeting House in St Martin's Lane. So Alys accompanied him to Berlin in 1895, when he was working on the *Geometry* and again, later in the same year, when he returned with the more specific intention of studying German Social Democracy. It was during the first visit to Germany that Russell resolved not to take up any profession, but to become a writer. He was at that time in a sufficiently comfortable financial position to take such a decision. But perhaps what is more important is the light this throws on his comfortable fit into the social pattern. Upbringing is hard to overcome and even twenty-seven years later, with his second wife Dora, a small dispute arose[1]:

> Bertie asked me to tie up a parcel for him. As I happened to be busy I suggested that he might tie it up for himself. 'I have never' he said with great dignity, 'tied up a parcel in my life and I am not going to begin now'.

What is interesting about Russell's 1895 decision is that, though he did not hold fast to it in intention, circumstances dictated that he should fulfil it in practice.

After the Fellowship election, Russell began to read much more widely, and it was also at this period that his close friendship with Whitehead began. In 1895 he visited the United States with Alys, to meet her family, and whilst there he lectured at Bryn Mawr on non-Euclidean Geometry,

and Alys gave addresses in favour of endowment of motherhood, combined with private talks to women in favour of free love. This caused a scandal and we were practically hounded out of the college.[2]

Since Alys's ideas were certainly developed since her marriage, this might be taken as the first of many tussles between Russell and various Establishments.

The Trinity Fellowship did not carry any great burden of duties, but in 1898 'Alys and I began a practice, which we continued till 1902, of spending part of each year at Cambridge.'[2] I have also mentioned in Chapter I the Leibniz lectures which had to be delivered. 1899 brought the Boer War, and Russell, as a Liberal Imperialist, at first supported it. But as the war progressed he changed his position completely and developed a strong, but strictly rational, pacificism. That is to say, he never took up an absolute pacifist position, believing, for example in 1939, that war might be the lesser evil. But both in 1899 and in 1914–18 he could detect no important cause or principle to justify the horror.

I have already mentioned the great importance of the 1900 trip to Paris and the meeting with Peano. But in the following year two separate incidents are worthy of note. The first is mentioned by Russell:[2] the Whiteheads and the Russells were sharing a house in Cambridge. Mrs Whitehead was suffering very much from heart trouble. On one occasion, when she was in particular pain, Russell records

the sense of the solitude of each human soul suddenly overwhelmed me. Within five minutes I went through some such reflections as the following: the loneliness of the human soul is unendurable; nothing can penetrate it except the highest intensity of the sort of love that religious teachers have preached; whatever does not spring from this motive is harmful, or at best useless; it follows that war is wrong, that a public

school education is abominable, that the use of force is to be depre-
cated, and that in human relations one should penetrate to the core of
loneliness in each person and speak to that.

Whilst this revelation had little direct influence on Russell's
philosophical writings, it affected his other activities profoundly. Evidently his years of exact analytical thinking had
been the greater strains for his underlying, essentially religious, temperament. He remained, however, no friend to any
kind of organised theism.

The other incident in 1901 was the attendance at Russell's
lectures on logic of Philip Jourdain. He corresponded with
Russell till 1919 on logic and foundational problems, and
according to Grattan-Guinness[3] 'It seems certain that Russell did not correspond with anyone else about his work in
such great detail.' Jourdain was one of a family of ten; his
eldest sister Eleanor who became Vice Principal of St
Hugh's, Oxford, is known for her book with Annie Moberley, her Principal, in which they describe a visit to Versailles
in 1901 at which they 'saw' Marie Antoinette and her court.
Miss Moberley's father was friendly with Cantor's father,
and his wife was Cayley's aunt. Such is the smallness of
European intellectual circles. The importance of Jourdain
for Russell lies in the number of letters that have been preserved. I have already had occasion to refer to them, as
collected in.[3]

From 1901–2 onwards work had begun towards *Principia
Mathematica*, but the contradictions began to emerge. And a
parallel development was taking place in Russell's personal
life. Each must surely have aggravated the other. 'I realised
that I no longer loved Alys.'[2] The other side of the revelation
which came with Mrs Whitehead's pain was an uncomfort-
able honesty in personal relations which meant that the
change could not be concealed. Both partners went through
great misery, though 'I was determined that no difficulty
should turn me aside from the completion of *Principia
Mathematica*.'[2] However 'In 1905 things began to improve'
and this was the case on the intellectual side too. Russell's
theory of Descriptions, with which this chapter begins, was a
first step towards a solution of the contradictions, and the
Theory of Types, with which it ends, was the second step,

and the one that allowed *Principia Mathematica* to be completed.

3.2 Russell's paper *On Denoting*[4] appeared in *Mind* in 1905. It may not be fanciful to draw a comparison between the work of Russell, always a very scientific philosopher, and the activity in physics. For 1905 was also the date of publication of three papers by Einstein, one on the Brownian motion, one on radiation which was important in the development of the quantum theory, and the famous *On the Electrodynamics of Moving Bodies* which set up the special theory of relativity.

As Robert Marsh notes in the editorial matter of *Logic and Knowledge*,[4] Russell's paper bears little relation to the rest of the contents of the volume about which

> One would assume . . . that the conflict between idealists and pragmatists over the nature of truth was the most important thing in the world.'

By contrast, *On Denoting* deals ostensibly with a purely linguistic matter. It is about a question that is of importance in both natural language and in formalised languages. Russell does not draw that distinction – indeed it could be argued that a sharp distinction, unblurred by the ideas that natural language was trying to approximate formal, or *vice versa*, did not appear till Carnap and Tarski, in about 1935.

Russell himself called the paper his 'finest philosophical essay'. Certainly I shall argue that the ideas in it are the key to all his subsequent thought. I shall, accordingly, discuss it, and its context, in considerable detail.

As he says early on in the paper, the general lines of the theory had been referred to already in the *Principles of Mathematics*[5] but the detailed theory there was 'nearly the same as Frege's' and quite different from this one. Whether or not Frege would have accepted the sameness of the earlier theory, it is certainly the case that a warm and friendly correspondence[6] had taken place between the two from June 1902 to the end of 1904. The theory in the 1905 paper was grealy influenced by this: Russell's acquaintance with Frege's ideas was no longer that of a hasty meeting. And if he failed to come to a full understanding and agreement, this will be seen to be the result of a different philosophical starting-point. It might well be said that, at least to some extent, *On Denoting* is not criticising Frege but Russell's own earlier views, which he thought were Frege's. But what is very clear, as Quine says,[7] is that with this paper

> . . . a reformed Russell emerges . . . fed up with Meinong's impossible objects. The reform was no simple change of heart; it hinged on his discovery of a means of dispensing with the unwelcome objects. The device was Russell's theory of singular descriptions, . . . it involved defining a term . . . by providing equivalents of all desired sentences containing the term.

In this section I shall begin my description of the paper by considering the problems which it is intended to solve. Then I shall go on to explain the central role that Russell attributes to the notion of a *variable*. This notion had earlier been examined by Frege and so, in §3.3, I begin to consider Frege's approach, which is closely connected with his related distinction between *Sinn* and *Bedeutung*. In §3.4 I turn to a more exhaustive consideration of variables in mathematics, since this formed a model for the understanding of their use in logic by both Russell and Frege. It transpires, however, that Russell, in stating the importance of the notion of variable, has stated less than the whole truth. It is not just the use of a variable x, which may or may not possess a property expressed by a predicate φ. Rather it is that of a quantified variable, expressing such sentences as 'For all $x, \varphi x$' which is important, and this raises two ontological questions which are dealt with in §3.5: the question of the existence or otherwise of such variables, and the question of the various notions of existence which the use of such quantified variables are intended to express. In §3.6 I return to considering the details of Russell's paper, and deal with his analysis of denoting phrases, Then §3.7 deals with his demonstration that his theory does solve the problems. To end Russell's paper, I consider in §3.8 at some length his rejection of Frege's *Sinn und Bedeutung* and explain why I cannot agree with Russell here. Finally, in this section, in §3.9, I describe the 'substitutional theory' which was the most direct application of *On Denoting*, and which contained some seeds of the

theory of types with which Russell was to make his ultimate
attack on the paradoxes.

The 1905 paper begins by defining a *denoting phrase* by a
reversal of the procedure in the earlier discussion; that is, it
is now defined as 'a phrase such as any one of the following:
a man, some man, any man, every man, all men, the present
King of England, the present King of France . . .' In the
Principles, it will be recalled, a concept is said to denote if,
when it occurs in a proposition, the proposition is not about
the concept 'but about a term connected with a certain
peculiar way with the concept'. This definition evidently suf-
fers from two defects; to *occur in a proposition* is far from
unambiguous. Indeed, it will transpire in the discussion of
both *Principia Mathematica* and of the mutual influences of
Russell and Wittgenstein, in Chapter 4, that the question of
an object or a concept occurring in a proposition needs careful treatment. More seriously, at the present juncture, *a
certain peculiar way* is far from precise. Of course, in the
Principles this definition is helped along by an explanation,
viz., that denoting usually arises by one of six words (all,
every, any, a, some, the), and this is essentially the definition
chosen in the paper. As well as being tidier, the second
version is better suited to the style of *Mind* in 1905, even if it
carries a linguistic taint which must then have seemed novel.

Russell's next step is to remark that a phrase is denoting
solely in virtue of its form, so that he regards denoting as a
logical property. But he then goes on at once to link it with
epistemological properties, distinguishing between *acquaintance with* a thing and *knowledge about* it. It is the second
kind which is stated by a denoting phrase; the first comes by
a presentation of the thing. Thus acquaintance comes from
perception; knowledge about through thought. These distinctions, important in this paper, become even more so in
considering Russell's later work. As Gödel has remarked[8]

> What strikes one as surprising . . . is Russell's pronouncedly realistic
> attitude . . . The fact that Russell does not consider this whole question
> of the interpretation of descriptions as a matter of mere linguistic con-
> ventions, but rather as a question of right and wrong, is another exam-
> ple of his realistic attitude . . .

I shall illustrate this at some length from Russell's paper of five years later, *Knowledge by Acquaintance and Knowledge by Description*.[9] He begins this by explaining that he is concerned to answer the question of what it is that we know when we know propositions about 'the so-and-so' without knowing what it is. For example, 'The candidate with most votes will be elected'. This is knowledge by description; knowledge by acquaintance is intended to refer to a direct cognitive relation, say with sense-data. This is meant quite strictly, so that we are not acquainted with physical objects or with other people's minds. We can distinguish ambiguous descriptions ('a so-and-so') and definite descriptions (the so-and-so); to say that the so-and-so exists means that there is just one object fulfilling the description. Thus proper names are usually descriptions.

> The fundamental epistemological principle in the analysis of propositions containing descriptions is this: Every proposition which we can understand must be composed wholly of constituents with which we are acquainted.

For example, Julius Caesar cannot be a constituent of one of my propositions; in all such cases we substitute a description. The reason that

Scott is the author of *Waverley*

is valuable, whereas

Scott is Scott

is only a case of the law of identity is explained (in rather the same way as by Frege) by noting that the two sentences have the same denotation but different meanings. The denotation is not a constituent of the proposition except in the case of proper names, for we may know the proposition but not be acquainted with the denotation (which, indeed, as for the 'round square', may not exist). The importance of this analysis of 'the author of *Waverley*' shows up when we want to say

The author of *Waverley* is the author of *Marmion*

for the 'is' asserts identity, but the meanings of the two phrases are not identical:

the only escape is to say that 'the author of *Waverley*' does not, by itself, have a meaning, though phrases of which it is a part do have a meaning.

What then is the precise theory in *On Denoting* which Russell is to put forward, and what is it to do? The answer to the second question is, that it is to deal with the three related problems of reference. These problems are (i) the nature of empty reference, if we are regarding denoting phrases 'as standing for genuine constituents of the propositions in whose verbal expressions they occur.' For then we are put in the position of asserting that the present King of France both exists (as a 'genuine constituent') and does not exist (because France is a republic) and this conflicts with the law of contradiction. This is, in Quine's phrase 'the old Platonic riddle of nonbeing. Nonbeing must in some sense be, otherwise, what is it that there is not?'

(ii) The problem of identity and the substitution of identical terms. For if we assert that 'Scott was the author of Waverley', then it seems to follow that we may substitute 'Scott' for 'the author of Waverley' in any sentence in which it occurs without affecting its truth-value. But if we make this substitution in the original sentence, it becomes 'Scott was Scott', a particular case of the law of identity, 'a is a', and so uninformative.

(iii) The related difficulty, in the case of empty reference, over the law of excluded middle. For this seems to imply that exactly one of 'The present King of France is bald' and 'The present King of France is not bald' must be true, yet if we list those people who are bald and those who are not bald, the present King of France will not occur in either list.

As to the first question, Russell declares boldly

I take the notion of the *variable* as fundamental; I use 'C(x)' to mean a proposition in which x is a constituent, where x the variable, is essentially and wholly undetermined.

Before I go on to explain how Russell's theory tackles the problems of reference, I need, then, to say something about earlier discussions particularly that of Frege, which influenced Russell, and also about the new problem introduced by the concept of a *variable*.

I turn to these matters in §3.3, but I conclude this present discussion by drawing attention once more to the continuity of Russell's thought. It is not immediately apparent that *On Denoting* is a study of a particular problem in treating relations. For, instead of seeing a relation holding between x and y, in the way suggested by the notation xRy, it is also possible to see it as a suitable property, say R^* of the pair (x, y). Thus, $R^*(x, y)$ holds if and only if xRy. This means that there is no sharp distinction between the theory of relations and that of predicates, or propositional functions. The whole theory of *On Denoting*, being based on expressions like C(x), will include as a special case the corresponding results on relations.

3.3   As early as 1892 Frege[10] says 'Equality gives rise to challenging questions . . . Is it a relation? A relation between objects, or between names of objects?' He has preferred the second alternative in his 1879 *Begriffsschrift* since a = a and a = b are obviously statements of differing cognitive value and this seems to rule out the first alternative. This is evidently an elliptical reference to problem (ii) above. Again, in a geometrical example, if a triangle is considered with the three lines joining each vertex to the mid-point of the opposite side – call these three lines *a*, *b*, *c* – then, since it is known that the three lines meet in a point, the phrase 'point of intersection of *a, b*' refers to the same point as the phrase 'point of intersection of *b* and *c*'. The two phrases are differ-

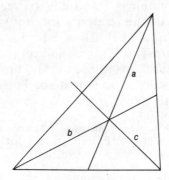

Figure 13

ent modes of presentation of the point; and so it is natural, and this is the crucial step in Frege's argument, to think of *any* sign as corresponding (a) to the thing it designates (here, the point), which may be called its *reference* (see note 9 again), (b) to its mode of presentation, which Frege calls its *sense*.

What makes Frege's argument obscure here is a lack of symmetry between the treatment of sense and reference. The reference, being an object, is defined quite precisely; but the sense is not so defined. All that is really provided by Frege is a criterion for when the senses of two signs are the same or different, not a statement of what the sense is. The situation is very like that criticised by Russell in Cantor's treatment of cardinal numbers: and it is odd that Russell does not recognise it and deal with it in the same way. I shall return to this below.

Russell is certainly intending to take most of Frege's argument on board; but, as their correspondence shows, there is an important difference. For Frege, starting from this assumption about any sign, applies it in particular to a sentence or proposition which he regards as a complex of signs. The main line of Frege's argument is, firstly, that a sentence such as a = b contains a thought, so, secondly, this thought must be either its sense or reference. This was the sticking point for Russell in Frege's argument. Russell accepted that sense and reference could be distinguished in this way for proper names, but he considered sentences as exceptional, and propositions even more so since they do not contain signs, but things. Returning to Frege's argument, the thought cannot be the reference for, if it were, the substitution difficulty (iii above) arises. Substitution gives another sentence of the same reference; and yet the thought changes between a = b and a = a. So, thirdly, the thought must be unchanged by substitutions and so, Frege concludes, can only be the truth-value. So

> . . . all true sentences have the same reference and so, on the other hand, do all false sentences. From this we see that in the reference of the sentence all that is specific is obliterated.

Russell found himself, as I said, unable to accept this application of an analysis based on proper names to propositions. He writes to Frege in February 1903,[6]

> I have read your essay on sense and reference, but I am still in doubt about your theory of truth-values, if only because it appears paradoxical to me. I believe that a judgment, or even a thought, is something so entirely peculiar that the theory of proper names has no application to it.

Frege's attempts to counter this in later letters do not actually tackle the main point, which had already arisen between them in October 1902. He wrote then to Russell,[6]

> Your example of propositions like 'p ε m ⊃ p' prompts me to ask the question: 'What is a proposition?' German logicians understand by it the expression of a thought, a group of audible or visible signs expressing a thought. But you evidently mean the thought itself. This is how mathematicians tend to use the word.

Frege here has in mind, presumably, the mathematicians' use of such words as *theorem*, which is, of course, synonymous with a proved proposition, though the words have acquired different overtones in mathematics. They certainly would not regard the theorem of Pythagoras as identical with a statement of the theorem. Frege continues: 'I prefer to follow the logicians in their usage'.

As Quine says,[7]

> Frege's three-way distinction between the expression, what it means, and what if anything it refers to, did not come naturally to Russell.

Indeed, it never really reached him at all. Neither the earlier nor the later arguments convinced him. At the end of 1904 he wrote,[6]

> Concerning sense and reference, I see nothing but difficulties which I cannot overcome. I explained the reasons why I cannot accept your view in the appendix to my book, and I still agree with what I wrote there. I believe that in spite of all its snowfields Mont Blanc itself is a component part of what is actually asserted in the proposition 'Mont Blanc is more than 4000 metres high'. We do not assert the thought, for that is a private psychological matter; we assert the object of the thought, and this is, to my mind, a certain complex (an objective proposition, one might say).

Such different views about the nature of a proposition inevitably led Frege and Russell to different views on sense and reference. Russell could even accept Frege's attribution of both sense and reference to *any* sign (though it is not clear that he did) but still dissent in the case of propositions, which were not just the signs representing them.

3.4   As to variables, Russell seems at this stage to be perfectly happy with the concept of the mathematical variable. This concept is then capable of an easy extension to the idea of a logical variable (which may be a proposition) *provided the original concept is understood*. Now mathematicians have always been exceedingly sloppy about their actual usage of variables, expecting the context to make clear the difference between, for example, the two *expressions*

$$x^2 + 5x + 6 = (x + 2)(x + 3),$$

and the assertion, which is to be understood as an identity, true for all values of x, and the *equation*

$$x^2 + 5x + 6 = 0,$$

whose solutions ($x = -2$ or $x = -3$) are sought.

They are also frequently careless (and were more often so in the nineteenth century) about the existential assumptions involved, leaving these to the context as well. So, of course,

$$x^2 + 5x + 6 = 0$$

has no solutions if x is to be a natural number, and therefore, if solutions *are* asked for, some larger number-system, for example, the integers, is automatically implied. The use of the word *imaginary* for quantities involving $\sqrt{-1}$ is a reminder of an earlier ontological confusion engendered by this carelessness.

But usage is not the question here, though it will appear later. Rather it is this: a basic problem of ontology is under consideration. The question is whether, for instance, the present King of France is to be considered as part of the furniture of the world. In this situation the ontological status of variables equally needs consideration. This point, too, had already been taken up, in mathematics, by Frege in 1904.[11]

He starts there from the related idea, in mathematical analysis, of *function*. The relation between the ideas is this: if one questions why the idea of variable ever needs to enter mathematics, the most satisfactory answer seems to be that it is used to express the idea of a function. Other uses can be derived from this one in a more or less natural manner.

The notion of function has been explained, Frege says, in two ways, either by means of the idea of a mathematical expression, or in terms of a variable. Examples would be, for $f(x) = x^2 + 5x + 6$, the two explanations (i) that the value of f for any number is derived by squaring, adding 5 times the number and adding 6, (ii) that the expression written for $f(x)$ gives the value of $f(x)$ for a variable x. It is clear that the difference is largely verbal; both ways of looking at the function use the idea of a variable, though the second is more overt and both are expressions of a rule for calculation. But, argues Frege, about variables, any variation occurs in time, and yet analysis has nothing to do with time. Besides, what varies? A magnitude – say, a length – but analysis deals with numbers, not magnitudes. How can there be variable numbers? And

> ... what is the difference between the variables that are said to be designated by 'x' and 'y'? We cannot say.

Frege's way out of this difficulty is discussed in his 1891 essay on *Function and Concept*.[12] He begins there with the idea of a function as an incomplete or unsaturated expression; he would write instead of the more usual expression above,

$$f = (.\,.\,.\,.)^2 + 5(.\,.\,.\,.) + 6.$$

Then

> An object is anything that is not a function, so that an expression for it does not contain an empty place.

The technical device for defining objects recalls Russell's earlier definition of points in geometry as the terms of relations. He must have felt Frege's approach congenial. Frege goes on to argue

A statement contains no empty place, and therefore we must take its reference as an object. But the reference of a statement is a truth-value. Thus the two truth-values are objects.

But, returning to mathematics, it is far from being merely a technical difficulty to point out that Frege's analysis runs into trouble over functions like $f(x, y) = x^2 - y^2$ of more than one variable. A modern way out, which would preserve Frege's argument by a technical trick, would be to define two functions p, q of the ordered pair (x,y) by

$$p((x, y)) = x, \qquad q((x, y)) = y$$

and then to define $f = p(\quad)^2 - q(\quad)^2$. But this would not have been acceptable to Frege, for even the concept of the ordered pair was not very clear before 1914, although it was widely used in analytical geometry. He would probably have taken refuge, as he does in his *Begriff und Gegenstand*,[13] in

> *Complete* and *unsaturated* are of course only figures of speech: but all that I wish or am able to do here is to give hints.

To return to the ontological question about variables, the point I wish to argue is this: there is indeed an ontological puzzle here but it is not the one with which we are concerned. Since any investigation that discusses the present King of France is bound to be concerned with considerable ontological subtleties, it is essential to keep the independent puzzle about variables out of the way. Now there is a way of doing this; it is to eliminate variables from the discussion altogether. This is not, of course, put forward as a convenient way of actually carrying out the argument. The important thing is to recognise the possibility of the elimination. Once that is clear, one can restore the more convenient treatment using variables with the reassurance that no mysterious ontological commitment is thereby produced.

This method of proceeding was, in fact, not clarified for half a century, so, in order to throw some light on it I am forced to be anachronistic and refer forward to what has been done since. This is the easiest way of seeing what the difficulties are. For the sake of this short explanation, I confine myself, as Frege did, to mathematical variables. I shall follow a small part of the treatment given by Curry and Feys in 1958.[14] Their discussion begins with a logical formula but it could equally be a mathematical one. In effect they ask about the meaning of such a statement as

$$x^2 - y^2 = (x + y)(x - y).$$

Certainly, they claim, the statement concerns neither the symbols 'x', 'y', nor any objects they denote. Rather, they say, what is asserted is a relation between the operations of addition, substraction and multiplication. The symbols, or variables, are convenient fictions for explaining this relation.

There is an analogy here, but also an important difference, from Russell's introduction of points in the *Geometry* and Frege's introduction of objects noted above. For Russell begins with relations as the primary objects; these relations then have to be filled out with terms. These terms are points. But for Russell this did not make the points fictions; it was only that the relations were logically prior. The reality of the relations, I think he would have argued, bring reality to the points as well. Frege would have said something similar. If one does not take this rather Platonic view, a fresh difficulty arises. Could it be that this embodiment of the relation in terms of these new entities could bring in *more* than intended?

The only way to answer this question is to try to see whether it is possible to eliminate the variables. This suggestion was made by Schönfinkel in 1924.[15] His approach was a very formalist one: that is, he tackled the problem of elimination of variables in a formal language, regarding the expressions in the language simply as strings of symbols. But although the whole climate of ideas in Schönfinkel's approach is therefore completely alien to both Frege and Russell, his analysis is just as valuable. For suppose, as I shall show, that it is possible to express all the results which use variables in mathematics (and the same for logic) in alternative forms without explicit use of variables. Then it will be clear that no spurious material has been introduced, and so it is quite safe to use the variables as a technique. They have not involved one in any ontological commitment; there is no need for an additional domain of variables, beside the domain of the natural numbers, in the real furnishing of the world.

Schönfinkel effected his elimination, over a considerable range, by means of two symbols called combinators; using a later notation these could be called S, K, where S converts any string xyz to xz(yz) and K converts xy to x. Let us use the arrow, →, as shorthand for 'converts to' so that

$$Sxyz \rightarrow xz(yz),$$
$$Kxz \rightarrow x.$$

It would be misleading to use equality, since other established conventions would cause this to lead to severe confusions over substitution.

The whole subject was carried much further by Curry from 1929 onwards, and by Church, from a slightly different point of view, beginning in 1932. Curry introduced some further combinators:

$$Ix \rightarrow x,$$
$$Cxyz \rightarrow xzy$$
$$Wxy \rightarrow xyy,$$
$$Bxyz \rightarrow x(yz),$$

as well as

$$\psi xyzw \rightarrow x(yz)(yw),$$

though these combinators are not all independent. Of course the combinator technique is a complex and unusual one and I shall not need to enter into all its ramifications. But one or two points must be mentioned. It is important to realise that combinators do not act only on variables but on other combinators if these are present; and also to realise that it will be necessary, in evaluating a conversion, always to start with the most left-ward combinator. Brackets round combinators, or round variables, simply mean that the bracketed symbols are to be treated as a single element.

I do not think it is possible to appreciate the subtlety of this elimination of variables without attending to at least one detailed elimination. The example of $x^2 - y^2$ mentioned above is not sufficiently easy, so I consider instead four of the properties of a number-system that I mentioned in the last chapter, viz.,

$$x + y = y + x, \qquad xy = yx,$$
$$x + (y + z) = (x + y) + z, \qquad x(yz) = (xy)z.$$

I omit the remaining property, $x(y + z) = xy + xz$, since this needs considerably more ingenuity to express without variables. These properties are, as I said above, not properties of the variables x, y, z but of the two operations A, M of addition and multiplication. We cannot now use brackets in the way we have just done in expressing the properties, since, as already explained, we need them for a somewhat different purpose with the combinators. So we plump instead for a bracketless notation, writing

$$\text{Axy} \qquad \text{for } x + y$$

and

$$\text{Mxy} \qquad \text{for } xy,$$

when the four properties become

$$\text{Axy} = \text{Ayx}, \qquad \text{Mxy} = \text{Myx},$$
$$\text{AxAyz} = \text{AAxyz}, \qquad \text{MxMyz} = \text{MMxyz}.$$

Such a bracketless notation, often called Polish notation because of its use by the famous Polish school of logicians in the 1930s has been quite widely used in logic. Here I am using it in arithmetic. The only reason that it has never until recently commended itself there is that there is already a conflicting place-value convention to do with writing digits next to each other, as 21, to denote 'twenty-one'. So that although A23 is quite unambiguous, and is a symbol for 5, A123 might be $12 + 3 = 15$ or $1 + 23 = 24$. But I can use Polish notation here since I shall not be substituting particular numbers and so no confusion will arise. The advent of hand-held calculators, some of which are programmed in Polish notation, has now provided practical evidence that the convention can work in arithmetic.

The first two of the four formulae can be expressed by employing the combinator C. For, from its definition,

$$\text{CAxy} \rightarrow \text{Ayx},$$

and so the first formula is

$$Axy = CAxy.$$

Evidently the variables no longer play any role, so that this equation may equally be written as

$$A = CA.$$

The other one of the first two formulae is similarly equivalent to

$$M = CM.$$

In much the same way,

$$CAxAyz \rightarrow AAxyz,$$

so that the other two formulae are equivalent to

$$AA = CAA, \qquad MM = CMM.$$

It may be argued that nothing has been achieved here since, although no variables appear in the final versions of the formulae, combinators occur, and the behaviour of the combinators was originally defined by using variables. This argument is, perhaps, valid as an opposition to the simplified version of the theory given here, but I have used variables to express it only to avoid a long digression. In fact, it would have been possible to set up a complete theory of combinators to stating a sufficient number of axioms which they satisfy. These axioms then define the behaviour of the combinators, without using variables. That is to say, the axioms give the meaning when the combinators *are* applied to strings of variables. For the meaning of a combinator is its use.

If it is granted that such a complete theory of combinators can be set up, then it follows that this analysis is not simply a re-interpretation. Instead it is a demonstration that the ideas concerned are quite independent of the variables usually used to express them.

Of course it is not claimed that anything of practical value is achieved by this elimination of variables. The final result is a good deal less transparent than the original. But the important point is that the variables are exhibited as harmless fictions, and so they bring no ontological commitment with them, for the relations can be expressed without them. Indeed, recalling the motivation for the theory of descriptions coming from the consideration of the paradoxes, it is worth remarking that the relatively weak logical system of Curry and Feys is still strong enough to contain Russell's paradox. The technical details of this are too far from my present topic to be worth pursuing.[16] But since Russell's paradox can appear without variables it may be conjectured that, at least as far as its discussion is concerned, no great harm can come from adopting the convenience of using them.

3.5 If variables can be eliminated, then, Russell can be cleared of any charge of prior ontological commitment by introducing them. But, on the other hand, it becomes puzzling how a convenient fiction can play the part of the fundamental concept of the theory. The answer to this puzzle lies in the next sentence of the paper: for having introduced the propositional function $C(x)$, he considers the two notions 'C(x) is always true', 'C(x) is sometimes true'; and evidently the vital concept is not just that of a variable, but that of, to use the modern term, quantifying a propositional function. In the notation used later in *Principia Mathematica*, and still widely used, the two notions would be written as

$$(x)C(x), \qquad (\exists x)C(x).$$

Russell chooses to take the first of these, together with the notion of *negation* ($\sim p$ to mean that p is false), as basic. Then the second is definable in terms of the first by

$$(\exists x)C(x) \quad \text{if and only if} \quad \sim(x)(\sim C(x)).$$

He abbreviates $(x)C(x)$ as $C(\text{everything})$, with similar abbreviations for $(\exists x)C(x)$, $(x)\sim C(x)$, and then remarks

> *Everything, nothing* and *something* are not assumed to have any meaning in isolation, but a meaning is assigned to *every* proposition in which they occur.

In the same way

... denoting phrases never have any meaning in themselves, but every proposition in whose verbal expression they occur has a meaning.

This seems at first an odd approach; but less so when one compares it with the tenor of the better kind of Cambridge mathematics at this time. G. H. Hardy in his *Pure Mathematics*,[17] evidently building on a continuing tradition, takes just the same line about *infinity*, when he says:

Later on we shall learn how to attach a meaning to other phrases involving the symbol ∞, but the reader will always have to bear in mind (1) that ∞ *by itself* means nothing, although *phrases containing it* sometimes mean something. (2) that in every case in which a phrase containing the symbol ∞ means something it will do so simply because we have previously attached a meaning to this particular phrase by means of a special definition.

The general idea of quantification is, of course, very old, but in 1905 quantifying a propositional function was somewhat more recent. Frege in his *Begriffsschrift*,[18] having employed the symbol ⊢A for the judgment A, that is, for the judgment that A is true, introduces

$$\vdash\!\!\!\!\!\smile\!\!\!a\!\!\smile\!\!\!\!\!- \varphi(a)$$

for what we have just written as $(x)\varphi(x)$. And since he has, by then introduced ⊢⊤— A for the judgment that A is false, he has the notation

$$\vdash\!\!\top\!\!\!\smile\!\!\!a\!\!\smile\!\!\top\!\!\!- \varphi(a)$$

for $(\exists x)\varphi(x)$. But it would be wrong to assume that in 1905 ideas on quantification were at all rigid, or particularly clear. For example, twelve years later (and after the publication of *Principia Mathematica*) Hermann Weyl[19] was proposing a logical system, based on the notion of atomic propositions which represent facts and which can be combined in various ways. These combinations included three usual logical compositions (negation, or, and) and three others:

(a) identification, so that from φxy is derived $Fx = \varphi xx$,
(b) substitution, so that from φxyz is derived

$$Gxy = \varphi xy\alpha$$
(for some fixed α)

(c) quantification, so that from φxyz is derived

$$Hxy = \varphi xy^*.$$

the * representing an empty place (compare Frege!). The interpretation to be given here was existential quantification, so that, in the notation used above,

$$Hxy = (\exists z)\varphi xyz.$$

Recognizing, then, the important role played in Russell's theory by quantifying a propositional function, I must complete my argument about the ontological harmlessness of variables by taking up again the question of their elimination and of Russell's ontological commitment. The question of 'quantifiers without variables' is much less clear than was my earlier discussion on combinatory logic. If, for example, we refer again to the standard work of Curry and Feys,[14] we find that the whole book contains no existential quantifier, in contrast to the earlier theory of Church where

the existential quantifier is introduced in such a way as to imply that sets or other abstract objects exist.

Rather the approach of Curry and Feys is to take any free variable as universally quantified, which is, in effect, what I did in my example of the four conditions which a number-system must satisfy. For in taking $A = CA$ as representing $Axy = Ayx$, that is $x + y = y + x$, the motivation is that the statement is to be read as holding for all x and y. In the notation used above, we should really write

$$(x)(y)(x + y = y + x).$$

Mathematicians habitually leave the expression of such universal quantifiers to the context; and even logicians often employ the convention of not writing initial universal quantifiers. But to recognise that such initial quantifiers can be taken for granted (and so present no problem) does not carry the argument very far, as can be seen from such an expression as $(x)(\exists y)(z)\varphi xyz$. It is much more difficult to express such statements without variables, but not impossible. To quote Ayer:[20]

> Whether [the] logical constants are bound to include the signs for quantified variables is a matter of debate . . . [That they are theoretically dispensable] is, in fact, the conclusion at which Professor Quine arrives in his paper *Variables explained away*.

I shall not follow Quine's path here but I shall pursue the policy of removing variables, as far as possible, by a rather simple technique. And it will be found that this simplified elimination of variables is adequate to deal with the sentences that occur in *On Denoting*.

Now the core of the trouble here is evidently the need for an existential quantifier. It is one thing to define this in terms of the universal quantifier by $(\exists x)\varphi x$ if and only if $\sim(x)\sim\varphi x$; but it is quite another to think of this in terms of such an emotive term as *existence*. Grattan-Guinness has drawn attention to at least five senses of existence which occur in Russell's correspondence (particularly with Jourdain) about this time. The first is the conventional existence of an individual in the normal existential quantification $(\exists x)\varphi x$. The second, which is different, refers to the existence of a reference for a denoting phrase. Russell symbolises this by

$$E!(\exists x)(\varphi x),$$

which can be rephrased as

$$(\exists b)[\varphi x \quad \text{if and only if} \quad x = b].$$

The symbol $(\exists x)$ (where $\exists$ is the Greek 'iota' upside down) is the same quantifier as that introduced in Chapter 2, with the interpretation 'the (unique) x such that . . .' It could be defined in terms of the others by

$$(\exists x)\varphi x = a \quad \text{if and only if} \quad [\varphi a \ \& \ (x)(\text{If } \varphi x, \text{ then } x = a)].$$

In some ways the symbolism here tends to underestimate the importance of the ideas. But Reichenbach,[8] for example, sees as Russell's main technical improvement in logic the fact that his

... concept of propositional function extends the concept of *class* to that of a relation ... Using the iota-symbol introduced by Peano, Russell showed the way to the understanding of the definite article 'the', and the similar particles of speech.

Thirdly, Russell asserts existence of a class or of a propositional function by a conventional existential quantifier, $(\exists u)$. But a fourth variant, in the case of classes, arises in the discussion of paradoxes, and of whether or not a class u, does indeed correspond to a propositional function, φ. He writes Eu to mean $(\exists\varphi)(x \, \varepsilon \, u$ if & only if $\varphi x)$. Fifthly, existence of a class may refer to its non-emptiness, so that $\exists!u$ is to mean $(\exists x)(x \, \varepsilon \, u)$. In this section, and later, it will be important to bear in mind the particular kind of existence implied by Russell's context.

It is perhaps relevant to point out, once again, a difference in emphasis over apparently similar logical positions between Russell, the more formalist logicians and others, and the mathematicians. This difference rests on Russell's preoccupation with truth, indeed, with certain truth, rather than with consistency. An example of this, from as late as 1946, is in his reply to his critics in,[8] about the truth or otherwise of the law of excluded middle. He writes,

> My argument for the law of excluded middle and against the definition of 'truth' in terms of 'verifiability' is not that it is impossible to construct a system on this basis, but rather that it is possible to construct a system on the opposite basis, and that this wider system, which embraces unverifiable truths, is necessary for the interpretation of beliefs which none of us, if we are sincere, are prepared to abandon.

And as for excluded middle so for the rest of logic.

3.6   It is time to leave the exploitation of Russell's underlying concepts and turn to the details of the theory. I shall give these as he presents them, and re-interpret the examples, as appropriate. He takes the various denoting phrases in turn. Such a denoting phrase as 'I met a man' is to be rendered in terms of two propositional functions. C denotes meeting so that Ca means: *I met a*, and H denotes humanity. In *Mind* of 1905, of course, only the male half is implied. The denoting phrase is then rendered by the statement:

$$(\exists x)(Cx \ \& \ Hx).$$

The point here, as Russell says, is that, if this is true, then it is also the case that I met some definite man: but that is *not* what I seek to assert here. The phrase 'All men are mortal' is analysed, with acknowledgement to Bradley's view of it as a hypothetical, using Mx for 'x is mortal', as

$$(x)(\text{If } Hx, \text{ then } Mx).$$

So far as these two examples go, there is no real problem in removing variables. It will of course be necessary to introduce the concept of a propositional function C holding for everything, as Russell does. A convenient abbreviation would be $\bar{C}$, so that $\bar{C}$ is equivalent to $(x)Cx$. Then an existential statement is given by:

$$(\exists x)Cx \quad \text{if and only if} \quad \sim(x) \sim Cx,$$

which would now read $\sim \overline{\sim C}$. We could abbreviate this as $\dot{C}$, so that $\dot{C} = \sim \overline{\sim C}$. Then the first sentence can be analysed as $\dot{K}$, where $K = C \ \& \ H$, and the second as $\overline{L}$, where

$$L = \text{If } H, \text{ then } M.$$

The phrases some men, any man, every man are of course translated in exactly the same symbolic form, and so no new considerations arise. The remaining interpretation, and this is the most interesting and difficult, concerns phrases containing 'the', because this involves uniqueness. This affords, as I said above, the most important example of Russell's analysis of the basic logical concepts. The example of 'The father to Charles II was executed' asserts, according to Russell, the existence of a unique man, who was father to Charles II. We ought to ignore the accidental element of uniqueness implied by what we know of the property of being a father. It also asserts that he was executed. So it should be rendered

$$(\exists x)[Bx \ \& \ Ex \ \& \ (y)(\text{If } By \text{ then } y = x)],$$

where Bx stands for 'x begat Charles II' and Ex for 'x was

executed', or, in terms of the iota symbol, $E\{(\imath x)Bx\}$.

There is no doubt that Russell saw this at the time, as I would now, as the important aspect of the paper; in 1907 he wrote to Jourdain[14]

> You know that my paper 'On Denoting' is summed up in the following definition . . .

$$\psi\{(\imath x)(\phi x)\} . = : (\exists c) : \phi x . \equiv_x x = c : \psi c \quad Df,$$

which is equivalent to that written above. And writing to him on somewhat similar lines in 1906 (and enclosing a copy of the paper) he goes on to say

> Thus $(\imath x)(\phi x)$ by itself has no meaning; but any proposition in which it occurs has meaning . . . We put
>
> $$E!(\imath x)(\phi x) . = : (\exists b) : \phi x . \equiv_x . x = b \quad Df.$$
>
> If this condition is not fulfilled, we say that $(\imath x)(\phi x)$ is a non-entity: but there is not anything which is a non-entity, there is merely a phrase that fails to describe anything.

Gödel[8] remarks on the preference one may give to Russell's theory over Frege's because

> By defining the meaning of sentences involving descriptions . . . he avoids in his logical system any axioms about the particle 'the', i.e. the analyticity of the theorems about 'the' is made explicit . . . Frege, on the contrary, has to assume an axiom about 'the', which of course is also analytic, but only in the implicit sense that it follows from the meaning of the undefined terms.

To what extent do the variables play an irreducible part here? Taking the most explicit form

$$(\exists x)(Bx \ \& \ Ex \ \& \ (y)(\text{If } By \text{ then } y = x))$$

it is clear that

$$\text{'If } By \text{ then } y = x\text{'}$$

is a propositional function of *two* variables, derived from B, say B^*xy. This shows up a defect of our earlier notation, for we have (through defining it for the case of one variable only) omitted to say how to specify the variables. A partial answer to this, which still lacks the whole flexibility of the quantifier notation but will serve for the present examples, is to write $\overline{B^*}_1$ $\overline{B^*}_2$ for, respectively, $(x)B^*xy$, $(y)B^*xy$, with similar usage for dots and then the explicit form is

$$\dot{K} \text{ where } K = B \& E \& \overline{B^*}_2$$

Moreover there is no problem over having used variables to define B^* in terms of B, for it could be done in terms of combinators in this way: If, in terms of Schönfinkel's K, D = BK then we can call D an extension of B. In terms of variables, Dxy holds if and only if BKxy holds, that is, if and only if Bx holds, so y plays no important part. Suppose also that we use the alternative notation Exy for x = y. We can then define

$$B^* = (\text{If BK, then E}),$$

for this gives, reintroducing variables, B^*xy if and only if (If Bx, then x = y). I infer that the variables again do not play any essential role here.

The important consequence of this analysis is that if Charles II had more than one father, every proposition of the form L where L = B & $\overline{B^*}_2$ & F (F being *any* propositional function) would be false, so that all statements about the present King of France (or about the round square or the golden mountain) are false.

As Pears[21] sums it up

> though the definite description looks as if it has to denote an entity, it really entails a proposition . . . (only) if the proposition happens to be true, the definite description will succeed in denoting the entity which it aims at denoting.

3.7 This concludes Russell's analysis of all denoting phrases. It will have been observed that the rather simplified combinational technique has enabled me to eliminate the variables throughout the discussion. As a consequence, I can argue that the ontological puzzles that the concept of variables generates are of no relevance for Russell's discussion. In the following continuation of my account of Russell's paper, then, I shall be able to use variables freely, as he did.

Russell's next step is to show that the three problems of reference are satisfactorily dealt with by the theory. The case of the round square, for example can be analysed in terms of functions R,S for round and square. Put T = R & S. The round square is then (⌐ x)Tx. The problem that arises here concerns the law of contradiction, since one seems to be able to assert both R{(⌐ x)(Tx)} and ~R{(⌐'x)(Tx)}, the second of these arising from the implicit assumption that 'If Sy then ~Ry'. The answer to this problem given by the theory is that

$$\psi\{(\, ⌐\, x)(Tx)\} \; means \; (\exists x)\{Tx \; \& \; (y)(If \; Ty \; then \; y = x) \; \& \; \psi x\}$$

and this second expression is always false, both when $\psi = R$ and when ψ ~R. The same analysis deals with the baldness of the present King of France (ψ is then baldness and T the French throne). And, of course, as well as dealing with the difficulties raised against the law of contradiction, it deals equally well with the law of excluded middle. For the negation of the false proposition 'The round square is round' is not the other false proposition 'The round square is not -round' but the true proposition 'It is not the case that the round square is round'. In the notation just used, the negation of R((⌐ x)(Tx)) is

$$\sim[R(\, ⌐\, x)(Tx)], \quad not \quad (\sim R)[(⌐\!\mid\!x)(Tx)].$$

This way of dealing with empty reference Russell rightly sees as far superior to that of Meinong, who supposed that the round square was a genuine but 'non-subsisting' object, and so was landed with difficulties over the law of contradiction. Russell's own comment on his own earlier Meinongian views was that he had shown

> a failure of that feeling for reality which ought to be preserved even in the most abstract studies . . . Logic must no more admit a unicorn than zoology can.

Frege's treatment in terms of sense and reference[22] is noted by Russell as avoiding this difficulty and as having the further advantage of explaining why it is worth asserting identity in 'Scott was the author of Waverley'. For only the references, and not the senses, of 'Scott' and 'the author of Waverley' are the same. But this is explained equally well by the new analysis; for if S is the property of being Scott and W that of being the author of Waverley, the analysis is

$$(\exists x)[Wx \ \& \ Sx \ \& \ (y)(\text{If } Wy, \text{ then } y = x)],$$

that is, K, where $K = W \ \& \ S \ \& \ W^*_2$. And so the suggested substitution is evidently not valid.

As far as the three stated difficulties are concerned, then, Russell's theory and Frege's seem equally useful. But Russell then goes on to analyse what he sees as Frege's distinction between sense and reference and to conclude that it cannot be maintained, and this is in some ways the most difficult part of the paper. Gödel[8] has explained succinctly the hazards of following Russell's view of Frege too closely:

> According to Russell, what corresponds to a sentence in the outer world is facts. However he avoids the term 'signify' or 'denote' and used 'indicate' instead . . . because he holds that the relation between a sentence and a fact is quite different from that of a name to the thing named. Furthermore, he uses 'denote' instead of 'signify' for the relation between things and names, so that 'denote' and 'indicate' together would correspond to Frege's *bedeuten*.

The first difficulty Russell raises is over empty reference. 'The King of England is bald', written in 1905, is a statement, not about the sense of 'The King of England', but about its reference. viz., Edward VII. But 'The King of France is bald' cannot be about the reference of 'The King of France', since the phrase has no reference. That seems to make it nonsense; 'but it is not nonsense, since it is plainly false.' So either, like Russell we abandon the idea that it is the reference of denoting phrases which is involved in propositions containing them or we have to provide a reference in cases where it seems to be absent, by inventing non-subsisting objects which do not obey the law of contradiction, like Meinong, or, like Frege, by providing a purely conventional reference. So the 'present King of France' has as reference, for Frege, the null class, and 'the only son of Mr —' has the class of all his sons.

So Russell argues. It may or may not be the case that Frege would have taken this view, but he is a good deal less forthcoming about empty reference in *On Sense and Reference*,[10] where he allows such 'special stipulations' in mathematics but also rests his case on rather the opposite philosophical position:

> A logically perfect language should satisfy the conditions, that every expression grammatically well-constructed as a proper name out of signs already introduced shall in fact designate an object.

Wittgenstein's 'The limits of my language are the limits of my world' is indeed anticipated here. Russell is not sure that Frege's view leads to logical error, but he is content to point out that it is artificial and 'does not give an exact analysis of the matter'.

3.8   There still remains an ambiguity in the Russell ontology. One can either simply suppose that phrases without reference fail to refer to any existing object; so some objects previously listed as existing are completely struck off. Or one can say that a phrase which had been thought of as naming an object fails to do so, but specifies a property instead, so that the ontological status of what the phrase implies has been changed. This ambiguity does not affect the way in which the theory solves the puzzles. But it is not the empty reference difficulty over sense and reference which is crucial for Russell but

> certain rather curious difficulties, which seem in themselves sufficient to prove that the theory . . . must be wrong.

Evidently these are the 'difficulties that I cannot overcome' of Russell's 1904 letter to Frege. The important question is whether they are true difficulties in Frege, or lie in Russell's interpretation, or misinterpretation, of Frege's theory. It is my view that they are indeed produced by Russell's misunderstanding, and that this misunderstanding could have been avoided by a notational improvement which Russell might have been expected to recognise. I do not know why he did not do so.

   These difficulties arise when one tries to talk about the sense and reference of particular phrases. Russell proposes (as a 'natural mode' of procedure) to use inverted commas to specify that he is considering the sense of a denoting phrase as opposed to its reference. In this he follows Frege's convention.[10] But whereas Frege proposes this convention in relating his concepts of sense and reference to everyday speech ('If words are used in the ordinary way, what one intends to speak of is their reference ... a word standing between quotation marks must not be taken as having its ordinary meaning'), Russell is concerned with a definite notation, which he is then going to show leads to puzzlement. For a phrase C has, according to Frege, both sense and reference. If 'C' is to stand for its sense, it is confusing to use C for its reference taken alone, notwithstanding ordinary usage. I shall propose a better notation below. Meanwhile, I shall try to present Russell's argument as clearly as I can.

His examples are:

  (a) The centre of mass of the solar system is a point. 'The centre of mass of the solar system' is a denoting complex.
  (b) The first line of Gray's *Elegy* states a proposition. 'The first line of Gray's *Elegy*' is a denoting complex.

Russell's argument now consists of pointing to a difficulty that arises when one wishes to talk about the sense or the reference. The sense of the first line of Gray's elegy, Russell argues, is the same as the sense of 'The curfew tolls the knell of passing day', but the sense of the 'The first line of Gray's elegy' is not. It may help to extend this example a little in a way not given by Russell:

  (c) The first line of Gray's *Elegy* has eight words. 'The first line of Gray's *Elegy*' has six words.

Similarly, Russell argues, with reference. We do not get the reference we want. If C is defined as the denoting complex in (b), above, then

$$C = \text{'the first line of Gray's } Elegy\text{'}$$

and the reference of C is: The curfew tolls the knell of passing day. But we meant to have as reference: the first line of Gray's *Elegy*.

He sums up the difficulty in speaking of a denoting complex by saying:

The moment we put the complex in a proposition, the proposition is about the denotation [reference]; and if we make a proposition in which the subject is 'the meaning of C', [that is, its sense] then the subject is the meaning if any of the denotation, which was not intended.

He follows this argument with a more abstract version and concludes that 'C' and C are different entities, but 'C' refers to C;

but this cannot be an explanation, because the relation of 'C' to C is wholly mysterious; and where are we to find the denoting complex 'C' which denotes C?

Moreover, he goes on, if C occurs in a proposition, it is not only the reference that occurs, and yet the sense was meant to be put into 'C'.

This is an inextricable tangle and seems to prove that the whole distinction of meaning and denotation has been wrongly conceived.

Russell's problem has a curious status. He is arguing that the sense-reference distinction cannot be maintained because, although it is perfectly possible to explain the distinction clearly, it is not possible to apply this in particular cases. The problem is, in fact, a notational one, and this, as is often the case with notational difficulties, conceals a philosophical distinction. I have argued above that, if 'C' is to denote the sense of C, it is confusing to let C denote the reference. Such a confusing notation arose from the absence in Frege[10] or in Russell of a clear definition of the sense of a phrase. Frege, it is true, remarks in a footnote

In the case of an actual proper name such as 'Aristotle' opinions as to the sense may differ. It might, for instance, be taken to be: 'the pupil of Plato and teacher of Alexander the Great'.

But it could be taken otherwise and

such variations of sense may be tolerated, although they . . . ought not to occur in a perfect language.

And in the text, he remarks

The same sense has different expressions in different languages or even in the same language.

In Frege's example of 'Aristotle', what would count as tolerable variations of sense? And, again, in Russell's example (b)?

The best clue comes perhaps from Russell's example (a). The reference of 'The centre of mass of the solar system' is evidently a certain point of the heavens. The sense is contained in the set of rules which it implies to astronomers for calculating where the reference (the point) is. But of course there is not a unique set of rules. The situation is a little like the Frege geometrical example. The calculation can be done in many different ways. So evidently the sense is not to be thought of as any such set of rules, but as something they have in common. This is appealing to a 'Principle of Abstraction' of a form very reminiscent of Cantor's definiton of a cardinal number. It is very surprising that Russell did not see that the same way out of the difficulty would work here. That is, the sense can be defined as the class of all such sets of rules. In the case of Russell's example (b) the rules are those designed to allow us to find the line. They may instruct us to page x of Palgrave's *Golden Treasury* or to page y of the *Oxford Book of English Verse*, and so on. The class of all such rules is the sense, and the reference is the line of poetry. This suggests a preferable notation. If C is a denoting phrase, we can let its reference be C_r and its sense C_s: so that C_s is a class of rules. This deals with the notational question.

But Russell also has a second problem which arises from his stipulation, which does not seem to be derived from Frege, that the relation of sense and reference

is not merely linguistic through the phase: there must be a logical relation involved, which we express by saying that the meaning denotes the denotation,

that is, that the reference of the sense is the reference of the phrase. What is this 'reference of the sense' if, as I argue here, C_s is a class of rules? Evidently one is to choose *any* element of C_s, pursue the rules and finish with the reference, and evidently it *will* be the reference of C. That is, one is defining $(C_s)_r$, or C_{sr}, by

$$(x)(x \; \varepsilon \; C_s \quad \text{if \& only if} \quad x_r = C_{sr})$$

and, from the way the rules are constructed, we know

$$(x)(x \; \varepsilon \; C_s \quad \text{if \& only if} \quad x_r = C_r),$$

so that $C_{sr} = C_r$.

There is also an apparently symmetrical argument, which Russell gives, with sense and reference interchanged. This argument cannot, I think, be saved. For it argues that 'if we speak of "the meaning of C", that gives us the meaning (if any) of the denotation.' Now Russell might here be using meaning to translate *Sinn*. In that case his contention would also state that $C_s = C_{rs}$ is meaningless, and yet C_s is quite clear. So this Russell argument must be using meaning in some other sense, and confusing it with *Sinn* in the later part of the paragraph. This I take to be closely related to Geach's point[10] that, in *On Denoting*,

> Russell had excusably, but wrongly, conflated Frege's distinction between *Sinn* and *Bedeutung* with his own distinction between what an expression "means" and what it "denotes" . . . Frege's distinction between *Sinn* and *Bedeutung* was largely (I think entirely) derived from puzzles about indirect-speech clauses; no such considerations are used in PM to justify the distinction between meaning and denoting.

The only substantial point remaining seems to be summed up in Russell's implied question: what denoting phrase has as its reference the phrase 'the first line of Gray's *Elegy*'? The answer is, a phrase such as 'The phrase which characterises the members of the class C_s'. That there is such a phrase is a property of the class C_{sr}. This notational clarification together with the explanation of $C_{sr} = C_r$, so that their relation is no longer 'wholly mysterious,' disposes of Russell's 'rather curious difficulties'. The difference between Russell's theory of descriptions and Frege's sense and reference theory can be seen, then, in terms of the successes of Russell's theory in providing a better understanding of empty reference. The explanations of the use of identity by the two are different, but equally acceptable. But, of course, empty reference was the whole driving force behind the theory of

descriptions: with the intention of application to the paradoxes. I now turn to that.

3.9   The impact of the thought of *On Denoting* in *Principia
Mathematica* is much less clear than it might be, for in the
intervening period Russell's thought had developed in various ways. But the letters to Jourdain show that Russell
regarded the theory of descriptions as 'dealing with' the contradictions and we now know how this was to be from papers
unearthed by Grattan-Guinness in the Russell archives.[23]
These relate to Russell's 'substitutional theory' on which he
was working in Spring 1906. He describes, in a letter to Lucy
Donnelly,[2] how he worked on it while staying in Clovelly:
'My work goes ahead at a tremendous pace, and I get intense
delight from it.' But in the *Autobiography* he adds a footnote
'It turned out to be all nonsense'. Here Russell is unduly
hard on himself. I shall describe the substitutional theory
briefly, following the description in.[23]

The general idea behind it is again the question of variables and their possible elimination if doubt should arise
about the ontological commitment they bring. But Russell's
method of elimination is considerably less formalistic than
the one I have described. He asks himself exactly what function a variable plays in logic. In, for example, $(x)\varphi x$, any
object a (of appropriate kind) may be substituted for x (and,
in each case, a true proposition, φa, will result). So that
$(x)\varphi x$ may be looked on as an appropriate label for all the
propositions φa, φb, ... And similarly $(\exists x)\varphi x$ says
something else about the aggregate $\{\varphi a, \varphi b, \ldots \}$ viz. that
some of the propositions are true. Suppose, now, doubt
should arise about variables because, for instance
$R = \hat{x}(\sim x \, \varepsilon \, x)$, the class in Russell's paradox, is defined by
using them too freely. Then one could deal with the aggre-
gate more directly by selecting one member, φa say, as a
representative. Any other one can then be derived simply by
a substitution; φb comes from writing b for a in φa.

If this programme can be carried out, then no classes,
relations, propositional functions or variables will be
needed; it will be sufficient to have propositions p, q, ...

(with truth-values) and constants a, b, . . . representing individuals. In Ayer's words[24]

> . . . the generous Platonism . . . is pared away to the point where even such comparatively respectable entities as classes and propositions appear as logical fictions . . .

Though it is well to bear in mind, in reading Ayer, just what is implied by *logical fiction*. As Pears remarks,[21] the notion relates to a particular, deep, logical analysis of a phrase. If the analysis is less than comprehensive, then something more must be put in, in order to reconstruct the whole of what is popularly meant by the phrase. If, as may be the case, there is not cogent reason for supplying this extra material, Russell expresses this by saying that the thing in question need not exist, is a logical fiction.

The basic idea in the substitutional theory is that of a denoting phrase, $p \mid a$, which means 'the result of substituting a in p by'.

And

$$p \mid a : x \,!\, q,$$

or alternatively

$$p \; \frac{x}{a} \,!\, q,$$

is to mean that q is the result of substituting a in p by x, or, in a more natural use of language, the result of substituting x for a in p. Here x is simply used as a letter, not as a variable (since there are no variables). Multiple substitutions can be handled by a natural extension of the notation, so that, for example, one can write

$$p \mid (a, b) : (x, y) \,!\, q.$$

The incomplete expressions $P \mid a$, $p \mid (a, b)$, . . . are called *matrices*, and of course the matrix $p \mid a$ plays much the same part in the theory as that played by a class in the usual discourse. For x to belong to this class is the same as $p \mid a : x$ being true. In the same way $p \mid (a, b)$ is a binary relation, R say; where

$$xRy \quad \text{if and only if} \quad p \mid (a, b) : (x, y).$$

There is, however, another way of looking at p | (a, b), as a class of classes, by taking b, a in succession. The substitutional theory recommended itself so strongly to Russell as a cure for the paradoxes because of the way in which, although a single letter *may* be introduced for a class or a relation, this will not always be significant. For p | a : x is significant only if x is an individual; and in that case it may be translated into the old notation as x ε S. But S ε S would have come from the meaningless expression p | a : (p | a), and so cannot arise.

It will not be necessary to consider the remaining details of the substitutional theory, other than to remark that the theory is a very bold one, that allows propositions to be substituted for individuals and *vice versa*. The failure to distinguish these is one of its defects; but although it had others too it is certainly a better theory than the later Russell thought. He wrote to Jourdain in 1906:

> I decided not to publish the paper I read at the London Mathematical in May; there was much in it that wanted correction, and I preferred to wait till I got things into a more final shape.

He had, in fact, sent it for publication in May and, after some delay, both referees recommended acceptance, but then Russell withdrew.

Section 2: The Theory of Types

3.10   The next steps in Russell's development are expressed with deceptive simplicity:

> In 1906 I discovered the Theory of Types. After this it only remained to write the book out.

Whitehead was busy with his teaching duties, so the main labours fell to Russell. There was really more giving and taking than Russell suggests in[2] but there is no reason to doubt his statement that

> I worked at it from ten to twelve hours a day for about eight months in the year, from 1907 to 1910.

Although it is not relevant to my argument, I must quote also his remark that

> The University Press estimated that there would be a loss of £600 on the book, and while the Syndics were willing to bear a loss of £300, they did not feel they could go above this figure. The Royal Society very generously contributed £200, and the remaining £100 we had to find ourselves. We thus earned minus £50 each by ten years's work. This beats the record of *Paradise Lost*.

But although Russell's description of the discovery of the theory of types is deceptively simple, *Principia Mathematica* is more truly in the nature of a long, worked-out development of a single theme. It is fortunate that Russell published the essential features of his 1906 discovery in a paper[25] called *Mathematical Logic as based on the Theory of Types*. Just as I noticed, in Section 1, the coincidence of date between *On Denoting* and the fundamental papers of Einstein, so here it is even more striking to note that 1908 also saw the appearance of Zermelo's paper on the foundations of set theory[26] and Brouwer's[27] on the unreliability of classical logic. I shall discuss Russell's paper in this section and reserve a description of *Principia Mathematica* for Chapter 4.

Russell begins the paper with a description of the known paradoxes, now more numerous than before. I discuss this in §3.11. He sees the common feature of these as one of illegitimate self-reference, as I explain in §3.12. In §3.13 I deal with his distinction between *all* and *any*, which is seen by him as the same as one between real and apparent variables. The idea of quantified variables as giving rise to denoting phrases, just as in *On Denoting*, is described in §3.14, and this gives rise to the notion of a range of significance. This is used to construct the theory of types, as I explain in §3.15. Then §3.16 considers Russell's 'axiom of reducibility'. The rest of Russell's paper concerns technical developments in mathematical logic, which it is more convenient to leave until Chapter 4, since they are further developed in *Principia Mathematica*. But I draw the chapter to a conclusion in §3.17.

The clue to the understanding of Russell's thought in 1906

is the substitutional theory mentioned in §3.9 above. As I said there, although a single letter may always be introduced for a class, this introduction may not always be significant. The idea of the theory of types is to capture this loss of significance in certain substitutions, without committing oneself to the whole apparatus of the substitutional theory. The title of the paper deserves some comment. It refers to *mathematical logic*. The correct emphasis is on the second of the two words, notwithstanding the austere pages of the American Mathematical Society's Journal in which it is to be found. The aim of the paper, as stated by Russell at once, is to solve the paradoxes, especially that of Burali-Forti. But he also includes other, purely logical, ones, and he remarks about the theory that

> it has also, if I am not mistaken, a certain consonance with common sense which makes it inherently credible. This, however, is not a merit upon which too much stress should be laid; for common sense is far more fallible than it likes to believe.

He then goes on to list the contradictions with which he is to deal.

3.11   Russell begins his list of paradoxes with the contradiction of the Cretan, which appears apparently unnoticed in St Paul.[28] If Epimenides, a Cretan, says that all Cretans always lie, this statement which he makes can neither be true nor false. Then, after mentioning Russell's paradox, in the form I have considered in Chapter 2, Russell goes on to look at another version of it expressed in terms of relations. It is not clear whether Russell thought that this alternative version was essentially a different one or not. But he is at pains, in a letter to Jourdain[3] in 1905, to stress

> It is not from the assumption 'that a class can always be an element of another class' that contradictions result.

He goes on to construct 'my contradiction', calling the class that exhibits it w.

> You can't escape this by saying that w is not a member of any class; for

to say it is *not* a member of w is proved to be equivalent to saying it *is* a member of w.

The statement in terms of relations dodges this point, at least in part.

This version considers relations between relations. There is evidently nothing inherently strange about the possibility of relations between relations. If R is the relation which holds between two natural numbers n, m when m = 2n, and S is that which holds when m ⩾ n, it is natural to describe R as stronger than S since, if nRm, then nSm, but not necessarily conversely. And it is also natural to use some notation, say Q, for the relation 'stronger than' and to write RQS. But suppose, in particular, that T stands for the relation between *any* relations R,S that R does not have the relation R to S, so that

$$(R)(S)[RTS \quad \text{if and only if} \quad \sim(RRS)].$$

Then taking the relation T for each of the arbitrary relations R,S leads to the self-contradictory statement

$$TTT \quad \text{if and only if} \quad \sim(TTT).$$

Russell follows this with Berry's paradox which concerns the number of syllables in the English name of a natural number (three, for example, for the natural number 'one hundred'). The paradox arises by considering the phrase 'the least integer not nameable in fewer than nineteen syllables'. This seems to represent 111,777, as a little experiment will show. But the phrase itself consists of eighteen syllables, and so, if the phrase can be interpreted as a name, a contradiction results.

The next two contradictions differ from those just described in the way in which they make explicit use of Cantor's theorem P(S) > S. I have drawn attention in Chapter 2, and also above, to the detailed proof of this. This proof is rather abstract in the general case and it may perhaps be useful to spell out a particular version of it here. This particular version is the one applicable when S is the class of natural numbers. Instead of proving directly that P(S) > S, I shall prove that T > S, where T is a subset of P(S). This then provides a proof of Cantor's theorem, but it has the advantage of proving it for the special case in which I am particularly interested viz., that in which T represents all finite or infinite decimals between 0 and 1. Any such decimal is made up of a collection of natural numbers, that is, it consists of a member of the class of all sub-classes of S. Such a class of decimals can also be described as the class of real numbers between 0 and 1. The Cantor proof proceeds by supposing that there is a 1:1 relation between S and T; I can call this a *numbering-off* of the elements of T. I could imagine such a numbering-off to take some such form as this, where the underlining should for the present be ignored:

1. 0.75432 . . .
2. 0.52000 . . .
3. 0.82745 . . .
. . . .

I then construct an infinite decimal, 0.838 . . ., by taking each underlined figure in turn and adding one to it. The underlined figures are the first digit of the first element of the list, the second of the second element and so on. And if one of these digits should be a nine, the rule of 'adding one' has to be modified to 'replacing 9 by 0'. Then this new decimal has not been listed, for it differs in its first digit from the first in the list, in its second digit from the second in the list, and so on. So the assumed complete numbering off and listing cannot be complete after all.

Russell uses this result in discussing the transfinite ordinals. He considers the definitions of the various ordinals. Any such definition is a finite collection of English words; that is, a finite sequence of the twenty-seven symbols a, b, c, . . ., y, z and 'space'. The cardinality of all such finite sequences is no greater than that of the natural numbers S. This fact can be proved by listing all such sequences, beginning with the shortest, and, in the list of the finite number of such sequences of a particular length, carrying out the listing in strict alphabetical order. Thus, in this listing, the first twenty-seven places are occupied respectively by a, b, c, . . ., z, *, (writing * for the space), and then follow aa, ab, ac, . . ., a*, ba, bb, . . ., b*, . . ., *a, *b, . . ., **, aaa, aab, . . ., and so on. Since one can list *all* such sequences, whether they make sense or not, and since the class of actual definitions are a sub-class of this list, it follows that there are only as many definitions of infinite ordinals as there are natural numbers. But, as Cantor's theorem shows, there are more infinite ordinals than that, so some of them must be undefinable. Amongst these Russell takes for granted that there must be a least one. But since this is then definable as 'the least non-definable ordinal', a contradiction results.

He next describes Richard's paradox, which has much the same structure. It arises by considering the class of all decimals definable in a finite number of words. This class can, as I have just said, be numbered off by the natural numbers, whereas the class of all decimals cannot. But the rule for constructing the decimal in Cantor's proof could be used here to construct a decimal which is not definable. And yet the rule does define it, and in a finite number of words. Russell concludes his list with Burali-Forti's paradox.

3.12 Russell argues that the common feature of these paradoxes is that of *self-reference* or *reflexiveness*.

> The remark of Epimenides must include itself in its own scope . . . In the case of names or definitions, the paradoxes result from considering non-nameability and indefinability as elements in names or definitions . . . something is said about *all* cases of some kind, and from what is said a new case seems to be generated, which both is, and is not the same kind.

But self-reference is not wholly to be avoided in mathematics, any more than in ordinary discourse. As Quine has said, 'the tallest person in this room' defines a person unambiguously and unparadoxically, although there is self-reference. A slightly more interesting example is Quine's 'The typical Yale man'. Here the concept is defined only by reference to all Yale men; it is best, perhaps, to interpret it as in a given year. By studying all such men in terms of colour of hair, parental income, IQ, birth-place and so on, the concept of the typical one can be put together. But when this has been done, it is entirely possible that an actual Yale man answering to this description may exist.

Both of these examples are really picturesque illustrations

of certain self-reference constructions that arise frequently in statistics. There one often considers a collection of numbers which may, for example be measured values of some physical entity. Suppose each measurements of the number of children in a particular collection of families are

$$\{0, 1, 2, 2, 3, 2, 3, 2, 2, 1, 0, 0, 2, 3\}.$$

Statisticians distinguish, amongst other measures of the collection, the *mode*; that is, the element which occurs most frequently. The mode, in the example given is 2. They also consider the *mean* or average, which would be $26/15 = 1.73$. The mode must be a member of the collection. The mean is usually not, though it is perfectly possible that it might be. But each of these numbers is defined in terms of the whole collection and the new number defined 'both is and is not of the same kind', without any paradox arising.

I mention these doubts about the real seriousness of self-reference in order to point up the subtlety of Russell's principle for avoiding it. He puts it like this:

> If, provided a certain collection had a total, it would have members only definable in terms of that total, then the said collection has no total.

Now this is a way of avoiding the paradoxes, but, as Russell says at once, it is purely negative and it is of no help in rectifying those errors that it points out.

> It is impossible to avoid mentioning a thing by mentioning that we won't mention it.

So one has to construct a logic which cannot mention the forbidden things and this point is really the crucial beginning of the Russell-Whitehead *logicism*, although it had already been hinted at in[5]. Unfortunately, logic as it existed in 1908 was in a state quite inadequate for such a weight of development to be put on it. For this reason much of the paper I am discussing is concerned with a clear formulation of logic and this is even more so with *Principia Mathematica* two years later.

3.13   The next section of Russell's paper is headed *All and any*. The distinction he seeks to make here is not one which I think is of importance any longer. The need to make it has been obviated by the way in which mathematical logic is now elaborated. Indeed, though it was still present in the first edition of *Principia Mathematica*, it was abolished in the second. But the discussion is important for following Russell's later argument, so I will consider it critically. Russell argues that variables in mathematics may be *real* or apparent. He considers the detailed form that Weierstrass gives for a definition of continuity of a function f of a single variable x, f(x).

Continuity means for mathematicians, as for everyone else, the absence of sudden jumps in the values f(x) of a function of x when x changes smoothly. Weierstrass expressed this in a formal way as follows: a function f is called continuous at a point a if a certain situation arises in what might be thought of as a game. In this game a number, ε, greater than zero, is chosen by one player. Continuity is the name given to the situation when whatever fixed value of ε is chosen, it is always possible for the other player to win by choosing a number δ. This number has the winning property in the game. This winning property is that f(x) is nearer to f(a) than ε for all x nearer to a than δ. It does not matter for my purpose why it was necessary for Weierstrass to capture this apparently simple concept in such a complex construction. It is sufficient that mathematicians have accepted that this is the way to proceed.

In terms of notations we have used already, f is continuous at a if

$$(\varepsilon)(\exists\delta)[\delta = g(\varepsilon) \ \& \ (y)[\text{If } |a - y| < \delta, \text{ then } |f(a) - f(y)| < \varepsilon]],$$

where I have used the notation $|u|$ for the absolute value of u, $|u| = u$ if $u \geqslant 0$, $|u| = -u$ if $u < 0$. Now Russell argues that, as is shown by the notation, ε, δ are apparent variables, in the sense that the statement is not about ε or δ. And, he claims, this is shown by the fact that the statement is made about *all* positive values of ε and about the existence of *some* value of δ. This reference to δ is a little more complicated. But there is an implicit reference to all values of δ in the sense that the quantifier $(\exists\delta)$ can be defined as stating that it is not the case that, for all values of δ, the later part of the statement, in square brackets, is false.

But, Russell further argues, the statement *is* about f and a; for, of course, it is intended to state the continuity of f at a. But it is not interpreted by mathematicians as a special, singular statement. It states what it means for *any* function f to be continuous at *any* point a. So f, a are called real variables. Russell attributes this distinction to Frege. And he gives, as Frege's reason for making it, the same reason as in mathematics generally viz. that real variables are necessary for logical deductions. Russell means by this the following: if p, q are any propositions of which one has proved p and has proved also the proposition 'If p, then q', then q may be deduced. This is indeed the classical logician's *modus ponens* and it is also a common method of procedure in mathematical proof. But if one has proved $(x)\varphi x$, and one has also proved (x) (If φx, then ψx), it is possible to deduce ψx by *modus ponens* only by first deducing If φx, then ψx, in which x has become a real variable.

I take Russell's two related points in reverse order. It is indeed true that *modus ponens* will not suffice in the deduction mentioned. But the question of what are valid modes of logical deduction is part of the very investigation which Russell is proposing. And there is no reason why:

If $(x)\varphi x$, and if (x)(If φx, then ψx), then (x) ψx

should not be included. Returning to the first point, it is clear that the distinction between apparent and real variables does exist. But it is a distinction which refers to the way in which the statement of continuity has been fitted in to the rest of the sentence, not about the statement itself. The statement is about when f is continuous as a. It would be more correct to write

f is continuous at a if and only if Q,

where Q stands for the whole previous phrase beginning $(\varepsilon)(\exists\delta)$. And if this is agreed then it would be even appropriate to write

(f)(a)(f is continuous at a if and only if Q),

and in this form f, a are evidently apparent variables as well.

The importance of the distinction between *all* and *any*, which Russell connects with apparent and real variables, is however, very important for him, though for quite a different reason. It may be, he argues, that a phrase containing *any* is legitimate when the corresponding phrase with *all* replacing *any* leads to self-reference. He believes that it is permissible to say 'p is true or false, where p is any proposition', whereas to say that 'all propositions are true or false' is to enunciate a new proposition, over and above all those implied in the *all*. And he applies similar considerations to the laws of logic:

> There is no one proposition which *is* the law of contradiction (say); there are only the various instances of the law.

In terms of notations that we have used already, the law of contradiction, 'not both p and not-p' can be written

$$\sim(p \ \& \ \sim p),$$

the implication being that this is the case for any p. But Russell would not condone

$$(p)(\sim(p \ \& \ \sim p))$$

since the quantifier (p) would then range over all propositions, including the law of contradiction and so there would be self-reference. It is essential to this distinction that $\sim(p \ \& \ \sim p)$ is not a proposition; it is a form which becomes a proposition only when p is replaced by a definite proposition. To sum up, I conclude that the distinction between *all* and *any* is really the important one for Russell; that between real and apparent variables relates only to the manner of expression.

3.14 In Part III of the paper Russell goes on to consider the meaning to be given to what he calls *generalized propositions*, but which we would call propositional functions quantified by *all* or *some*. He raises a number of cogent objections to the view that 'all men are mortal' has a clear unambiguous meaning. Firstly, he argues, what if there are no men? He compares this situation with Bradley's analysis of the phrase 'Trespassers will be prosecuted', the truth of which cannot depend on whether there are any trespassers or not. He adopts Bradley's view that the correct analysis is as a conditional, so as

$$(x)(\text{If } Hx, \text{ then } Mx)$$

but the difficulty then arises about the range of x. Now *all men* is a denoting phrase in the sense of[4], so has no meaning in isolation. Moreover the proposition containing it is not about 'all men'. Indeed, even if 'all men' denoted a definite object, it is obvious that we do not desire to attribute mortality to it. So we must return to the conditional above and the question of the range of x. It is not possible to restrict x to range only over men, for then the 'If Hx' would be unnecessary, and we could simply deduce that $(x)Mx$, a proposition which is certainly false. On the other hand, if x were allowed an unrestricted range, the way would be open to introduce 'all propositions . . . and such illegitimate totalities'. So we seem inevitably to be pushed into some kind of 'Universe of discourse' doctrine, which would assert that the above proposition holds whenever x ranges over some class i, a class which must include the class of men. But inevitable as this may seem, it will not do; for then we are to interpret the above statement as

$$(x)(\text{if } x \; \varepsilon \; i, \text{ then: if } Hx, \text{ then } Mx).$$

But this new statement now raises precisely the same difficulties again on its own behalf.

Russell has now exhausted all possibilities inherent in that line of argument, so he begins again. If we hold fast to Bradley's analysis as a conditional, it is clear that, if we need to exclude any values of x, it is not values of x that would make the proposition false, for there are none. This is because, if x is a man, x is mortal: but if x has some value not a man, then the 'If Hx' part of the conditional is false and this means that the whole phrase 'If Hx, then Mx' is true whether x is mortal or not. So if it is necessary, as we know it is, to exclude some x's, it must be those x's which would make the proposition meaningless, not false. The argument therefore forces

Russell into the doctrine that any function φ, such as

$$\varphi x = \text{If } Hx, \text{ then } Mx$$

has a *range of significance*, and that $(x)\varphi x$ refers to all the x in that range. Russell prefers to put it in the form 'If Hx, then Mx, always', where *always* means: for all values of x for which the function is significant. Later he puts it more succinctly like this: $(x)\varphi x$ means that all values of the function φ are true, not that φ is true for all values of x, since some values of x may make φ meaningless.

3.15   The way is now clear for Russell, in his Section IV, to introduce 'The Hierarchy of Types'. A *type* is defined as the range of significance of a propositional function. Then the requirement of no self-reference can be put in the form

Whatever contains an apparent variable must be of a different type from the possible values of the variable.

The function is said to be of a *higher* type. Now any proposition containing an apparent variable x, as for example $(\exists x)Cx$, presupposes another, Ca, from which it can be derived by substituing x for the term a. Here Russell evidently has very much in his mind his recently discarded substitutional theory. Since there are only a finite number of apparent variables, they can all be removed in turn, so exhibiting the proposition as arising from repeated substitution of apparent variables for terms in an *elementary proposition*, that is, one with no apparent variables. The terms of elementary propositions are called *individuals* and they form the first or lowest type. It is not necessary, for this analysis, to know what the individuals are, since it is only the *relative* types of variables that are important. However, a difficulty does arise at this point. By applying the process of changing terms into apparent variables, a process called *generalization* by Russell, new propositions result. This process is legitimate only so long as no individuals are propositions.

That this is so is to be secured by the meaning we give to the term *individual*.

Russell proposed to define it as something devoid of complexity, which then prevents it being a proposition. But, of course, a definite metaphysical assumption is being made here, for individuals have already been defined as the terms of elementary propositions and so this new, so-called definition must really be interpreted as a statement about how the world is. It is in fact identical with the statement picked out by Wittgenstein[29] as crucial to the logicist position

> 2. What is the case, the fact (die Tatsache) is the existence of atomic facts (Sachverhalten). (See §4.19 for comment on this particular translation of Wittgenstein.)

I believe that logicism, the doctrine that logic provides a secure foundation for mathematics, stands or falls by the possibility of some such analysis. This fact about logicism is often ignored, but it is its most profound feature. A slightly unsympathetic commentator, Pollock,[30] remarks

> At one time logicism was an extremely popular theory and was regarded as being very profound, thanks largely to the efforts of Russell . . . Prior to 1931 it was simply assumed by most people that logic was axiomatisable. In fact, it was generally supposed that logic had been axiomatised by Russell himself in *Principia Mathematica*. Consequently, logicism was interpreted as lending considerable support to the conventionalist theory of mathematical truth.

As a historical statement, Pollock's may be correct. But the implication inherent in 'was regarded as being very profound' etc. ignores the sense in which it was indeed profound. That lies, once again, in Russell's view of logic as true, not as a conventional system. Something like the same distinction occurs in Russell's letter to Jourdain[3] in 1908 about Zermelo's paper.[26]

> I thought his axiom for avoiding illegitimate classes so vague as to be useless; also, since he does not regonise this theory of types, I suspect that this axioms will not really avoid contradictions . . . For I feel more and more certain that the solution lies in types . . .

Grattan-Guinness remarks about this letter:

he was referring to his method not as a way of avoiding the paradoxes but *the* way of *solving* them.

A major confusion seems to be present in Russell's actual setting up of the hierarchy of types. The way in which he proceeds involves a substantial new departure from the simple theory of the *Principles of Mathematics*. Modern logicians would distinguish between the *simple* and the *ramified* theories. The two basic postulates of the simple theory are:

1. Every propositional function φx has, in addition to its range of truth, a range of significance.

2. Ranges of significance form types, so that if x is in the range of significance of φx, there is a class of objects, the type of x, which also belong to the range of significance no matter how φx may vary.

From 1908, however, there is added the vicious circle principle.

3. No totality can contain members which are definable only in terms of this totality.

To put this into effect, it is not sufficient merely to distinguish between entities of type 0, 1, 2 . . . A further classification has to be made in each type: suppose that in the definition of an entity of given type there is a bound variable of type n but none of higher type. The *order* of the entity is then defined as n+1. The entities of lowest order are called *predicative*, and all others are *impredicative*. The need for this ramification lies in the Richard paradox.

The paper is confusing, however, because this ramification of the theory is not presented as a new basic assumption, but merely as a more convenient way of putting things. Russell begins with the simple theory. The elementary propositions together with those containing individuals as apparent variables are *first order propositions* and so are of the second type. One can then generalise and form new propositions in which first order propositions become apparent variables, and this gives second order propositions, that is, of the third logical type. The application of this distinction to the Cretan paradox is straight forward. When Epimenides, having had his logical grammar corrected, says 'All first order statements made by me are false' he is uttering a second order statement. This is the basic notion behind the theory of types.

In practical applications, however, continues Russell it is 'more convenient' to translate all this in to a hierarchy of functions rather than of propositions. As a guide to this Russell returns again to this recently rejected substitutional theory, in which, of course, he can remove all apparent variables 'except individuals and propositions of various orders' by expressing functions by matrices. But, he concedes, although possible, this is technically inconvenient and so, instead, p is replaced by φa, p | a; x by φx. In this re-writing p and a, which were apparent variables, have been replaced by one apparent variable, φ. This is legitimate only so long as the values of φ are all of one type.

This therefore is held to require a slightly different restatement of the hierarchy of types, more appropriate to functions. This revised version is in fact the one now usually described as the ramified theory of types. A function φ taking individuals x into first-order propositions φx is called a *first order function* and is written φ ! x. Then a function φ involving a first order function ψ as apparent variable is called a second order function. The specially tidy case in which a function φ of one variable has order exactly one higher than its argument is called *predicative*. This term is extended to functions of many variables by defining as predicative those functions which are predicative in one of the variables when the others are specified. This 'revised presentation' of the theory of types is more convenient for the later paradoxes, especially Richard's. However, as Ramsey pointed out, Richard's paradox is really a linguistic not a mathematical one. The elements of Russell's theory which are intended to get rid of the linguistic paradoxes are of no use in mathematics. So it would be possible to eliminate such features without spoiling the foundations of mathematics. The ramified theory of types is such a feature.

3.16 Russell's Section V *The axiom of reducibility* is in some ways the most interesting of the paper, since it presents its material with a directness and cogency which is lacking from some later versions. The limitations of the ramified theory of types are demanded, so Russell argues, by the need to avoid the paradoxes. Yet now these same restrictions put us in the position of no longer being able to refer to 'all properties of x'. It is one thing for the logician to warn against the way in which such a usage may lead to the introduction of a new property, and so a reflexive fallacy. But something very like 'all properties of x' is demanded in mathematics. To take only one example, the fifth of Peano's axioms, the axiom of induction, is expressed, perhaps loosely as

For all properties φ of the natural numbers,

if $\varphi 0$, and if (x) [when φx, then $\varphi x'$], then (x)φx.

So some way has to be found, argues Russell, by which we may talk about all properties φ. We need to reduce the order of φ, without affecting the truth-values of the function.

Now common-sense, which was after all a guide to the original formulation of the theory of types, does this in practice by the introduction of classes. The statement φx is rendered precisely by the alternative x ε α, where α is written for the class $\alpha = \hat{x}\varphi x$. But the new statement is now a first order statement, for it contains no reference to 'all functions of such and such a type'. Russell states his belief that this advantage of classes, that they reduce the order of a statement, is in fact their only advantage. Be that as it may, it seems to him that there is definitely no advantage in assuming the real existence of classes, for the contradictions prove that, if they were to exist, they would be very unlike individuals. It is only individuals that we really know how to handle. So, instead of assuming the real existence of classes, Russell proposes to assume only what would be useful if it followed from their existence. The device is, of course, a typical mathematician's stratagem for reducing the strength of assumptions without impairing the conclusion. Russell puts it in the form:

Axiom of Reducibility Every propositional function is equivalent, for all its values, to some predicative function.

By this means, argues Russell, statements about 'all first order functions of x' succeed in capturing most of the results which would otherwise have needed 'all functions'. It is just the results where only the truth or falsehood of the functions concerned is relevant which are captured, and it is exactly those results which are needed in mathematics. For example, Peano's fifth axiom need now be stated only for first order properties, φ.

Moreover the paradoxes listed do not reappear after this lightening of the yoke of the theory of types. For in the paradoxes something more than truth-values is relevant or else, even with the axioms of reducibility, the statement is still meaningless according to the theory of types. As an example, the axiom of reducibility does *not* assert that 'Epimenides asserts ψx' is equivalent to 'Epimenides asserts $\varphi \,!\, x$'.

There has been much discussion about the rôle played by the axiom of reducibility in Russell's system. It certainly raises a doubt, in the following way: a particular set of paradoxes has been listed and logic has been restricted in such a way as to avoid them. It is then too weak to support mathematics. The axiom of reducibility strengthens it again but not so much as to reintroduce any of the paradoxes on the list. What if there are other paradoxes however? Can we be sure that they will not be reintroduced? Ramsey, for example, thought there was no reason why the axiom of reducibility should be true, and he proceeded, instead, to develop an alternative approach. In this approach he put finite and infinite classes on the same footing. *All* mathematical truths are truth-functional combinations of atomic functions of individuals or of atomic propositions. It is just that we have an accidental inability to write propositions of infinite length. Otherwise we could simply render $(x)\varphi x$ as

$$\varphi a \;\&\; \varphi b \;\&\; \varphi c \;\&\; \ldots$$

With this approach there is no longer any need for the axiom of reducibility. As Carnap says,[31] Ramsey declared

the forbidden impredicative definitions to be perfectly admissible. They contain, he contended, a circle but the circle is harmless, not vicious . . . The totality of properties already exists in itself . . . [But] Such a conception, I believe, is not far removed from a belief in a platonic realm of ideas which exist in themselves, independently of *if* and *how* finite human beings are able to think them.

Ramsey's approach, moreover, gives no clue about how we might actually prove the consistency of these infinite operations, and indeed he was converted in 1929 to a more finitist approach, leading to the rejection of any actual aggregate. An opposite approach, of more recent date, is that of John Myhill.[32] His treatment is a technical one, but its approach may be judged from this quotation:

> The purpose of this chapter is to vindicate the axiom of reducibility, not in the sense of adducing fresh grounds for believing it, but in the sense of demolishing once and for all an argument (by Ramsey, Chwistek and Copi in particular) . . . (this argument suggests it) is as though a man had built a wall around himself to keep out his enemies and then, finding himself in need of a door, had knocked out parts of the wall and let them all in again. We shall show that they are wrong.

3.17   I shall not deal here with the later sections of Russell's paper. In them he returns to the point (§3.12) that a reconstructed logic is necessary for the positive side of the doctrine. The nature of this reconstructed logic is more or less the same as is to be found in *Principia Mathematica*. It will be described in the next chapter. It will be sufficient here to draw attention to three points.

The first one is a technical one, concerning Burali-Forti's paradox. All the paradoxes, with the exception of Burali-Forti's paradox of the largest ordinal, disappear very readily when the theory of types is understood. The proof that Burali-Forti's paradox can be dealt with, however, is possible only when a secure theory of ordinals has been constructed. Russell's theory for this is, essentially, that put forward in his *Theory of Relations*, but now modified to take account of the theory of types. An ordinal number is a class of relations. The relations in the class generate similar well-ordered series. So the number is of a different (higher) type than the constituent individuals; and so the corresponding generation 'no longer leads to any totality of *all* ordinals'. If one considers all ordinals of one type, there are always other, greater, ordinals of higher type. This is Russell's explanation of why, although any segment of the ordinal series is well-ordered, one cannot say that the whole series is well-ordered. For the *whole series* is only a fiction, there being no whole, but only separate elements. This was a substantial change from Russell's view in a letter to Jourdain[15] in 1905 when, after early doubts,

> I agree now that the series of all ordinals is well-ordered.

The second point may be passed over briefly. The part of Russell's paper I am omitting includes a section dealing with the *multiplicative axiom*. This is so-called because it is used in defining multiplication of cardinal numbers. It states that, given a class of mutually exclusive classes, there is at least one class consisting of exactly one member of each of the mutually exclusive classes. Since one can picturesquely describe this in terms of making a 'choice' of one element from each class, it is usually called the *axiom of choice* by mathematicians. It is used in very many other constructions with infinite systems. Russell's view is that it is best not to assume the axiom,

> but to state it as a hypothesis on every occasion on which it is used.

The third point to which I want to draw attention concerns Russell's final paragraph of the paper. In it he remarks on the fact that the theory of types raises 'a number of difficult philosophical questions' about how it should be interpreted, and he promises to deal with those in a later paper. It is not very clear what difficult questions Russell has in mind here. Perhaps he is particularly concerned with the impact of the theory on ontological questions: one could puzzle, for instance, on whether objects of different type should be seen as occupying different realms of existence. At all events, Russell's attention was taken from direct consideration of those problems by three different influences. The first of these was the immense labour of working-out and writing out *Principia Mathematica*. The second was the arrival of Wittgenstein in Cambridge in 1912 and the critical study which he made of the logicist programme. Russell saw this criticism as so serious as to hold up the whole programme.

The third was Russell's increasing interest in politics, initially in general, but from 1914 onwards over pacifism. He had already been interested, in Cambridge, over the question of Free Trade. After the 1906 Election, protection was no longer a burning issue and Russell took up the cause of women's suffrage (though non-militantly, since he was already a pacifist). It is of interest to note how he describes his gradual change of opinion on women's suffrage.[2]

> Gradually, however, I became convinced that the limited enfranchisement of women which was being demanded would be more difficult to obtain than a wider measure, since the latter would be more advantageous to the Liberals, who were in power.

The main body of suffagists were opposed to this because, although it enfranchised more women, this was not on exactly the same terms as men. Russell was well able to concede a point of principle, so long as it led to substantial gains. He stood for Wimbledon at a by-election in 1907, but without success. At the 1910 election he spent much time assisting Philip Morell. This led to important developments in his personal life, for one result was that he met Lady Ottoline Morell. But this was not an event with philosophical importance. From 1910 onwards, however, the problem of war became a major preoccupation.

His initial view on the question is made very clear in a passage quoted by Jo Vellacott,[33] when Russell had been considering William James's essay in which he supposed that people want war as a mystic rite. Russell's view then was

> Men's energies need an enemy to fight, but all progress demands that the enemy should not be human.

Vellacott remarks on Russell's ability both to agree with James and also to 'bury it . . . comfortably in Liberal optimism'. But when, towards the end of August 1914, he wrote to Ottoline Morell about the disaster which had come about, he saw that his essential task was to try to think out how wars come about, how to avoid them

> and then, after the peace do all one can to bring other people round.

Other developments had taken place. There had been an

expectation in 1910 that Trinity would elect him to a permanent fellowship. This did not transpire. Russell supposed that it was because of his agnosticism. But he was appointed a college lecturer in mathematics, for five years, which carried the same salary.

In 1910 he published *Philosophical Essays*; this included work on ethics. And in 1911 his paper on knowledge by acquaintance and by description exploited the philosophical consequences of the distinction drawn in *On Denoting*. In January 1912 Wittgenstein arrived in Cambridge. I shall say more about that in Chapter 4. In 1914 Russell was invited to give the Lowell lectures in Boston, and there met T. S. Eliot. The lectures form *Our Knowledge of the External World*, whilst the poetical bonus comes in Eliot's *Mr. Apollinax*.

But the war led to his expanding his energies more on political writings. When a prosecution was pending in 1916 over a *No Conscription* pamphlet, Russell (falsely) claimed to be the author. He was convicted, and fined. In 1916 Trinity College was able to turn against him for his rational views. Not only was he cut off from the University which had meant so much to him. For the rest of his working life he was cut off from normal ways of philosophising through teaching the young. His main philosophical activity had to lie with the books he wrote. It is impossible to estimate the difference this isolation may have made to the form and content of his later work. It is true that, once the younger Fellows had returned from the war, a demand arose for his reinstatement. He accepted, with leave of absence in 1920–21. But by 1921 he had married a second time and thought that, if he took up his appointment, it would embarrass his friends. So he resigned.

Meanwhile, in 1916, the President of Harvard, Lowell, invited Russell to a full-time lectureship. The Foreign Office prevented him from leaving Britain. Had he gone it is interesting to speculate on the effect on American philosophy. Perhaps it would have reached its present active state many years earlier. But in any case the effect on Russell's work would undoubtedly have been great.

I have leaped ahead here in trying to capture the very large number of new influences that were brought to bear on

Russell after *Principia Mathematica* in 1910. I have done this to explain why its completion is an end to one particular development. In the next chapter I shall begin with a description of what *Principia Mathematica* actually does. Then I shall take up the mutual influences of Russell and Wittgenstein.

Synopsis

The main lines of Russell's contributions to philosophy and to the philosophy of mathematics are now determined. Empty reference, the main driving force behind *On Denoting* had become a preoccupation with him, from its possible connection with the contradictions. It is not clear whether he was consciously aware of this connection at first, but if not, it developed quickly. The theory of descriptions removes problems of empty reference by making the meaningfulness of denoting phrases depend on the *truth* of a certain associated proposition.

The first fruit of this new approach to the contradictions is Russell's discarded substitutional theory, but shortly afterwards his *Mathematical Logic as based on the Theory of Types* provides the sought after foundation for mathematics as a consequence of logic, with one blemish. This blemish is that, by dividing variables up into different types, only a small and inconvenient fragment of mathematics is justified. To secure something like the whole corpus of classical mathematics, the axiom of reducibility has to be assumed. Given that, it will prove to be more or less straightforward to develop the ideas into the finished form of *Principia Mathematica*.

Notes

[1] Dora Russell, *The Tamarisk Tree*, Virago, London, 1977.
[2] B. Russell, *The Autobiography of Bertrand Russell*, Vol. 1 Allen & Unwin, London, 1967.
[3] I. Grattan-Guinness, *Dear Russell – Dear Jourdain*, Duckworth, 1977.

[4] B. Russell, *On Denoting, Mind* (n.s.) **14**, 479–493, 1905, reprinted in *Logic and Knowledge* (ed. R. C. Marsh), Allen & Unwin, London 1956.

[5] B. Russell *The Principles of Mathematics* Cambridge, 1903. (a second edition, Allen & Unwin, London, 1937).

[6] G. Frege *Philosophical and Mathematical Correspondence* (ed. B. McGuinness), Blackwell, Oxford, 1979.

[7] W. V. Quine in *Essays on Bertrand Russell*, (ed. E. D. Klemke), University of Illinois, 1970.

[8] P. Schilpp (ed), *The Philosophy of Bertrand Russell*, Library of Living Philosophers, Cambridge, 1946.

[9] Reprinted in *Mysticism and Logic*, 1918, Penguin, London, 1953.

[10] G. Frege, *Zeits für Philosophie und phil. Kritik 100*, 25–50. 1892, reprinted in English as *On Sense and Meaning* in *Translations from the Philosophical Writings of Gottlob Frege*, (ed. P. Geach and M. Black), Blackwell, Oxford, third edition 1980. These translators prefer *meaning* to *reference* for Frege's *Bedeutung*. I have retained the earlier *reference* in most cases, since, as they admit, in ordinary English *meaning* is often what Frege calls *Sinn*.

[11] G. Frege in *Festschrift Ludwig Boltzmann gewidmet zum sechzigsten Geburtstage*, pp. 656–666, Leipzig, 1904. Translated as *What is a function?* in the Geach and Black volume.[10]

[12] G. Frege, in an address to the Jena *Gesellschaft für Medizin und Naturwissenschaft* 9.1.1891. Translated as *Function and Concept* in the Geach and Black volume.[10]

[13] G. Frege, *Vierteljahrschrift für wissenschaftliche Philosophie 16*, 192–205, 1892. Translated as *On Concept and Object* in the Geach and Black volume.[10]

[14] H. B. Curry and R. Feys, *Combinatory Logic* (Vol. 1), North-Holland 1958.

[15] M. Schönfinkel, *Math. Ann.* **92**, 305–316, 1924.

[16] The technical details are to be found in[14]. It may be mentioned here, though, that an important part is played by the so-called *paradoxical combinator* $Y = WS(BWB)$. This generates paradoxes in a logical context but it is possible to see easily that it has peculiar properties by evaluating its effect on any variable x. For

$$WS(BWB)x \rightarrow S(BWB)(BWB)x \tag{1}$$
$$\rightarrow BWBx(BWBx) \tag{2}$$
$$\rightarrow W(Bx)(BWBx) \tag{3}$$
$$\rightarrow Bx(BWBx)(BWBx) \tag{4}$$
$$\rightarrow x(BWBx)(BWBx) \tag{5}$$

Comparison with (2) shows that, in turn

$$BWBx(BWBx) \rightarrow x(BWBx)(BWBx)$$
$$\rightarrow xx(BWBx)(BWBx)$$
$$\rightarrow xxx(BWBx)(BWBx)$$

and so on. This sequence is reminiscent of one presentation of Russell's paradox, in which one supposes R ε R. Then, from the definition, ~(R ε R). Therefore, from the definition, R ε R. So, from the definition ~(R ε R) . . . But, to quote Curry and Feys[13]

> It should be emphasised that we cannot say that Y . . . (is) meaningless in the sense that (it is) to be excluded from the theory . . . the theory of combinators is consistent in quite a strong sense.

The mathematical reader may also want to see the expression for $x^2 - y^2 = (x + y)(x - y)$. For convenience, adjoin the difference operator D, $Dxy = x - y$. In bracketless notation we have to equate DMxx Myy with MAxyDxy, that is, as MSAD(xy). The brackets can be inserted by the combinator B so we have to equate DMxx Myy with MB(SAD)xy. But the first term converts to $\psi D(WM)xy \rightarrow D((WM)x)(WM)y)$, so the identity becomes

$$MB(SAD) = \psi D(WM).$$

It may be also noted in passing that all the combinators can be defined in terms of a small number. For example, in terms of S and K it may be verified that

I = SKK, B = S(KS)K, W = SS(KI),
C = S(BBS)KK, $\psi = \varphi\ (\varphi\ (\varphi B))\ B(KK)$,

where φ = B(B(B(B(BW)C)(BB)))B.

[17] G. H. Hardy, *Pure Mathematics*, First edition, Cambridge 1908.
[18] G. Frege, *Begriffsschrift*, Halle/Saale, 1879. Chapter 1 is translated in the Geach and Black volume.[9]
[19] H. Weyl, *Das Kontinuum*, Zurich 1917.
[20] A. J. Ayer, *Russell and Moore – The Analytical Heritage*, Macmillan 1971.
[21] D. F. Pears, *Bertrand Russell and the British Tradition in Philosophy*, Collins/Fontana, London, 1967.
[22] Russell translates *Sinn* and *Bedeutung* as *meaning* and *denotation*. *Denotation* would serve just as well as *reference*, but I have rendered Russell's argument into *sense* and *reference* to agree with my usage with Frege. To render *Sinn* as *meaning* would lead to hopeless confusion, especially as Geach and Black[10] very reasonably use *meaning* for *Bedeutung*.
[23] I. Grattan-Guinness, *Ann. Science* **31**, 387–406, 1974, summarised by the author on pp. 74–77 of[3].
[24] A. J. Ayer, *Russell*, Collins/Fontana, London, 1972.
[25] B. Russell, *Amer. Jour. Math.* **30**, 222–262, 1908. Reprinted in J. van Heijenoort *From Frege to Gödel* Harvard, Cambridge: Mass. 1967 and also in R. C. Marsh, *Logic and Knowledge*, Allen & Unwin, London 1956.
[26] E. Zermelo, *Math. Ann.* **65**, 261–281, 1908.
[27] L. E. J. Brouwer, *Tijdschrift v. Wijsbegeerte 2*, 152–158 1908.
[28] St. Paul, *Epistle to Titus*, I,12.

[29] L. Wittgenstein, *Tractatus Logico-Philosophicus*, trans. C. K. Ogden, Routledge and Kegan Paul, London, 1922. Another translation by B. F. McGuinness and D. F. Pears, Routledge and Kegan Paul 1961. I have quoted from the Ogden translation but with one or two amendments of my own.

[30] E. D. Klemke (ed), *Essays on Bertrand Rusell*, University of Illinois, 1970.

[31] R. Carnap, *Erkenntnis* **2**, 91, 1931. Reprinted in P. Benacerraf and H. Putnam, *Philosophy of Mathematics*, Blackwell, Oxford, 1964.

[32] G. W. Roberts (ed), *Bertrand Russell Memorial Volume*, Allen & Unwin (Muirhead Library of Philosophy), London 1979.

[33] Jo Vellacott, *Bertrand Russell and the Pacifists in the first world war*, Harvester, 1980.

CHAPTER IV

1911–1927 The solution completed

Section 1: *Principia Mathematica*

4.1   So far I have described a number of Russell's earlier books and papers. There are two threads which run through these and which I have repeatedly mentioned. These two threads are:

  (i) The need to substantiate the truth of mathematics by constructing it from logic, whose truth was acknowledged,

 (ii) the strengthening of logic by a fully-developed theory of relations.

The first thread is closely related to an epistemological point; we can, it is held, know the truth of mathematics, because we know the truth of logic. The second thread is similarly related to an ontological point; the reality of relations substantiates the corresponding reality of their terms. These two threads are both present in the peak of Russell's achievement, *Principia Mathematica*,[1] which is the subject of Sections 1 and 2 of this chapter. This remarkable book pulls together all the ideas I have drawn from the earlier works and tried to weld them into a whole. To some extent it is confused. The magnitude of the task makes this unsurprising. Instead of emphasising any confusions I prefer to stress the way in which the book shares the property of two other books, not so different in their dates. It poses and answers one apparently simple question, about the truth of mathematics, in just the same way that Frazer's *Golden Bough* and Marx's *Das Kapital* pose and answer one question.

There are therefore two aspects of *Principia Mathematica*, one of which tends to be neglected. The evident aspect, which cannot be ignored by anyone who opens the book, is the technical, logical one. A detailed argument is used to construct, firstly, the natural numbers and their arithmetic, as in the *Logic of Relations* as I described in Chapter 2 Section 1. The book is complete in the sense that no prior knowledge is essential to read it. Everything is explained; though naturally there is the usual trade-off between prior knowledge and ability. The reader with no prior knowledge must be one of quite exceptional ability. The argument is carried on beyond elementary arithmetic to the construction of the rest of arithmetic, and of mathematical analysis. Every detail in the logical argument is set out in a fully formalised language, and ordinary English is avoided as much as possible to avoid ambiguities.

It is conceivable that in 1911 other people than Russell could have carried out such a technical construction. Hilbert and the formalist school might, for example, have seen the construction of mathematics from logic as a means of assuring the consistency of mathematics, assuming that of logic. Russell's approach was different because of his concern over the truth of logic and mathematics, and this concern is the other aspect of *Principia Mathematica*. This aspect is less evident, for there is little mention of truth in the text, but the idea is taken for granted. That it is taken for granted may be seen by considering what Russell says about mathematics in other places. For example, in *Mysticism and Logic*, in an essay dated 1901 he says,

> We start, in pure mathematics, from certain rules of inference, by which we can infer that, *if* one proposition is true, then so is some other proposition.

Two years later, in *The Principles of Mathematics*, he writes,

> Pure mathematics is the class of all propositions of the form 'p implies q', where p and q are propositions containing one or more variables, the same in the two propositions, and neither p nor q contains any constants except logical constants . . . In addition to these, mathematics *uses* a notion which is not a constituent of the propositions which it considers, the notion of truth.

In *The Problems of Philosophy* in 1912 we find, in a discussion which is mainly about Kant and the synthetic *a priori*, a description of the logicist programme and

> It seems strange that we should apparently know some truths in advance about particular things of which we have as yet no experience; but it cannot easily be doubted that logic and arithmetic will apply to such things.

The examples could be multiplied. It is clear that Russell throughout attached considerable importance to truth. It is less clear just what he meant by truth, and how he saw the truth of logic. About this he is disarmingly frank in *Portraits from Memory* when he writes, on his eightieth birthday.

> I may have conceived theoretical truth wrongly, but I was not wrong in thinking that there is such a thing, and that it deserves our allegiance.

In his early life he was not disposed to believe that true logical statements were analytic, since this would imply that they were trivial. He takes this point up in *The Principles of Mathematics*:

> It seems clear that there must be some way of defining logic otherwise than in relation to a particular logical language. The fundamental characteristic of logic, obviously, is that which is indicated when we say that logical propositions are true in virtue of their form . . . I must confess, however, that I am unable to give any clear account of what is meant by saying that a proposition 'is true in virtue of its form.' But this phrase, inadequate as it is, points, I think, to the problem which must be solved if an adequate definition of logic is to be found.

Later Russell agreed with Wittgenstein's analysis that the theorems of the propositional calculus are tautologies, but whereas Wittgenstein extended this logic as a whole, Russell went over to the view that theorems in quantification theory were analytic.

Correspondingly, Russell's view of truth in general underwent changes. At the beginning of the century he saw truth as an undefinable attribute of some propositions. Later he went over to what he called a correspondence theory of truth, in the sense that the arrangements of the objects in a proposition corresponded with their arrangement in reality.

Later still he tried still further variants. So it must be admitted that the sense in which Russell understood the truth of logic, or mathematics, to be established is not completely clear. My aim in this book is not to clarify it, but to exhibit this concern for truth as the guiding thought behind the earlier books, as it is for *Principia Mathematica*. The concern can be traced back to his early desire for certainty of knowledge. Pure mathematics seemed the most promising field to start with, and this led to the quixotic attempt which culminated in the book.

And now, turning to the details of *Principia Mathematica* I begin by a brief summary of the first edition relating it to the works of Russell that I have discussed in previous chapters. Here is to be a book whose whole aim is to provide a secure foundation for mathematics on the basis of logic. Logic and mathematics are to be shown as truth, not merely as a consistent formal system. This continues the emphasis already to be found in the *Foundations of Geometry*. In the method to ensure this one can trace two influences. The first of these is Leibniz's *Characteristica Universalis*, the second the need for a positive doctrine to follow the restrictions, generated by the theory of types as explained in Chapter 3 §2. The necessary preliminary formulation of logic is a development of that in *Mathematical Logic based as on the Theory of Types*[2] which I omitted in my earlier description. Here it is dealt with in §4.1 to §4.3. There are certain unsatisfactory features of Russell's approach, and some alternatives to avoid these are discussed in §4.4 and §4.5. The distinction between apparent and real variables from *Mathematical Logic* is taken up next, together with other discussions on quantified propositional functions. This carries very much further the discussion that began on *On Denoting* and it allows the formulation of Leibniz's identity of indiscernibles. These are described in §4.6 and §4.7. In §4.7 I also mention briefly Russell's introduction of types and the axiom of reducibility. These follow closely the corresponding sections of *Mathematical Logic*.

Russell goes on to classes and relations, but with particular reference to the results on relations that have no analogue for classes. The work in the early *Logic of Rela-*

tions is extended considerably, and the arithmetic of cardinals is set up in much the same way as there. I describe these developments in §4.8 and §4.9. The succeeding part of *Principia Mathematica* is largely a fully worked-out application of the ideas that I have just listed. In §4.10 I describe what distinction Russell is able to draw between finite and infinite quantities, an extension of the distinction mentioned in Chapter 2. Finally, §4.11 describes the construction of mathematical analysis and the real number system. This last is the way in which Russell defeats Leibniz's 'labyrinth of the continuum' and strives to lay to rest the problem of irrationals which beset the Pythagoreans.

It could be argued then, that the principal philosophical ideas of *Principia Mathematica* have already been discussed in previous chapters, particularly Chapter 3. Though there is truth in this, I would not draw the conclusion that no further attention need now be paid to that book. This is for two reasons. Firstly, it seems to me that no true appreciation of Russell is possible without understanding the main lines of his major contribution. But, secondly, the details of *Principia Mathematica*, as one progresses through it, throw up enlightenment about a number of points in Russell's thought, in addition to the principal themes of denoting and types. Accordingly I shall now go on to give a fuller description of the contents of this least accessible of Russell's works. In this description I shall concentrate on the material of Volume 1 to a considerable extent, but not exclusively.

The reason for this is one mentioned earlier. Russell is prone to continuing with any successful line of argument well on into the orthodox mathematical developments to which it leads, and naturally this occurs more in the later volumes. Indeed, it is explicitly stated in[1]

> In making deductions from our premises, we have considered it essential to carry them up to the point where we have proved as much as is true of whatever could ordinarily be taken for granted. But we have not thought it desirable to limit ourselves too strictly to this task.

In what follows, I shall refer the authorship of the joint work to Russell. This is not meant to imply any lack of respect for Whitehead's significant contribution. It is merely intended to serve two purposes; shortness, and emphasis on the fact that our study of the book is being carried out exclusively for its position in Russell's thought.

It would, indeed, be tempting to speculate on how different the book would have been if various outside influences had not prevented the cooperation between the two authors in the later part of Volume 2 and in Volume 3. Russell shows a tendency to be excessively formalistic and Whitehead seems to restrain this. That is, of course, a result of the partnership, for Whitehead by himself is very obscure and not, I believe, so deep. But Russell seems, at this stage, very much the typical mathematician, needing someone to interact with, to bring the abstraction down to earth. It would be tempting, but fruitless.

The most readily available edition of *Principia Mathematica* is the second, of 1927, but the main text of this is the unchanged text of the first. The editions differ only in detailed suggestions for revision to the first edition, that come in a thirty-page introduction to Volume 1. This introduction contains many remarks of great interest. I defer consideration of it to Section 2 of this chapter, for it provides a view of how Russell thought the work was affected by the criticism of Wittgenstein, to whom I shall turn in Section 3. The main work comes in three volumes, and is divided into six parts I, II, . . . VI. Each part is divided into between three and six (lettered) sections. These sections in turn are divided up into shorter portions, somewhat like chapters, which are numbered off with an asterisk, as *1, *23, ... This numbering is not consecutive but begins afresh in each section. Thus in part I, section A contains *1 to *5, and section B then starts with *9, finishing with *14. Section C begins with *20 and so on. This provides room for additional numbers to be inserted if required. Generally, the word *number* is used for these shorter portions. The propositions in any one number are numbered on a decimal basis, following Peano, in which the most important propositions have the shortest decimals. To take a detailed example in *2, the proposition *2.5 has some analogous results numbered *2.51, *2.52, and a corollary of this last one is then numbered *2.521, before another, related, result appears as *2.53. So much for the technical structure of the presentation, which was adopted to make possible the elaborate cross-referencing involved in writing out very full proofs.

Part I is called *Mathematical Logic* and contains five sections. Here Russell is taking up the point[2] that the negative side of the restrictions used to avoid vicious circle fallacies needs to be balanced by a positive construction of logic. Part I is said to deal with

> such topics as belong traditionally to symbolic logic, or deserve to belong to it in virtue of their generality.

This summarises what Whitehead and Russell had found the situation to be; that logic itself was in such a primitive state that it needed construction in any case, even without the need to avoid the contradictions. Here, of course, as earlier, I must stress that the construction being carried out is not a free creation of a formal system, but an analysis of an objective, true, but previously imperfectly formulated, logic. In the introduction:

> It is not claimed that the analysis could not have been carried further; we have no reason to suppose that it is impossible to find simpler ideas and axioms by means of which those with which we start could be defined and demonstrated. All that is affirmed is that the ideas and axioms with which we start are sufficient, not that they are necessary.

*1 begins by listing the basic notions: *elementary propositions*, which are described as propositions which do not contain variables. The example given of such a proposition is 'This is red', where 'this' is something given in sensation. Combinations of elementary propositions p, q by negation, disjunction or conjunction give respectively not p, p or q, p & q, that is, $\sim p, p \vee q, p \& q$. These are also to be counted as elementary. Propositions, it is held, may be asserted, or merely considered. If p stands for the unasserted proposition, the sign $\vdash .p$ is to denote the asserted form. The dot plays the part of a bracket and need not concern us at present. The other part of the sign $\vdash$, is derived from Frege's *Begriffsschrift*,[3] and is attributed to him. For Frege it is, as it were, the left-hand end of the 'trees' of propositions that grow across the pages of *Begriffsschrift*, and so on the same

Russell

footing as the indentations of branches to denote quantifiers as in §1.5 above. Here it is a single isolated symbol.

If one were to adopt, as Russell certainly would not, a modern division between the symbolic formal system and the natural informal language, or meta-system, used to talk about the structure of the formal system, then the assertion sign would be difficult to place. Russell gives one example which will serve to illustrate this. It uses, in anticipation, the notion of implication, which is to be introduced later. Russell develops Peano's inverted C sign into the symbol $\supset$ for *implies*. The example is that $\vdash (p \supset q)$ means 'it is true that p implies q', whereas $(\vdash p) \supset (\vdash q)$ means 'p is true; therefore q is true'. Here it seems evident that $\vdash$ is part of the system in the second proposition, but in the first it plays the part of an assertion in the meta-system. But, in any case, as I have said earlier, Russell, with his insistence on truth, would not accept the idea of any such division into system and meta-system.

I return for a moment for the use of dots for brackets. This is just an ingenious use, devised by Peano, of readily available printer's symbols to prevent the symbolism from becoming too clumsy. The convention is that, when a certain number of dots follow a symbol, the symbol applies to everything until one reaches an equal number of dots or the end of the sentence. Dots may also precede an implication sign, with a similar convention going backwards. The two examples given above are written by Russell as

$$\vdash : p . \supset . q$$

and

$$\vdash . p . \supset \vdash . q,$$

but the first of these could equally be written

$$\vdash . p \supset q.$$

The additional number of dots will be needed when compound propositions occur, as in

$$\vdash : p \supset {\sim}p . \supset . {\sim}p.$$

A little experience is sufficient to allow these formulae to be read as easily as if they were written with brackets; and it is, of course, essential to get a close acquaintance with Russell's notation in order to understand the ideas.

4.2   It has been necessary to enter into some details of notation in order to understand quotations, but, with the exception of certain aspects of the assertion sign, these are of no importance in the argument. I return now to the matters of content.

Assertion of a propositional function is referred to briefly; this is really a reappearance of the distinction[2] between real and apparent variables. Here the main use of it is in the interpretation of such a propositional function as

$$\vdash . \, p \supset p.$$

If, as intended, this is to be interpreted as the classical logician's *law of identity*, 'if p, then p', then it must be read as applying to *any* elementary proposition p.

> By leaving p undetermined, we obtain an assertion which can be applied to any particular elementary proposition.

Then the notations ~p and p ∨ q are introduced to correspond to the negation of p and the disjunction, 'p or q or both'. In terms of these the conditional, or, as Russell always calls it, *implication* is defined by

$$*1.01 \quad p \supset q . = . \, {\sim}p \vee q \quad Df$$

Two further remarks on notation may be made here. The proposition could have been written

$$p \supset q := : \, {\sim}p . \vee . q,$$

but this more cumbersome form with extra dots has been avoided by adopting the convention that negation applies only to the immediately following elementary proposition and does not extend beyond any other connective. So that ~p. ∨. q can be written ~p ∨ q, and if one wishes to negate p ∨ q one must write out, *in extenso* ~. p ∨ q. The second remark concerns the abbreviation Df at the end, which indicates that the sign of equality is to be read as 'is defined to mean'.

At this stage in his development Russell would have accepted quite generally a thesis that is perhaps indubitable in mathematics. This is the thesis that when we gain knowledge by description of properties and relations, we already need some *a priori* knowledge about the properties denoted by the words in the description in order to understand their meanings, and this *a priori* knowledge is provided by definitions of the words. This thesis goes back a long way. Russell saw it in Hume, though Wittgenstein ascribes it to Socrates. Outside of mathematics there are evident difficulties about this thesis. Other ways than definition will serve to make clear the meaning of a word. Russell saw the general thesis as one about how philosophers should strive to improve their subject, to make it more scientific.

Finally it should be remarked that the operation ⊃ is the standard conditional which is now more often denoted by →. It would be more usual to read p ⊃ q as 'If p, then q' and so to avoid misconceptions and irrelevant argument about material implication, modality and so on. Russell's contention, which would not, I think, be seriously contested, it that in mathematics the only relevant implication is the conditional. This is notwithstanding the slightly curious fact that, if p is false, then p ⊃ q is true, whatever q may be.

The next step is to set up a means of inference. The modern view of this is that both axioms and rules of inference are needed, the former belonging to the system, the latter to the metasystem. Since Russell would not accept this distinction, he lumps them together and calls both *primitive propositions*, marking them Pp in the text. The first one, which

> We cannot express . . . symbolically, partly because any symbolism in which p is variable only gives the *hypothesis* that p is true, not the *fact* that p is true.

is that anything implied by a true elementary proposition is true. This, like other references to elementary propositions, is qualified by a promise to extend the results to other than elementary propositions in *9. The second is a variant of this for propositional functions, and is much more like the traditional *modus ponens*: If ⊢ φ x, where x is a real variable, and ⊢ . φx ⊃ ψx. then ⊢ ψx. But, as so often with Russell, there is considerably more subtlety involved here than later developments might suggest. For the primitive proposition refers to a real variable x. The assertion of φx is for any x for which φx is significant. Similarly ⊢ .φx ⊃ ψx is for values of x giving it significance. These may, then, not be the same class of values of x as before. Now the theory of types has a principle that, if there is any value a of x such that both φa and ψa are significant, then the range of values of x is the same in each. Russell argues that, if ⊢ φx ⊃ ψx, there must be values a for which φa ⊃ ψa is significant, and so for which φa, ψa are both significant. Then, using the principle, the primitive proposition both ensures that the ranges of x for φx, ψx are the same and also states a practical consequence.

4.3   The next stage is to set out those further primitive propositions that would now be called axioms. Those are five in number:

$$p \lor p . \supset . p$$
$$q . \supset . p \lor q$$
$$p \lor q . \supset . q \lor p$$
$$p . \lor . q \lor r : \supset : q . \lor p \lor r$$
$$q \supset r : \supset : p \lor q . \supset . p \lor r$$

In quoting these I have omitted their numbers, the assertion signs and the mark Pp of being an elementary proposition, since these are relevant only in the detailed deduction, which I do not intend to carry out. The first one, for example, actually occurs in the form:

$$*1.2 . \vdash : p \lor p. \supset . p \quad Pp.$$

These five axioms are followed by explicit statements that the class of elementary propositions is closed under negation and disjunction. That is to say, if p, q are elementary, so are ∼p and p ∨ q. This is merely a statement of what constitutes an elementary proposition. There is also an 'axiom of identification of real variables' of the form

*1.72. If φp and ψp are elementary propositional functions which take elementary propositions as arguments, $\varphi p \vee \psi p$ is an elementary propositional function.

Like the version of *modus ponens* described above, this is to prove useful in connection with the theory of types.

Most people would not now choose these five axioms as a basis for the propositional calculus. For one thing, they are not independent. The fourth one was shown by Bernays[4] to be derivable from the other three, though admittedly by a long and arduous derivation. But a more serious objection is the rather arbitrary selection of propositions which has been made. The five chosen as assumptions are, it is true, intuitively obvious, given the interpretations of the connectives, but they are not more intuitively obvious than many of those later to be deduced. They are simply five found by Whitehead and Russell as adequate for providing proofs of all the others; but this adequacy itself is known only as the result of experience, and is not formally proved.

A clue to what was omitted here by Russell is provided if we ask how we would know when we had all the other true propositions, at least of the propositional calculus as it is dealt with in *1—*5, that is, in section A of Part I. For the characteristic feature of propositions is that they have a truth-value and so must be either true or false. And the characteristic feature of the propositional functions generated by negation or disjunction is that they are truth functions. The truth value of φp depends only on the truth value of p, when φ is a truth function.

It is more convenient to use the symbols 1, 0 for *true, false* and to denote the truth value of any proposition p by $|p|$. Then the truth value of $\sim p$ is $|\sim p|$ which is 0 if $|p| = 1$ and 1 if $|p| = 0$. Similarly $|p \vee q| = 1$ unless both $|p| = 0$ and $|q| = 0$. It then follows from the definition of implication that $|p \supset q| = 1$ unless both $|p| = 1$ and $|q| = 0$. This method of dealing with the propositional connectives originated later with Wittgenstein,[5] though there are hints of it already in Chapter 1 of Frege's *Begriffsschrift*.[3]

Now an asserted proposition or propositional function must always have the truth-value *true*, and it is precisely those that can be asserted. For example, $|p \vee p. \supset . p| = 1$

always. One can see this as follows: suppose that it were possible that $|p \lor p. \supset .p| = 0$. Then both $|p \lor p| = 1$ and $|p| = 0$. But if $|p| = 0$, then $|p \lor p| = 0$; so, in fact, no situation can actually arise when $|p \lor p. \supset . p| = 0$.

If we call a compound proposition, A, a *tautology* when $|A| = 1$ for all possible truth-values of its constituents, the situation in the propositional calculus is that tautologies and only tautologies may be asserted. Since, moreover, it is easy to see that the methods of inference, applied to tautologies, yield tautologies, and since also the five primitive propositions are tautologies, it follows that the system proposed in *Principia Mathematica* fulfils half of the condition stated. For any proposition which is asserted because it has been derived from the axioms must be a tautology. But it is not made clear whether the system fulfils the other half of the condition, that is, whether the axiom system is strong enough for all tautologies to be derivable. Evidently if certain axioms were struck out it would not be possible for all necessary deductions to be carried out in it. In fact the system *is* strong enough and this fact can be proved without too much difficulty, though a good deal of labour is involved. I shall later give a sketch of how this can be done, without bothering about the details. To do this it will be necessary to look more closely at the idea of setting up an axiom-system for propositions.

4.4   As usual with Russell there is a more subtle point in this that needs consideration. The connectives ~, ∨ have been explained by him, but the explanation of their meaning is not to be used in proving results. It is merely an explanation intended to make the reader more happy in following the deductions in the system, because he can see an intuitive good sense behind them. So the question arises of how the meaning of the connectives actually enters the system. The answer to this can only be, that the axioms listed must exhibit this meaning, and this is one of their functions. If one does not wish to be so subtle as this there are at least three different approaches which can be made to the propositional calculus. I shall begin by describing Quine's.[6] Then I shall describe a new one which is a philosophical compromise between Quine's no-nonsense position and that of Church.[7] Finally I shall describe the Church approach.

If one is content to define the meaning of p ∨ q, for example, simply by specifying its truth-value:

$$|p \lor q| = 1 \quad \text{unless both} \quad |p| = 0 \text{ and } |q| = 0,$$

then one can, following Quine,[6] simply *define* the class of all true propositions of the system to be the class of all tautologies. Quine would say, of course, that all *theorems* are tautologies. I have referred to true propositions to agree with the spirit of Russell's system. There is no need for a list of axioms. Those listed in *Principia Mathematica* are on a complete symmetrical basis with all the other proved propositions. A deduction of A, for Quine, then has a simple standard form. One merely verifies that any arbitrary assigning of truth values to the constituents of A cannot make $|A| = 0$. So, for example, if A is

$$q \supset r : \supset : p \lor q . \supset . p \lor r,$$

it is exhibited as a theorem in the following way. Suppose that there were an assigning of truth-values to p, q, r such that $|A| = 0$. Then, from what was said above about $|B \supset C|$, this assigning makes $|q \supset r| = 1$ and $|p \lor q . \supset . p \lor r| = 0$. The second of these requires $|p \lor q| = 1$ and $|p \lor r| = 0$, which together require $|p| = |r| = 0$, $|q| = 1$. This gives $|q \supset r| = 0$, contrary to the previous requirement, so we have reached a contradiction. Hence no such assigning exists, and so $|A| = 1$ always, or, in Russell's language, ⊢A. The realisation that Russell's system could be looked at in this way came with Wittgenstein.[5]

Quine's position is actually the conflation of two closely related ones. He believes in removing all doubt about propositions by including the fact that they have two truth-values from the beginning. He then believes in removing all doubt about connectives by giving precise rules for their truth-values, since they do generate truth-functions. It is possible however, to take Quine's view about propositions, and not go so far as he does about the connectives. That is, one can ask the question; What collection of axioms would be adequate to characterise the connectives used by Russell, given explicit use of the two-valuedness of propositions and given also the stated rules of inference? The purpose of the last clause in the question is to restrict the possible interpretation that can be given to ⊃, because *modus ponens* leads from $|p| = 1$, $|p \supset q| = 1$ to $|q| = 1$, so that if, in fact $|q| = 0$ and $|p| = 1$, it must be the case that $|p \supset q| = 0$. There are, doubtless, many different selections of propositions that will serve to characterise the connectives, given the two-valuedness. I shall content myself by showing the way that the two simplest of Russell's axioms will suffice for this.

What is to be shown here is that certain axioms are sufficient to characterise the two-valued truth-tables for the connectives. I begin with the first of Russell's axioms:

$$p \lor p . \supset . p$$

Here I am taking for granted his definition of ⊃ in terms ∨, ~. If I did not do this, another investigation would be needed. It could still be carried out, but would have no relevance to *Principia Mathematica*. What we know already is that, if $|A| = 1$, $|A \supset B|$ is in fact $|B|$. This is the condition of agreement with *modus ponens* as a method of inference. If, then $|p| = 0$, Russell's first axiom can be a tautology only if $|p \lor p| = 0$, and, since we are dealing with a truth-function, it follows that $|p \lor q| = 0$ for $|p| = 0$ and $|q| = 0$.

Turn now to the axiom

$$p. \supset . p \lor q$$

and consider the case when $|p| = 1$. In that case $|p \lor q| = 1$ as well, so that we now have most of the values of $p \lor q$ and can construct a small table:

	p ∨ q	q: 0	1
p	0	0	
	1	1	1

So far we have paid no attention to the negation and the extent to which ~p is characterised by the axioms. Only four possible tables for negation can be drawn up:

		a	b	c	d
			~p		
p	0	0	1	0	1
	1	1	0	0	1

of which (b) is the expected one and (a), (c), (d) are, we hope, to be ruled out as a result of the axioms.

We can reject (a) at once, since it makes $\sim$p = p and therefore p $\supset$ q. = . p ∨ q. This is forbidden by the fact that the bottom line of the table for p ∨ q would not be (0, 1), as it has to be (to preserve inference) for p $\supset$ q. Similarly if (d) is chosen, then |p ∨ q| = 1 whatever the values of p, q and this again conflicts with the necessary zero in the tables for p $\supset$ q. Finally, suppose that (c) is chosen, so that the values of |$\sim$p ∨ q| are determined by q alone and are those in the (so far partially completed) top line of the table for p ∨ q. Then since these values, which are those of p $\supset$ q, do not depend on p, they must be (0, 1), so that the usual table for p ∨ q has been completed, and also |p $\supset$ q| = |q|. But this will not do, for then |p ∨ p. $\supset$. p| = |p| and so, if |p| = 0, this is not a tautology. Hence (c) must also be rejected, and the only allowed table for negation is the usual one:

p	~p
0	1
1	0

If this negation table is used with what is already determined of the tables for $\sim$, ∨, it is clear that all the entries in the usual tables are determined.

The interest in this demonstration is not that the two particular axioms

$$p \lor p. \supset . p$$
$$p. \supset . p \lor q$$

and the definition

$$p \supset q . = . \sim p \lor q$$

have any particular virtue. Similar results could doubtless be shown for other combinations of Russell's axioms. What is of interest is that, if the two-valuedness of propositions is taken fully into account, considerably less than Russell's whole set of axioms will suffice to characterise the connectives.

4.5   I turn to the third view of the propositional calculus associated particularly with Alonzo Church. This approach takes the statement that the axiom system is to be adequate to prove every tautology and only those as the preeminently desirable condition that the axiom-system must satisfy, and one, indeed, which determines, in a fairly unique manner, the actual structure of the axioms. I shall sketch here only the first steps in the construction of the axiom-system on this basis, since to do more would lead me too far astray. Details of the whole construction can be found in Church's *Mathematical Logic*,[7] though, for technical reasons, he prefers to operate there with a system without negation, and to insert instead a constant false proposition f. I shall begin the description in a system more near to Russell's but I shall differ by taking $\supset$ as the basic connective from which, with negation, the others can in due course be defined.

Since Church seeks to establish the adequacy of the axiom system for proof, he finds it necessary to say precisely what is meant by proof in his system. Apart from substitution of one proposition by another, the only substantial rule of proof in *Principia Mathematica* is *modus ponens*. The first result that Church's approach requires may be called the *Deduction Theorem*. It states that if, from the assumption of A, a proof of B can be found, then a proof of $A \supset B$ may also be found. I shall use the symbol $\vdash$ to indicate proof, so as to avoid confusion with Russell's assertion sign. Here we are dealing with a formal system, and the sign $\vdash$ is not in the system, but in the meta-system. The expression A, B $\vdash$ C will denote that C is provable from the assumption of A and B having been already proved. One usually omits mention of the axioms. A and B here are specific assumptions, perhaps introduced at a particular point of the argument. In particular, $\vdash$ C denotes that there is a proof of C from the axioms, that is, that C is a *theorem*.

The deduction theorem states, then, that if A ⊢ B, then ⊢ A ⊃ B, and, indeed, more generally, that if A, B, C, ..., K, L ⊢ Z, then A, B, C, ..., K ⊢ L ⊃ Z. In order to construct an axiom-system for which the deduction theorem must hold, consider a proof in the system. It consists of a chain of statements

$$P, Q, R, \ldots, V$$

where V is the conclusion, and each P, Q, R, ... in the chain is related to *earlier* ones by

(a) quoting an axiom
(b) quoting one of the specific assumptions A, B, C, ...
(c) substitution
(d) *Modus ponens*.

This is a restatement of the idea of proof expressed above, but (a), (b) have been added, as they obviously should be.

The proof of the deduction theorem takes the form of showing that, when there is a chain concluding in V = Z, there is also one concluding in V′ = L ⊃ Z. This can be done one step at a time by utilising one crucial fact about proofs. This fact is that, at every stage of a proof, the proof up to that stage is in fact a complete proof of the last statement made. Accordingly, a sequence of propositions

$$L ⊃ P, L ⊃ Q, \ldots, L ⊃ Z$$

is written down. This is not a proof, as it stands, since successive terms are not related by *modus ponens* or substitution in the way that has been described. But one can formulate just the necessary axioms that will always enable this to be 'filled-in' by extra steps to make it into a proof. A more detailed investigation[8] shows that it is sufficient to have as theorems or axioms in the system

$$p ⊃ p.$$
$$p . ⊃ . q ⊃ p,$$
$$p . ⊃ . q ⊃ r : ⊃ : p ⊃ q . ⊃ . p ⊃ r.$$

The deduction theorem will then hold.

Conversely, if the deduction theorem holds, these three

results must be true in the system. For example, it is evident that

$$p, q \vDash p,$$

for the proof consists simply in quoting p. The deduction theorem would then yield

$$p \vDash q \supset p,$$

and a second application of it gives

$$\vDash p . \supset . q \supset p.$$

Similar arguments serve for the other two.

I leave my description of Church's construction of an axiom system at this point. The next steps would be to introduce negation and, having done so, to show how to construct proofs of tautologies. It is necessary here only to see that such a construction can be carried out.

As a result of this investigation one finishes with a system of axioms which is certainly adequate for deriving every tautology, and only those. Since any theorem of *Principia Mathematica* is a tautology, it follows that every theorem and axiom of *Principia Mathematica* is derivable in Church's system. Conversely, the axioms of Church's system are amongst the theorems of *Principia Mathematica*, a fact that can be verified simply by thumbing through the pages of proved theorems in that book. So it follows that all the theorems of Church's system are theorems of *Principia Mathematica*. The two systems are therefore equivalent. The benefit of this investigation is two-fold. In the first place, it establishes that all tautologies are provable in *Principia Mathematica*. Secondly, it formulates a rationally chosen set of axioms suitable for deriving tautologies. In this way the arbitrariness in choice of axioms exhibited by *Principia Mathematica* can be removed.

4.6   I return now to the actual development of logic given by Russell. I shall be able to deal with it very shortly, because the details, in the sketch above of a alternative approaches, will serve to illustrate it equally well. After some immediate deductions from the axioms in *2, conjunc-

tion or the logical product as it is here called, is introduced in
*3. Russell uses a dot for this, so that the definition of *p and
q* is:

$$\text{*3.01} \quad \text{p. q.} = . \sim(\sim\text{p} \lor \sim\text{q}). \quad \text{Df.}$$

This is an unfortunate notation, since confusion can arise
about a dot signifying conjunction and one which is used as a
bracket. I propose to vary Russell's notation at this point
and to write p&q for what he would write as p.q. Then *4
introduces logical equivalence:

$$\text{*4.01.} \quad \text{p} \equiv \text{q: =: p} \supset \text{q. &. q} \supset \text{p,}$$

and Section A concludes in *5 by proving various miscellaneous propositions, including slightly unusual ones such as

$$\text{*5.1} \quad \text{p & q.} \supset . \text{p} \equiv \text{q.}$$

Section B deals with apparent variables, since the distinction between real and apparent variables in *Mathematical
Logic as based on the Theory of Types*[2] was still important to
Russell at the time of the first edition. *9 introduces the
notations (x).φx, ($\exists$x).φx, and x is called an apparent variable. If a proposition has not apparent variables, it is called
elementary.

> For reasons explained in Chapter II of the Introduction, it would seem
> that negation and disjunction and their derivatives must have a different
> meaning when applied to elementary propositions from that which they
> have when applied to such propositions as (x).φx or ($\exists$x).φx.

It will be necessary to spend a little time on this rather
curious assertion.

The Chapter II mentioned here is, in fact, a remodelled
version of *Mathematical Logic*[2] and the point made by Russell comes up in his discussion of types. He begins by observ-
ing straightforwardly that, since (x).φx involves the function
φ, it is impossible for it to serve as an argument for φ, and so
φ((x).φx) is meaningless. But then Russell suggests that the
principle just enunciated may have exceptions. It is to avoid
such exceptions that Russell proposes this variation in the
meaning of truth-functions. He argues for possible excep-

tions in the following way. Suppose $\varphi p = \sim p$ and consider $(p).\varphi p$ which asserts that all propositions p are false. Since this proposition is, presumably, false, it seems we *can* assert $\varphi((p).\varphi p)$ in this case. Yet, of course, $(p)\varphi p$ purports to be a proposition about all propositions and this is forbidden by the vicious circle principle. Russell therefore proposes to get out of this difficulty by supposing that 'false' has different meanings 'appropriate to propositions of different kinds'.

He supports this with the example of any function φ, and one of its values φa. If φa is asserted, call the truth *first truth*. If $(x).\varphi x$ is true, this should mean that any φx has first truth, and so we can say $(x).\varphi x$ has *second truth*. Similarly $(\exists x).\varphi x$ has second truth if there exists some x for which φx has first truth. He applies this to the case when $\varphi p = \sim p$. If φp means that p has first falsehood, φ applies only to the sort of proposition which has first truth or first falsehood. Then $(p).\varphi p$ has second falsehood and so the symbol $\varphi((p).\varphi p)$ becomes meaningless, and

Thus the apparent exception to the principle that $\varphi((x).\varphi x)$ must be meaningless disappears.

What is at issue here, evidently, is a penchant for quantifying over propositional variables as well as over mathematical ones, which is liable to lead to confusion. In the second edition Russell proposes to remove *9 and replace it by a new *8, which is printed in an appendix. Here real variables are rejected, and so is quantification over propositions in general. In the place of $\vdash.(p)fp$ Russell would now write $p = \varphi x$, and then

$$\vdash.(\varphi, x).\ f(\varphi x).$$

So there remains even in the second edition a freedom to quantify over both functions and variables.

But, to return to the first edition, *9 is intended simply to extend the axioms and rules for elementary propositions and their truth-functions to others. This extension is of course, to be carried out only so far as it is valid. Russell makes the revealing remark

From the purely technical point of view, the distinction between

elementary and other propositions may be ignored, so long as propositions do not appear as apparent variables.

This is the way which would be chosen in a more modern
presentation, in which one might begin, as Russell does, with
propositions. Then one would go on to consider first order
sentences, in which a propositional function occurs quantified over an ordinary mathematical variable. Then second
order sentences will include quantifications over first order
propositional functions, and so on.

This is not Russell's path, however. Instead he proceeds
on the basis of replacing propositional variables one at a
time. He concludes

We have now completed the proof that, in the primitive propositions of
*1, any *one* of the propositions that occur may be replaced by $(x).\varphi x$ or
$(\exists x).\varphi x$.

Indeed, as he explains in the introduction, it is proved that, if
the analogues of the primitive propositions hold for n apparent variables, they hold also for n + 1. This would normally
be taken by mathematicians as a 'proof by induction' that
they hold for any number of variables. But, Russell warns,

Mathematical induction is a method of proof which is not yet applicable, and is (as will appear) incapable of being used freely until the
theory of propositions containing apparent variables has been established.

So one can only use the procedure over and over again to
construct the proof for any particular number of apparent
variables. Here again we have the lack of distinction between system and metasystem causing trouble.

4.7   Whereas *9 concentrated on the primitive propositions, *10 takes up the extension of propositions involving
implication to forms like $(x).\varphi x \supset \psi x$. Then in *11 a corresponding further extension is made to forms with two vari-
ables such as $(x, y).\varphi(x, y)$, which is an abbreviation for
$(x)(y)\varphi(x, y)$. After this *12 introduces the (ramified)
hierarchy of types, very much along the lines of *Mathematical Logic*, and also the axiom of reducibility. This is stated in

the form

$$*12.1 \quad \vdash : (\exists f)(x) : \varphi x. \equiv . f ! x \quad Pp$$

with an appropriate generalisation to functions of more variables.

Once the axiom of reducibility is available Russell is able, in *13, to give a Leibnizian definition of identity, by indiscernability, in the form

$$*13.01 \quad x = y. = : (\varphi): \varphi ! x. \supset . \varphi ! y \quad Df.$$

Finally section B concludes with *14 on descriptions, which is essentially a technical use of the ideas of *On Denoting*. In this section the iota symbol is defined, somewhat on the lines that $\psi(\imath x)(\varphi x)$ is to mean

$$(\exists b)(x):. \varphi x: \equiv : x = b. \&. \psi b.$$

This is not quite adequate, however; for $(\imath x)(\varphi x)$ might occur as part of a larger proposition and it is not clear how much of this larger proposition is related to the $(\imath x) (\varphi x)$. Accordingly Russell proposes to call the proposition which is to be treated as the $\psi(\imath x)(\varphi x)$ the scope of $(\imath x)(\varphi x)$ and to mark the scope by prefixing it by $[(\imath x)(\varphi x)]$ together with the usual dots as brackets. The definition becomes

$$*14.1 \quad [(\imath x)(\varphi x)] . \; \psi(\imath x)(\varphi x) .=: (\exists b)(x):\varphi x.\equiv.x = b \; \& \; \psi b.$$

This complication in the formalism is avoided to a large extent, however, because usually the scope is the smallest proposition that it can be. In this case Russell proposes to omit the mention of the scope.

Section C then deals with classes and relations, and begins with *20 on classes. Russell stresses that the intention is to give a notation for classes without necessarily assuming their existence. The method for this is again modelled in *On Denoting*, as in *14. For Russell at this time, a class is simply all terms satisfying some propositional function, so that every propositional function determines a class by the rule

$$x \, \varepsilon \, (\hat{z}\varphi!z). =. \varphi x \quad Df.$$

The actual concept of class is then given by

$$*20.3 \quad \text{Cls} = \hat{x}\{(\exists\varphi). \; x = \hat{z}(\varphi!z)\} \quad \text{Df.}$$

But here, of course, the contents of the curly brackets have no meaning in isolation: the uses of expressions like it have been defined in particular contexts.

The function of definitions like *20.3 is somewhat obscure. As it stands, it purports to define the concept of a class. It does so in terms of the class of all objects which are equal to a class of objects satisfying a certain propositional function. In order to understand the concept *class*, it seems as if one must already understand what a class is. There is, as usual, more to be said. For the contents of the brackets contain $\hat{z}(\varphi!z)$, rather than $\hat{z}(\varphi z)$. The result is that the axiom of reducibility has been incorporated in the definition.

The immediate extension of the concept of class, which is evidently concerned with one variable, to two variables yields a corresponding theory of relations in *21. By now Russell feels happy to define a relation R as a class of couples, so that

$$xRy \; . = . \; (x, y)\varepsilon\alpha,$$

or, equally, in terms of a defining function. The class of relations is defined by

$$*21.03 \quad \text{Rel} = \hat{R}\{(\exists\varphi). \; R = \hat{x}\hat{y}\varphi!(x, y)\}.$$

So, in this notation

$$xRy. = . \; \varphi!(x, y)$$

Technical developments follow in *22, *23 under the heading of *Calculus of Classes*, *Calculus of Relations*. The first of these simply gives the definitions of $\alpha \subset \beta$, $\alpha \cup \beta$, $\alpha \cap \beta$ and also of

$$-\alpha = \hat{x}(\sim x \in \alpha).$$

Then the second lists the exact analogues for relations with the notations $R \subseteq S$, $R \cup S$, $R \cap S$, $\doteq R$. In *24 the universal class V and the null class Λ are defined by

$$*24.01 \quad V = \hat{x}(x = x) \quad \text{Df}$$

$$*24.02 \quad \Lambda = -V.$$

This number concludes with some results described as dealing with the existence of classes. This is a slightly misleading description, for this section, like the rest does not commit itself to the existence of any classes at all. What is meant here is that a class is not the null class. So, writing

$$\exists ! \, \alpha . = .(\exists x). \, x \, \varepsilon \, \alpha,$$

it is possible to prove such results as

$$\exists ! \, \alpha . \equiv . \, \alpha \neq \Lambda.$$

Exactly analogous results for relations come in *25.

4.8 Section D turns to the much more interesting results about relations which have no analogues for classes. The section begins with *30, on *descriptive functions*. This is the name given by Russell to functions such as the ordinary functions of mathematics. An expression such as 3^2 is the value of the square function $f(x) = x^2$ when $x = 3$. But $f(3)$ could be said to *describe* the number 9. Of course, propositions involving $f(3)$ are not the same as those involving 9, since $f(3) = 9$ conveys information, and $9 = 9$ does not. Thus is the author of Waverley returned to his origins. A descriptive function is defined by

$$R‘y = (\imath x)(xRy)$$

and the left-hand side may be read 'R of y'.

Then *31 deals with converses of relations, and *32 with technical details concerning images and inverse images of relations. Next, *33 deals with domains and converse domains of relations. What we have here is very much a reworking of the ideas described above in the *Logic of Relations*.[9] A clue to Russell's thinking is provided by one of his examples. He supposes R to be defined by

$$xRy . =. x < y$$

where it is supposed that x, y are natural numbers. Then the domain of R is evidently the class of all natural numbers, but the converse domain is the class of those natural numbers which have another natural number smaller than themselves. So it is the class of natural numbers excluding zero (compare §2.7).

In *34 the relative product R|S of relations is introduced, on the same lines as in the *Logic of Relations*. There are further developments of the calculus of relations, and then Part I concludes with a section E in which, for the first time, ideas of infinity appropriate to Cantor's theory are introduced. The section is entitled *Products and Sums of Classes*. The general idea can be seen as the generalisation of $\alpha \cap \beta$, $\alpha \cup \beta$ to a situation of an infinite class of α's. Call such a class of classes κ. Then the product and sum of κ are defined by

$$p`\kappa = \hat{x}\{(\alpha): \alpha \, \varepsilon \, \kappa . \supset . \, x \, \varepsilon \, \alpha\},$$

$$s`\kappa = \hat{x}\{(\exists\alpha): \alpha \, \varepsilon \, \kappa \, \& \, x \, \varepsilon \, \alpha\}.$$

The rest of Part I is concerned with kindred technical matters.

4.9   Part II is called *Prolegomena to Cardinal Arithmetic*. It is in five sections. Section A is on unit classes, and couples. It begins in *50 by writing identity and diversity as relations:

$$I = \hat{x}\hat{y}(x = y), \, J = \dot{-} \, I$$

so that

$$J = .\hat{x}\hat{y}(x \neq y).$$

Other notational matters are to define, in *51, $\iota = I$, so that

$$\iota`x = \hat{y}(y = x).$$

Thus $\iota`x$ is what is often written now as $\{x\}$, the class whose only member is x. As Russell says, the

> distinction between x and ι x is one of the merits of Peano's symbolic logic, as well as of Frege's.

Then in *52 the cardinal number 1 is defined, much as it was in the *Logic of Relations* as a class of classes:

$$\alpha \, \varepsilon \, 1. \equiv:. \, \alpha \neq \Lambda. \, \&:(x, y). \, x \, \varepsilon \, \alpha \, \& \, y \, \varepsilon \, \alpha .\supset . \, x =.y.$$

This form is a paraphrase of a proposition about 1 derived in *Principia Mathematica*. The actual definition used there is much simpler:

*52.01   1 = α̂{(∃x). α = ι 'x}   Df.

After some miscellaneous technical discussion in *53, couples are introduced in *54, and the definition

*54.02   2 = α̂{(∃x)(∃y). x ≠ y.&. α = ι 'x ∪ ι 'y}

provides the cardinal number 2. Then *55, *56 go on to discuss the ordinal number 2 which corresponds to the ordered pair (x, y) in just the way that the cardinal number corresponds to the unordered couple. It is a little hard to disentangle here the complications of the formalism from the ideas. In fact a significant improvement came shortly afterwards from Norber Wiener.[10] He is concerned to clarify the status of the axiom of reducibility, which occurs in *Mathematical Logic*[2] in two forms. One form is appropriate for functions of one variable and one for functions of two variables. Wiener constructs a definite one-to-one function of two variables whose value is a single variable. That is to say, Wiener constructs a function f,

$$f(m, n) = p,$$

such that any particular value of p on the right-hand side arises from a unique pair m,n. For example, if m,n,p are all natural numbers one example of such a function f would be

$$\tfrac{1}{2}(m + n)(m + n + 1) + n.$$

This is because, if one tabulates the value of f for pairs (m,n) one derives

m	n	p = f(m, n)
0	0	0
1	0	1
0	1	2
2	0	3
1	1	4
0	2	5
3	0	6
⋮	⋮	⋮

and so on.

Wiener's problem is to do this quite generally and he does this essentially by defining an *ordered pair*. Wiener's definition is more complicated than the one used now in mathematics (due to Kuratowski in 1921). That one would now be written

$$(x,y) = \{\{x\},\{x,y\}\},$$

and the right-hand side of this is, in Russell's notation,

$$\iota'x \cup \iota'(\iota'x \cup \iota'y).$$

The left-hand side, (x,y), is now called an ordered pair because, evidently.

$$(x, y) \neq (y, x)$$

although

$$\{x, y\} = \{y, x\}.$$

Section B goes on to describe sub-classes, the corresponding sub-relations, and relative types. I shall deal more shortly with these and later parts of *Principia Mathematica*. They are very much merely an elaboration of what is already inherent in the foundations, but a number of significant points need to be picked out. In section B the class of all sub-classes of α, which I called $P(\alpha)$ above, is called $\text{Cl}'\alpha$, so that

$$\text{Cl} = \hat{\kappa}\hat{\alpha}\{\kappa = \hat{\beta}(\beta \subset \alpha)\}.$$

There is a similar definition for relations:

$$\text{Rl} = \hat{L}\hat{P}\{L = \hat{R}(R \subseteq P)\}.$$

Then Russell goes on to definitions of relative types before proceeding, in section C, to define one-many, many-one and one-one relations, very much as in the Logic of Relations. And accordingly, just as there, the result which allows the definition of a cardinal number is now of the form

*72.66 $S^2 \subseteq S \& S = \check{S}. \equiv. (\exists R). R \in \text{Cls} \to 1 \& S = R/\check{R}.$

This has been derived from an earlier result which proves

that the entity α which arises in

$$x \text{ Sy} \supset (\exists\alpha). \ x\text{R} \ \alpha \ \& \ y\text{R}\alpha.$$

may be taken to be $\overleftarrow{\text{S}}\text{'x}$. But what was said in the *Logic of Relations* about the definition of cardinal number is now put in a more general form:

> This principle embodies a great part of the reasons for our definitions of the various kinds of numbers; in seeking these definitions, we always have, to begin with, some transitive symmetrical relation which we regard as sameness of number; thus by *72·64, the desired properties of the numbers of the kind in question are secured by taking the number of an object to be the class of objects to which the said object has the transitive symmetrical relation in question. It is in this way that we are led to define cardinal numbers as classes of classes, and ordinal numbers as classes of relations.

Two classes are said to be *similar* if there is a 1:1 relation between them.

In *73, which deals with similarity of classes, again following the *Logic of Relations*, the principal result is the one known to mathematicians as the Schröder-Bernstein theorem. This is given in the form

$$\alpha \text{ sm } \gamma \ \& \ \beta \text{ sm } \delta \ \& \ \gamma \subset \beta \ \& \ \delta \subset \alpha \ .\supset. \ \alpha \text{ sm } \beta$$

This is perhaps more transparent in the form which is now more usual; for any two classes α, β either α is similar to a sub-class of β or β is similar to a sub-class of α or both.

Section D of Part II introduces a subject that was to continue to trouble mathematicians for a long time to come. This is the question of selections, from a class of classes. What is now called *the axiom of choice* postulates that from a class of mutually exclusive classes a new class can be formed, which consists of one member from each of the original constituent classes. This is called the *multiplicative axiom* by Russell because it is used in the construction of multiplication.

I break off for a moment here to sketch in some background about this axiom. It has been expressed here in a manner which makes it sound very plausible. But it should be realised that this is deceptive for, in a situation in which Russell's paradox, or worse, may be lurking in any corner, it is necessary to be careful what form of words is decreed to define a class. Zermelo used the axiom as early as 1904, though it had been stated before that, in 1892, by Peano. Zermelo put it in another equivalent form.

In *85 the multiplicative axiom is proved to be equivalent to Zermelo's axiom that every class can be well-ordered. Well-ordering was described above in §2.10. Part II, and with it Volume 1, concludes with section E on *Inductive relations* and this is the extension to relations in general of the idea of mathematical induction as applied to the series of natural numbers. Here there is a specific acknowledgement to Frege's *Begriffsschrift* for a particular construction, that of the *ancestral* relation. This name arises from the fact that the ancestral relation, R_*, of a relation R corresponds to R in the same way that the relation "ancestor" corresponds to "father". Informally, then one can say that a R_*b holds if and only if there is a finite chain p, q, . . . r such that

$$aRp \ \& \ pRq \ \& \ . . . \ \& \ rRb.$$

But such a formulation, says Russell, is inadequate because the dots "represent an unanalysed idea". And we cannot avoid the dots by formulating the definition in some such form as "there exists a finite chain" because the notion of finiteness has to be defined in terms of the ancestral. For example, if S is the successor relation, so that 0S1, 1S2, . . . then a finite cardinal n is any one for which $0S_*n$. (It would only be possible to avoid this difficulty by constructing a theory which refrained from completed infinities altogether. But such a theory, though it might be entertained now, would have been rejected out of hand by Frege and Russell).

Instead the construction is made as follows. A class μ is called a hereditary class for R if $\check{R}\text{"} \subset \mu$, that is to say, if the successors of μ's are always μ's. Then it is possible to define the ancestral by a quantification over (hereditary) classes, in the form

$$aR_*z. \ \equiv. \ a \ \varepsilon \ C\text{"}R : \check{R}\text{"}\mu \subset \mu.a \ \varepsilon \ \mu. \ \supset_\mu. \ z\varepsilon\mu.$$

Russell concludes by remarking that 'The importance of the ideas dealt with in the present section is very great. The ideas dominate the treatment of finite and infinite, ...'. This is the conclusion of my exhibition of the constituent parts of Russell's thought as a whole in *Principia Mathematica*.

4.10   With Volumes 2 and 3 we find ourselves in an atmosphere much more of application of the basic ideas. For the sake of completeness I shall summarise them briefly. Volume 2 contains three parts of very different kinds. These are Part III on *Cardinal arithmetic*, Part IV on *Relation arithmetic* and Part V on *Series*. The first of these begins with what is really a set of qualifications to corresponding sections of Volume 1 in which all the manifold debts generated by the introduction of types are successively paid. Section A of Part III defines the cardinal number of α (which we denoted above by $|\alpha|$) as

$$\text{Nc}'\alpha = \hat{\beta}(\beta \text{ sm } \alpha),$$

noting now that this is to be found in Frege's *Grundlagen* of 1884. Here, too, the difficulty of the class as one or many, still lingering on from Peirce and Schröder, is finally cleared up. It is noted that, if x is an object, then $1 = \text{Nc}'\iota'x$, not Nc'x. And the cardinal number zero even allows a concise treatment of empty reference. One can write, for the King of France,

$$\hat{x}(\text{KF}x) \ \varepsilon \ 0,$$

but not KFε0. This second expression is not grammatical, but, if it were, it would be wrong, since it states something about the King of France, and there is no King of France. This section is also relevant to Cantor's paradox, for, in Russell's notation, what Cantor proved was that

$$\text{Nc}' \text{ Cl}' \ \alpha > \text{Nc}'\alpha.$$

The paradox arises when α is the universal class. But all that Cantor's result really proves is that, for the class of all classes α of one type there is a larger class Cl'α of higher type.

The important question of section A is the relation of a cardinal number of one type to one of another type. Such a relation is possible because the relation sm is *typically ambiguous*. For example, ι'x sm ι'y whatever types x, y may have. This ambiguity is derived from the corresponding ambiguity for $1 \rightarrow 1$ relations, and this in turn from the ambiguity involved in the definition of 1.

Then section B proceeds to the definition of addition and multiplication of cardinals, subject to the over-riding conditions that the definitions must hold equally for finite and infinite numbers, that the number of terms in a sum or a product may be infinite, and that the numbers need not be of the same type. The connections between addition and multiplication, as, for example,

$$x(y + z) = xy + xz,$$

can be established only with the help of the multiplicative axiom.

Section C goes on to discuss the ways in which finite and infinite cardinals may differ. I have omitted any discussion here about whether or not we should assume the existence of an infinite number of objects. As Benacerraf and Putnam[11] say

> Russell and his followers apparently regard the *possible*, if not actual, existence of infinitely many objects as self-evident, whereas for Hilbert and the formalists the consistency of this axiom must be *proved*.

In any case, a difficulty arises, for there seems to be two equally good ways of defining finite and infinite, and these can be proved identical only with another use of the multiplicative axiom. The first distinction is that between inductive and non-inductive cardinals, the inductive cardinals being those reached from zero by applications of the successor operation.

The other distinction is between reflexive and non-reflexive classes. A class is called reflexive when it is similar to a proper part of itself. I have already drawn attention to the reflexive nature of certain infinite classes by pointing to the example of the class of natural numbers. This is similar to the class of even natural numbers, which is a proper part of itself. It is straight forward to prove that an inductive cardinal is the cardinal of a non-reflexive class, and that a reflexive class has a non-inductive cardinal. But the multiplicative axiom is needed to ensure that every cardinal is either inductive or reflexive.

4.11 At this point in Volume 2 we are approaching the region, mentioned earlier, at which it would be possible to regard the task of laying foundations as finished and to leave the mathematicians to complete the construction of the upper walls. It is not possible to specify the point completely, but certainly from now onwards two things progressively happen. To a small extent, the chapters in *Principia Mathematica* are translations into the precise notation of results proved already, but, informally, in mathematics. To a larger extent, the results of *Principia Mathematica* have been taken over, or rediscovered, by mathematicians in the last sixty years. In either event it is unnecessary for me to say much in detail about these later sections. To quote Benacerraf and Putnam[11] again,

> Logicism had one great and undeniable achievement – it succeeded in reducing all of classical mathematics (by any reasonable standard excluding completeness) to a single formal system ... it should not be forgotten that if today it seems somewhat arbitrary just where one draws the line between logic and mathematics, this is itself a victory for Frege, Russell and Whitehead: before their work, the gulf between the two subjects seemed absolute.

Part IV is an attempt to generalise the ordinary arithmetic of ordinal numbers when the generating relation *less than* is replaced by some other relation. Then Part V, *Series*, is really a construction of the foundations of mathematical analysis. That is to say, it is a reconstruction of the properties of the real number system in much the style of Dedekind. The reader familiar with that subject can see the general flavour from this list of topics considered: maximum and minimum points, sequent points and limits, segments, convergence, continuous functions, well-ordered series, compact (= what we now call dense) series. The last three sections, D, E and F, of Part V are to be found in Volume 3. Here Russell says, in the introduction,

> The present volume continues the theory of series begun in Volume 2 and then proceeds to the theory of measurement. Geometry we have found it necessary to reserve for a separate final volume.

This volume was never written.

Volume 3 continues with part VI, called *quantity*. Here will be found a construction of the rational numbers from the integers on modern lines, followed by the introduction of the real numbers to provide limit points to sequences of rationals having no rational limit. Then section B goes on to *vector families*, in which directed quantities like displacements and angles find a natural place. Finally sections C and D relate the rational and real numbers to vector-families and so provide for measurement:

> A vector-family, if it has suitable properties, may be regarded as a kind of magnitude.

This concludes my brief summary of the later part of *Principia Mathematica*.

Section 2: The second edition

4.12 I have now described the main lines of the first edition of *Principia Mathematica* and it remains to note the changes made in the second edition. Many of these were a consequence of Russell's cooperation with Wittgenstein, with which I shall deal in Section 3, but it seems best to describe first of all the changes made in the second edition.

There is a certain difficulty which I will seek to put out of the way at the beginning. Russell takes the view, in the *Introduction to the Second Edition*, that

> The most definite improvement resulting from work in mathematical logic during the past fourteen years is the substitution in Part I Section A of the one definable 'p and q are incompatible' . . . due to Dr H. M. Sheffer.[12]

The wording has been chosen with care here. Russell's sentence as it stands could scarcely be challenged. But it is very questionable whether Sheffer's work, which I shall briefly describe below, is of any great conceptual importance. None the less, it produces notational simplifications later on in Russell's system, which Russell seems to regard as of philosophical importance. I will also argue that Wittgenstein attaches undue philosophical importance to Sheffer's invention. It will be necessary to disentangle the two threads of convenience of formation and conceptual innovation.

Sheffer[12] noticed that what he denoted by the *stroke* operation, p|q, served as a single truth-function from which all others could be defined. This is, therefore, an economy over the first edition system, which is based on the two connectives ~, ∨. The stroke function can be described by giving its truth-value:

$$|p|q| = 1 \quad \text{unless} \quad |p| = |q| = 1.$$

There are, in fact, two connectives which will each individually serve to generate all truth-functions. The other one is p ↓ q, 'neither p nor q', defined by

$$|p \downarrow q| = 0 \quad \text{unless} \quad |p| = |q| = 0.$$

I shall now sketch in Sheffer's proof of the adequacy of the stroke, p | q. A similar argument holds for p ↓ q.

One can define ~p = p|p. Moreover, since p|q could be expressed in Russell's terms by ~.p&q, and since also

$$p \& q. = :. \sim : \sim p. \vee. \sim q,$$

it follows that

$$p|q = \sim p. \vee. \sim q = \sim. p \& q$$

Thus

$$p \vee q. =. \sim p|\sim q,$$

and replacing ~p by p|p, ~q by q|q, we have as a definition of ∨:

$$p \vee q = (p|p) \mid (q|q).$$

Since ~, ∨ can both be defined by the stroke, the whole of the propositional logic in *Principia Mathematica* can be expressed. It is also possible to produce a neater axiom-system, consisting of a single, rather complex, axiom involving the stroke, and this was done by Jean Nicod.[13]

But, having said this, it is plain that it is only at the purely manipulative level that Sheffer's operation is an advantage. For whereas the notation of *Principia Mathematica* makes the minimum change to the order of ideas of a natural language consistent with precision and correctness, it is hard to imagine a way of thinking that would find it natural to express pvq as (p|p)|(q|q).

A much more valuable advance in the second edition is the realisation that the distinction between real and apparent variables is unnecessary, and correspondingly that there is never any need to assert a propositional function. In the first edition it was considered necessary to explain formulae like ⊢.fx, but this is now to be interpreted as ⊢.(x)fx. The notion of real variables is dropped, as I explained would be desirable in discussing *Mathematical Logic*.

The next point taken up is the axiom of reducibility. Russell's belief in this axiom has a slightly curious history. When it first occurs his arguments for it were very convincing and his conviction about its correctness was clear. I ought to stress here, once more, that *correctness* means more for Russell than for a formalist mathematician. The formalist would be content to know that the axiom of reducibility did not strengthen the system so much as to re-introduce contradictions. And, indeed, as a result of Gödel's work,[14] we know now that such an assurance cannot, in fact, be available for him. Russell is concerned here, as elsewhere, with truth. And, of course, if the axiom were known to be true, the consistency would be automatic.

By 1927, however, Russell says that improvement is obviously desirable. It is 'clearly not the sort of axiom with which we can rest content'. He refers in passing to Chwistek's attempt to dispense with the axiom, which involves sacrificing too much of mathematics. But he is much more impressed with

> another course, recommended by Wittgenstein for philosophical reasons. This is to assume that functions of propositions are always truth-functions, and that a function can only occur in a proposition through its truth-values . . . It requires us to maintain that 'A believes p' is not a function of p . . . .. We are not prepared to assert that this theory is certainly right, but it has seemed worthwhile to work out its consequences in the following pages.

The general point is further discussed in an appendix to

Principia Mathematica. I defer description of the appendix till §4.15, so as not to break into Russell's investigation.

The conclusion that Russell reaches in this investigation is that everything in Volume 1 remains true, though some proofs need changing, as does the theory of finite cardinals and ordinals. But severe problems beset all the infinite part of the theory. Since this is all needed in order to set up the theory of real numbers used in mathematical analysis, the sacrifice seems almost as severe as was Chwistek's.

4.13   The detailed formulation begins with *atomic propositions* of the form R(x), S(x, y). T(x, y, z). . . . Here R(x) is what would earlier have been written as φx, and S(x, y) is a relation, which might earlier have been expressed as xSy. T is a triadic relation between x, y and z and allowance has been made for higher order relations, if required. So more emphasis is now being placed, in true Russell tradition, on atomic facts, expressed through relations. Quine has warned[15]

> Not that Wittgenstein started Russell on facts. Russell was urging a correspondence between facts and propositions in 1912, when he first knew Wittgenstein. Russell was receptive to facts as entities because of his tendency to conflate meaning with reference.

It might be added that his continuing satisfaction with the reality of relations as a key to the construction of mathematics, and indeed of the world, played an important part.

Molecular propositions are constructed from atomic ones by means of logical connectives. Russell chooses the Sheffer stroke, and makes appropriate modifications to the theory of inference but I think there would be general agreement that this is no conceptual advantage over the usual connectives. An individual is now defined as anything that can occur as one of the x, y, . . . in an atomic proposition very much in the way that, in the *Geometry*, Russell was able to define points as the terms in relations.

An elementary function of an individual is defined next, and this echoes once more the lost substitutional theory of 1906. For Russell begins with an elementary proposition, that is, either atomic or molecular, with a constituent a. He writes this as φa. A propositional function is derived by considering 'a certain assemblage of elementary propositions'. This is the assemblage got from φa by replacing a by other individuals in succession. These are to be thought of as the values of a function φ, or φx.

It is worth remarking that the words 'replacing . . . in succession' occur in Russell's text and so are to be taken seriously. But evidently in this way the most complex propositional functions that can be defined have either a finite class of values or, at most, an enumerably infinite one. Such an analysis evidently stems directly from Wittgenstein's,[5] where $(x).\varphi x$ is regarded as shorthand for $\varphi a \,\&\, \varphi b \,\&\, \varphi c \,\&\, . . .$, just as $(\exists x).\varphi x$ is for $\varphi a \lor \varphi b \lor \varphi c \lor . . ..$ However Wittgenstein is reported by Moore[16] as holding in 1930–33 that

> he had been misled . . . having failed to see that the latter expression is not always a logical product, that it is only a logical product if the dots are what he called 'the dot of laziness'.

So it is reasonable to expect the resultant theory to be adequate for arithmetic but it is likely to run into trouble in trying to construct larger infinities than the natural numbers, or the rational numbers. Correspondingly, it is probably over-optimistic of Russell to hope that some other axiom may be found which will be adequate to save these later parts of his system. For the limitation has been applied at a very fundamental level in the formulation.

On the other hand one must sympathise with Russell, the empiricist, in the conclusion of the introduction:

> It might be possible to sacrifice infinite well-ordered series to logical rigour, but the theory of real numbers is an integral part of ordinary mathematics, and can hardly be the subject of a reasonable doubt. We are therefore justified in supposing that some logical axiom which is true will justify it.

Hermann Weyl, on the other hand, called in 1918 for a radical revision and weakening in the theory of real numbers,[17] for reasons not entirely dissimilar to those in Russell's introduction. But his call fell on deaf ears.

Once propositional functions have been defined, quantification is easy to formulate, and it is then possible to give the appropriate rules of inference. In particular, as well as rules involving the Sheffer stroke, the argument about apparent and real variables is finally put to rest by allowing the inference of (x).ψx from (x).φx and (x).φx $\supset$ ψx. The way is then clear to go on to the more difficult central thesis of the new approach, headed *IV Functions as variables*. The argument begins by considering again an expression φa. But now a is a constant, and φa is to be considered for different values of φ, giving different assemblages of elementary propositions. It proves necessary later in the argument to consider also functions whose values are not elementary propositions. Accordingly the notation φ ! x is used to indicate a function whose values are elementary propositions. It is now to be thought of as a function of two variables, φ and x. Quantifying, in the forms

$$(\varphi).\, \varphi\, !\, a, \quad (\exists \varphi).\, \varphi\, !\, a$$

gives new, non-elementary propositions.

The crucial assumption is now: *a function can only appear through its values*. This assumption amounts to saying that one can indeed think of variable functions φ in terms of an assemblage derived from φ ! a by considering other different properties ψ, ζ, . . . of a. Since it is evident that the idea is one of 'replacing in succession', similar restrictions on the size of infinities can be expected to arise to those noted above. The notion of quantifying over functions is extended to functions like Φx, defined by

$$\Phi x = (y).\, \varphi!(x, y),$$

but it is remarked that such a function as Φ need not be introduced if one can use an infinite conjunction or disjunction. Now such infinitary operations are not available without further *ad hoc* assumptions, even though, as Russell says

> We can work out results for any segment of the infinite conjunction or disjunction, and we can 'see' that these results hold throughout.

So further assumptions are naturally suggested and can be made and no difficulties arise so long as the variables involved in a function are not of higher order than the argument to the function.

Consider, however,

$$\Psi x = (\varphi) . \, f!(\varphi, x).$$

Then, of course, Ψ is a function of x but is not included amongst the possible values of φ on the right-hand side. Generation of new functions in this way provide new variables which can then generate further new functions, but no vicious circles can result, so long as we

specify what sort of φ is involved, whenever φ appears as apparent variable.

4.14 The effect of these changes on the theory of classes is two-fold. Since functions occur only through their values and all functions of functions are therefore to be understood in extension, it is no longer necessary to distinguish between functions and classes. For extensionality implies

$$(x) . \varphi x \equiv \psi x : \supset : f(\varphi) \equiv f(\psi),$$

and

$$f(\varphi) \equiv f(\psi) . \supset . \, \hat{x}\varphi x \equiv \hat{x}\psi x.$$

Thus classes, as distinct from functions, lose even that shadowy being which they retain in *20.

But, on the other hand, it becomes necessary to distinguish classes of different orders composed of members of the same order. For example, $\hat{x}(\varphi!x)$ must be distinguished from $\hat{x}\Phi x$. The result of this is that, although the general logical properties of classes survive, other results like

$$x \, \varepsilon \, p\text{'}\kappa . \equiv :(\alpha). \, \alpha \, \varepsilon \, \kappa . \supset . x \, \varepsilon \, \alpha,$$

involve a class, $p\text{'}\kappa$, of higher order than the order of any of the members of κ. Accordingly the situation will arise that $(\alpha). f\alpha$ will not serve to imply $f(p\text{ '}\kappa)$.

At this point Russell tries to show, by a rather long and technical deduction, that 'most of the fallacious inferences that seem plausible' can be reduced to a standard form which is in fact correct. A detailed investigation proves, for example, that the Schröder-Bernstein theorem survives in this reconstruction. On the other hand, the proof of Cantor's theorem $P(\alpha) > \alpha$ remains valid only for finite classes, when it is equivalent to the easily proved $2^n > n$. The reason for the failure is that a new entity is constructed in the proof. A hypothesis of a 1:1 correspondence between α and $P(\alpha)$ is made. The new entity is shown to have no mate in the correspondence, so the hypothesis is falsified and the proof is apparently complete. But this new entity which is constructed is of a higher order than the ones listed so that the proof fails. This failure can be seen clearly in the simplified version of Cantor's proof which I discussed in §3.11. For there, in order to show the non-enumerability of the decimal fractions, a supposed enumeration of them is made. Then the 'diagonal method' constructs a new fraction which was omitted from the enumeration. But this new fraction can be constructed only by using the whole of the previous aggregate. The general situation can be summed up like this: most of the proofs about classes aim to show that certain classes are similar, and these proofs survive. But those which purport to show *non*-similarity fail, except in the special case where one class is finite and the other is infinite.

To summarise this view of the second edition, I cannot do better than quote from Gödel's[18] very perceptive assessment:

> As to the question of how far mathematics can be built up on this basis (without any assumptions about the data – i.e. about the primitive predicates and individuals – except, as far as necessary, the axiom of infinity) it is clear that the theory of real numbers in its present form cannot be obtained. As to the theory of integers, it is contended in the second edition of *Principia* that it can be obtained. The difficulty to be overcome is that . . . the phrase 'every class' must refer to a given order . . . Now, in Appendix B of the second edition of *Pricipia*, a proof is offered that the integers of any order higher than 5 are the same as those of order 5, which of course would settle all difficulties. The proof as it stands, however, is certainly not conclusive.

4.15 It remains to take up the appendix in which Russell discusses the philosophical issues in believing that a function enters a proposition only through its values. He remarks, firstly, that it would be quite possible to decide, by fiat, that this restriction was true for mathematics. After all, it amounts only to saying that all mathematical concepts are taken in extension, never in intension. But, he remarks, there is the prior question of whether perhaps all functions of propositions are truth-functions. If f is any function of propositions, this amounts to

$$p \equiv q . \supset . fp \equiv fq.$$

This has, as a consequence of the definition of identity in *Principia Mathematica*, the consequence

$$p \equiv q . \supset . p = q,$$

so that there are only two propositions, the true one and the false one.

This was Frege's view, but it is one which cannot easily be accepted.

For example, the sentences

   A believes p,
   p is about A,

seem to be functions of p which are true for some true values of p and false for others. The first proposition is an example often discussed by philosophers, but the second is particularly important for Russell because the notation φx is used to denote a proposition about x. Thus the second sentence seems to be involved in setting up the logic of propositional functions.

Russell begins by distinguishing between the set of marks on paper, or sounds, which express a proposition, and 'a proposition as a vehicle of truth or falsehood'. Evidently the lesson of Frege's letters has begun to work, so that Russell is prepared to consider, in addition to the proposition, the expression of the proposition, but he is still concerned to distinguish the proposition from its expression. Now in logic the aim is to assert combinations of propositions which are true, whatever the truth-values of their constituents. And so, in asserting

$$\vdash : p \lor q . \supset . q \lor p$$

the truth-values of p, q do not enter, and neither do the structures of p, q. But when propositional functions enter and one asserts, for example,

$$\vdash: \varphi \,!\, a . \supset . (\exists x).\varphi \,!\, x$$

there is an essential difference from asserting

$$\vdash: \varphi \,!\, x \vee \varphi \,!\, y . \supset . \varphi \,!\, y \vee \varphi \,!\, x.$$

The latter is simply a direct inference from the earlier form with p and q in it. The former depends on the structure of the propositions, and so we are back to statements like 'A occurs in p'.

The essence of the succeeding argument is to deny that the sentences are indeed functions of p. Russell proceeds by replacing 'A believes p' by A asserts p', in order to avoid doubts about what constitutes belief. Then it is clear that A has asserted, not the proposition p, but a series of sounds. The corresponding analysis of 'A believes p' is complicated by psychological considerations but essentially A is shown as having had a certain succession of thoughts. The other sentence, 'p is about A', has to be analysed in a superficially different way, but a way which has an underlying similarity. The upshot of this analysis is that, when the notation $\varphi!x$ is used, it is a fact that x occurs in the proposition

> but we do not need to assert this fact; the fact does its work without having to be asserted.

Here the argument appeals to what Russell calls *Wittgenstein's principle*

> that a logical symbol must, in certain formal respects, resemble what it symbolises.

And it is to the mutual influences of Russell and Wittgenstein that I now turn.

Section 3: Wittgenstein

4.16 It is commonplace to remark that of all philosophical influences on Russell, that of Wittgenstein was most profound; and, conversely, that of all influences exerted by Russell, that on Wittgenstein was most important. This is not to deny that the later Wittgenstein is, at least on the surface, a very different philosopher from the earlier. But even there it is not fanciful to see much of his later development as freeing himself from a view formed very much by Russell, a view derived from an attempt to make philosophical sense out of the system of *Principia Mathematica* and expressed forcefully in the *Tractatus*.[5]

Wittgenstein had come to England in 1909 to study engineering in Manchester, but in January 1912 he came to Cambridge as an advanced student. This does not seem to have been the beginning of his interest in logic, or of his criticism of Russell's ideas. According to Grattan-Guinness,[19] Jourdain noted in April 1909 a visit Russell paid to him.

> Russell said that the views I gave in a reply to Wittgenstein (who had 'solved' Russell's contradiction) agree with his own.

The date is explicit and the handwriting confirms it, yet this is more than two years earlier than the usually accepted dated when Russell and Wittgenstein made contact. It is possible that Wittgenstein simply corresponded with Jourdain at this time. Certainly when Russell described[20] to Ottoline Morell taking Wittgenstein to meet Jourdain in 1913 the impression is of a first meeting.

Having come to Cambridge, Wittgenstein worked with Russell until the summer of 1913, or perhaps a little later. According to Russell,[20] at the beginning of 1914.

> He came to me in a state of great agitation and said 'I am leaving Cambridge, I am leaving Cambridge at once'. 'Why?' I asked. 'Because my brother-in-law has come to live in London, and I can't bear to be so near him'. So he spent the rest of the winter in the far north of Norway.

The initial effect of Wittgenstein on Russell was a negative one. Russell says in a letter to Ottoline Morell in 1916

> 'Do you remember . . . I wrote a lot of stuff about Theory of Knowledge, which Wittgenstein criticised with the greatest severity? His criticism, tho' I don't think you realized it at the time, was an event of

first-rate importance in my life, and affected everything I have done since. I saw he was right, and I saw that I could not hope ever again to do fundamental work in philosophy . . . Wittgenstein persuaded me that what wanted doing in logic was too difficult for me.

The reference is to a book that Russell was preparing in 1913. Six chapters were in fact published separately as articles,[21] but the book as a whole was abandoned.

The war broke off even contact by letter between Russell and Wittgenstein. But the negative mood of Russell's 1916 letter, which was perhaps coloured by the horrors of the war more than he imagined, was succeeded by a return to philosophy in which the ideas of Wittgenstein were assimilated. This return was aided, paradoxically, by the six month prison sentence which Russell received in 1918 for his continued pacifist activity. Whilst in prison he began *The Analysis of Mind* and *The Philosophy of Logical Atomism*. The second of these was the material for a course of eight lectures given in London in 1918. In an introduction to the written version[22] Russell describes them as

very largely concerned with explaining certain ideas which I learnt from my friend and former pupil, Mr. Ludwig Wittgenstein. I have had no opportunity of knowing his view since August 1914, and I do not even know whether he is alive or dead.

I do not need to deal with these lectures themselves in much detail. The introduction to the second edition of *Principia Mathematica*, which I discussed earlier in this chapter, gives a succinct account of the main ideas. It is, though, worth drawing attention to one part of lecture II, since it gives the clearest statement of one of the two main themes that I seek to present here. This is the theme of the ontological importance of relations. Here Russell, following the general lines of the second edition of *Principia Mathematica*, describes the hierarchy of atomic facts, which are expressed by atomic propositions $R(x)$, $S(x, y)$, $T(x, y, z)$, . . .

Atomic facts contain, besides the relation, the terms of the relation – one term if it is a monadic relation, two if it is dyadic, and so on. These 'terms' which come into atomic facts I define as 'particulars' . . . That is the definition of particulars, and I want to emphasize it because the definition of a particular is something purely logical.

So we have one more use of the device which defined points in geometry as the terms in spatial relations.

4.17   Early in 1919 events took a different turn. Russell received a postcard:[20]

> Dear Russell,
>   I don't know your precise address but hope these lines will reach you somehow. I am a prisoner in Italy since November and hope I may communicate with you after a three years interruption. I have done lots of logikal work which I am dying to let you know before publishing it.
>   Ever yours,
>   Ludwig Wittgenstein.

A month later, after having had replies from Russell, a longer letter 'posted by an Austrian medical student who goes home tomorrow' explains

> I've written a book called *Logisch-Philosophische Abhandlung* containing all my work of the last six years. I believe I've solved all our problems finally.

It must not be supposed that this book was written in the prison camp, difficult as that might be. Russell says[20]

> a month after the Armistice . . . I got a letter from him . . . saying that . . . he had been taken prisoner by the Italians, but fortunately with his manuscript. It appeared that he had written a book in the trenches . . .

The manuscript reached Russell in 1919 and he arranged for its publication in Ostwald's *Annalen der Naturphilosophie* in 1921, with an introduction by himself. Then Russell interested C. K. Ogden in publication of the English edition, in the following year, as *Tractatus Logico-Philosophicus*, in Routledge and Kegan Paul's International Library of Philosophy. Ogden translated it, and the edition again carried Russell's introduction. From this edition we can get a very good understanding of the mutual influences of Russell and Wittgenstein. In this section and §4.18 I shall consider Russell's introduction. Wittgenstein did not, in the end, agree with very much of what Russell wrote here, but it is an accurate indicator of the changes in Russell's thought produced by Wittgenstein. In later sections I shall then go on to consider those parts of the *Tractatus* that are evidently the result of a critical study of *Principia Mathematica*. I do not claim that this is a comprehensive way of studying the *Tractatus*. But I do claim that it provides a way into much of Wittgenstein's early thought, and I believe that, by clearing away the attack on the specific problems generated by one philosophical formalism, the rest of the book can be seen more clearly.

A similar line has been taken by Hao Wang, who says[23]

> It seems to me that much of Wittgenstein's *Tractatus* could be viewed as an attempt to explain the necessity of the logical propositions of the first half of the first volume of *Principia Mathematica*. The *Tractatus* provided a justification, if not correct at least of the right sort, of the sloppy formal system in *Principia*, and influenced more technical works such as those of Ramsey.

Russell begins his introduction by describing the *Tractatus* as a work, which starts from the principles of symbolism and the relations necessary between words and things, and which considers the conditions which would have to be fulfilled by a logically perfect language. Wittgenstein objected to this viewpoint. For him the *Tractatus* gave a way of analysing *any* language. Irrespective of their differing opinions the problem faced in the *Tractatus* is put this way by Russell: what relation must one fact (such as a sentence) have to another in order to be able to stand for it? According to Russell the 'most fundamental thesis' of the book is that the sentence and the fact must have some structure in common. This is a straightforward rendering of what Wittgenstein says. But the emphasis is, perhaps, a rather clear indication of Russell's advance since his correspondence with Frege. The sentence expressing the proposition and the proposition itself are now both under consideration.

The next step in the argument is the contention that language will not be able to say what the structure is, only to show it. The situation, in other words, is very like the question above about x being a constituent of φx. This particular case is indeed taken up explicitly by Wittgenstein as

4.1211   Thus a proposition 'fa' shows that in its sense the object a occurs, two propositions 'fa' and 'ga' that they are both about the same object.

Structure here is now analysed by postulating atomic facts, and molecular facts constructed from them. Then the proposition can be described as a *picture* of the facts, because the relations between things is mirrored by certain relations between the elements of the proposition. What the proposition says is not a philosophical statement, but a statement of physics, mathematics, geography, and so on. Philosophical matters, such as that the object a occurs in fa, cannot be said in the language but show themselves. Molecular propositions are built up from atomic propositions, as, for example, R(x) & S(x,y), and validity is determined by an explicit use of the tautology method noticed in §4.3 above. Then quantified propositional functions are generated, as in the second edition of *Principia Mathematica*:

$$(x)fx = fa \ \& \ fb \ \& \ fc \ldots,$$
$$(\exists x)fx = fa \lor fb \lor fc \ldots.$$

4.18   So far the introduction has given a straightforward summary of rather more than the first half of the book. Some scholars may differ about the emphasis, but not to an important extent. The next passage, however, is a valuable addition of Russell's at a technical level. It refers to a rather enigmatic passage in the *Tractatus*:

6. The general form of truth-function is:

$$[\bar{p}, \bar{\xi}, N(\bar{\xi})].$$

Russell remarks, rather laughably, that

Mr Wittgenstein's explanation of his symbolism at this point is not quite fully given in the text.

As Russell explains, $\bar{p}$ and $\bar{\xi}$ refer respectively to all atomic propositions, and to any class of propositions, and N($\bar{\xi}$) refers to the generalised Sheffer stroke operation. To be precise if $\bar{\xi} = \{\xi_1, \xi_2, \xi_3\}$, then $N(\bar{\xi})$ means $\sim\xi_1 \& \sim\xi_2 \& \sim\xi_3$. It will be noticed that N is not a *direct* generalisation of the Sheffer stroke, since for two propositions

$$N(p, q) = \sim p \& \sim q = p \downarrow q,$$

whereas

$$p|q = \sim p \lor \sim q.$$

But N is more convenient for Wittgenstein. The square brackets are another symbol which, though not fully explained by Wittgenstein, occurs elsewhere. For example,

6.03 The general form of the cardinal number is $[0, \xi, \xi + 1]$.

The notation evidently means that one begins with the first element, applies the operation typified in the third, and so derives an element of the second kind. Then one repeats the operation on these second kind of elements and so generates more elements of the second kind, and so on. This interpretation is confirmed by Wittgenstein's 5.2522, where he writes $[a, x, O`x]$ for the formal series $a, O`a, O`O`a, \ldots$ So Wittgenstein is really saying here that all truth-functions can be generated by repeated applications of the generalised Sheffer stroke. This statement is to be understood in the strong sense of including quantified statements, as I explained above.

Russell now turns to Wittgenstein's treatment of names. Different objects are given different names and the definition of identity by means of indiscernibles is rejected. This has a curious side-effect. It had previously been customary to talk about 'all there is' by means of a property which must belong to everything. So one defines the universal class by

$$V = \hat{x}(x = x).$$

But with the removal of identity, this method of speaking of the totality of things is removed. Russell accepts Wittgenstein's contention that any other method will be found equally fallacious. This leads to Wittgenstein's view that nothing can be said about the world as a whole, because we cannot get outside the world.

The next topic that Russell selects for discussion is Wittgenstein's reconciliation of 'A believes p' with the idea that compound propositions are truth-functions. The original reads:

> 5.542 But it is clear that 'A believes the p', 'A conceives p', 'A says p' are of the form " 'p' says p": and here we have no coordination of a fact and an object, but a coordination of facts by means of coordination of their objects.

Russell's gloss on this is to render it into much the same form as he was later to use in the second edition of *Principia Mathematica*. The two facts are the series of words used, and the fact they are supposed to express.

There are two final points in Russell's introduction to which I want to draw attention. He criticises Wittgenstein's theory of numbers. This was quoted above as 6.03. It is, in fact, the generation of natural numbers from zero by means of the successor operation. This may be thought unsurprising, for it is merely reiterating Dedekind and Peano. But Russell says

> No logic can be considered adequate until it has been shown to be capable of dealing with transfinite numbers.

Here is Russell very imbued with his own earlier struggles with Cantor, and with the undoubted (if flawed) success of the first edition of *Principia Mathematica*. He sees no reason why Wittgenstein's system could not be extended to this. Wittgenstein's next remark:

> 6.031 The theory of classes is altogether superfluous in mathematics.

shows with certainty, however, that such an extension would be against the whole spirit of Wittgenstein's approach.

The second point is connected with the distinction between what can be said and what can only be shown by the language:

> These difficulties suggest to my mind some such possibility as this: that every language has, as Mr Wittgenstein says, a structure concerning which, *in the language*, nothing can be said, but there may be another

language dealing with the structure of the first language, and having itself a new structure, and that to this hierarchy of languages there may be no limit. Mr Wittgenstein would of course reply that his whole theory is applicable unchanged to the totality of such languages. The only retort would be to deny that there is any such totality.

This passage is very interesting in showing the extent to which Russell had gone in 1921 towards accepting the possibility of considering the normal modern distinction between the language of a formal system and a meta-language (sometimes a natural language) used to talk about the expressions of the formal language, and about what they can do. This distinction was particularly difficult for Russell to accept, since his quest for truth made it natural to conflate language and meta-language. Two qualifications must be made about Russell's acceptance. In the first place, Russell was here proposing a particular way of understanding Wittgenstein's distinction between what can be said and what can only be shown. In the 1927 *Principia Mathematica* there is no trace of the distinction; he remains as wedded as before to a system which includes its own metalanguage. Secondly, I am not strictly correct in relating what Russell says to the modern distinction. The modern idea derives mainly from Hilbert, who will be discussed in Chapter 5. His idea was of a formal language with a metalanguage which was of a simpler structure. This simplicity meant that the metalanguage would not usually need formalisation. As a result, higher levels of the hierarchy would not usually be needed. It might in rare cases be necessary to formalise the metalanguage. In that case one further level would be needed, but that was all.

4.19 To end this chapter I turn to the consideration of those passages in the *Tractatus* that bear directly on the difficulties of *Principia Mathematica*, avoiding as far as possible the points already made in my description of Russell's introduction.

I think that the most important aspect of the argument from this point of view is:

2. What is the case, the fact, is the existence of atomic facts.

My argument here depends on translating Sachverhalten as atomic facts, which was the original published translation. There is an alternative view now that sees some such rendering as states of affairs as doing more justice to Wittgenstein's thought. I am not inclined to this view; for one thing, Sachverhalten has, amongst other meanings, the legal one of the facts of the case, and this does correspond as closely as any everyday usage could to the logical idea of atomic facts. Accordingly I prefer the old translation and then Wittgenstein's statement chimes in with what I have argued above, that atomic facts are essential to the system of *Principia Mathematica*. What Wittgenstein has done, I believe, is to see to underpin this with a logical metaphysical framework within which it makes sense;

1.1 The world is the collection of facts, not of things

and

1.2 The world divides into facts.

The spirit here, if not the details, is very much Frege's. In *Sense and Reference*,[24] he claims that

A logically perfect language should satisfy the conditions that every expression grammatically well-constructed as a proper name out of signs already introduced shall in fact designate an object.

Even mathematics may fail to achieve this perfection, for an infinite series may become divergent, as

$$1 + x + x^2 + x^3 + \ldots$$

does if $x = 1$. It then designates no object. Wittgenstein next goes on to define objects as the terms in atomic facts, and this was the path adopted by Russell in 1927.

This whole position can be summed up in this way: it is not a philosophy that seeks to talk about the real world. Rather, it defines the world as what can be handled by the system of *Principia Mathematica*. Then it seeks to investigate what properties this defined world must have to be capable of such description. Wittgenstein, in fact, has admirably captured the two essential features of Russell: logic and mathematics are true and they are about relations.

But there is a most important difference of emphasis. It could be put in this way, which is how Pears puts it:[25]

> Russell's thesis (is) that a complete analysis will only mention things that we have to treat as simple, and (Wittgenstein's) more extreme thesis, that it will only mention things that are intrinsically simple.

One can see this distinction in action, because Russell is careful never to claim that atomic propositions are independent of each other. An analysis might finish with 'A is red' and it might be such that this was atomic for Russell. Then the atomic proposition 'A is green is ruled out for Russell. But Wittgenstein says 'Atomic facts are independent of one another. For him, the propositions just mentioned, which could be atomic for Russell, could not both be atomic. It is, indeed, difficult to point to any actual proposition that is atomic for Wittgenstein, and it is this difficulty amongst others that made him change his mind about the *Tractatus*.

Wittgenstein gave up this extreme thesis in 1929. But, in the *Tractatus*, propositions are pictures of the facts by virtue of their structure. And so

> 3.3 In logical syntax the meaning of a sign ought never to play a role; it must admit of being established without mention being thereby made of the *meaning* of a sign;

This leads at once to the question of self-reference:

> 3.332 No proposition is able to say something about itself, because the propositional sign is unable to be contained in itself (that is the whole 'theory of types').

So Wittgenstein's position is that the ideal language will need no arbitrary theory of types to restrict its self-reference, because its accurate agreement with the world of atomic facts will ensure the impossibility of contradictions.

Of course, there is a price to be paid here. For, as Russell makes clear in the second edition of *Principia Mathematica*, such a language would allow the formulation of only a tiny fragment of mathematics (see §4.13, §4.14). It would even exclude from its formulation large sections of practical engineering mathematics like the calculus, and would fail to provide anything approaching what mathematicians would require. This objection would probably not have been regarded as very serious by Wittgenstein. He would have been content to jettison the mathematics. This is a possible point of view and one which would have been in keeping with such contemporary constructivist thought as that of L. E. J. Brouwer, who will be mentioned in Chapter 5. Brouwer went on to demand a new method which would replace the discredited classical one and so allow at least some of the classical mathematics to be reconstructed. Without this positive approach, the view I attribute here to Wittgenstein is for example, only a little more extreme than Weyl's view in *Das Kontinuum*.[17]

An attempt has been made to express this part of the *Tractatus* by a formal system, by R. Suszko,[26] under the title *Ontology in the Tractatus of L. Wittgenstein*. In the system it is proposed to introduce symbols for variables over *objects, propositions* and *possible situations*. Then operators are to correspond to *facts* or actual situations. This system does not yield any particular insight but it led Kreisel[27] to assess it by recounting how Wittgenstein told him, around 1950, that the essential features of the *Tractatus* were four-fold:

A proposition is determined by a possible situation, and the relation between the possible and the actual situation is like that between a model of a car accident in a courtroom and the actual accident.

Each proposition has a complete and unique analysis into atomic facts, and the model for such an analysis is the chemist's diagram of a molecule as atoms joined by bonds.

The assumption of the existence of objects is forced by the fact that even a false proposition must be about something, and its meaning cannot depend on what configurations happen to be realised. This point is taken up again by the later Wittgenstein,[28] when he argues that 'Excalibur has a sharp blade' does not cease to make *sense* if the parts which form the sword are broken apart.

The universe of objects is finite, though this seems to be at variance with what is said in the *Tractatus*.

As Kreisel concludes,

It may well be that the ideas of *Tractatus* are hopelessly inadequate for the kind of analysis Wittgenstein had in mind (as indeed he later maintained) . . . It goes without saying that a precise and thorough formal analysis of a coherent but false or inadequate philosophical view can have the same sort of interest as a precise mathematical treatment of a false physical theory.

Having dealt with the implications for *Principia Mathematica* of Wittgenstein's analysis of the world into atomic facts, a second, and perhaps less important question that he raises is the status of the logical connectives ⊃, v, ~. Here his position is less satisfactory. He first clears any preconception out of the way with

5.42 That v, ⊃, etc., are not relations in the sense of right and left, etc., is obvious.

5.461 The apparently unimportant fact that the apparent relations like v and ⊃ need brackets – unlike real relations – is of great importance.

The use of brackets with these apparent primitive signs shows that these are not the real primitive signs; and nobody of course would believe that the brackets have meaning by themselves.

I think that this argument misses its mark to some extent. It is perfectly possible to re-express the connectives in Polish notation, without brackets. That is, one can write Cpq for p ⊃q, and Apq for p v q. Usually one writes Np for ~p. Then, for example,

$$p. v. qvr : ⊃ : pvq. v. r,$$

becomes

$$CApAqrAApqr$$

The brackets prove unnecessary. Yet, of course, Wittgenstein's argument must be able to be salvaged, although it becomes harder to express. It is essential, in using the Polish notation, to know that C, A are binary operators, that is, to

know that they must be followed by *two* propositions to form
a new one, whereas N is a unary operator. So 5.461 could be
rephrased on the general lines that 'the need to know the
nature of C, A, N shows that these cannot be the real primitive signs'. And it is fairly clear that no other change of
notation will remove the burden of the argument.

However Wittgenstein goes on to argue that there is only
one logical constant, which is what all propositions, according to their nature, have in common.

That however is the general form of the proposition. And
I have explained this notion of the general form of the proposition in §4.18. Wittgenstein seems to be saying here that
the 'generalised Sheffer stroke' (see §4.12) is of more than
computational interest, because it allows the generation of
all propositions. This needs two qualifications.

First, it cannot be wholly correct to insist that the only true
connective is N(p, q), which Wittgenstein from confusion
describes in 5.101 as p | q, whereas it is p ↓ a. The important
point is that both the Sheffer stroke, p | q, and the N opera-
tion p ↓ q will serve equally well as a single generator of all
truth-functions. The only reason for Wittgenstein to prefer
N is a technical one which arises from a particular symbolisation he uses for connectives. This symbolisation consists of
writing down the truth-values of a compound proposition for
the successive cases where (p, q) is (11), (01), (10), (00)
respectively, in the notation explained in §4.3. In Wittgenstein's notation the whole expression p ↓ q or N(p, q) is written down as (0, 0, 0, 1). This turns out to be slightly more
convenient than the Sheffer stroke p | q which is (0, 1, 1, 1)
in the same notation. But the important point here is that
both the original Sheffer stroke, p | q, and the N operation
p ↓ q, will serve as a single generator of all truth-functions.

But perhaps we might agree that two alternative methods
of generating truth-functions were to be considered, one
involving the original Sheffer stroke and one involving N. So
to agree would be against the spirit of Wittgenstein's argument, but perhaps the argument could be moulded to suit.
Even then, there is a second qualification. For the argument
that these two operations generate all truth-functions relies
on generating them *in a series* by applications of one single

operation. But if, to put it picturesquely, two people were sat down to carry out this generation, both being given the same operation, it would not be the case that they would generate the truth-functions in the same order. For the generation depends on more than simply applying the stroke operation. For example ~p arises as p | p, so that a repetition is needed as well. And successive elements are got by choosing two groups A, B from amongst those already generated and forming A | B. Different choices could be made. Such a generation of a series is no more fundamental than a generation of all truth-functions by successive applications of ~ and v, as in *Principia Mathematica*. For the difference involved in using ~, v is only that, as well as choosing from already generated propositions, one chooses also between ~ and v.

A closely related point to this concerns the interaction between this formulation and the definition of quantified formulae as infinite conjunctions. For, in the infinite situation, the choices in the generation process have to be made from an enumerably infinite class α and so depend on all sub-classes of α. That is to say, the cardinal number of the class of choices is $|P(\alpha)|$. As Hao Wang[23] says, to propose to apply the operation N to a non-enumerable class is much too general.

This seems to be one of the instances where Wittgenstein treats the infinite case as no different from the finite case.

In the same reference Hao Wang goes on to interpret, correctly in my opinion, Wittgenstein's 6.1262:

Proof in logic is only a mechanical expedient to facilitate the recognition of tautology, where it is complicated.

as suggesting that there is a decision procedure for logic. We know now that there can be no such decision procedure even for first order logic. But, as Hao Wang concludes, Wittgenstein's error arises because

one can well expect logic to be decidable if it is thought that there is no essential difference between the finite and infinite cases.

A third and more valuable, criticism of *Principia Mathematica* is in connection with Frege's assertion sign. Wittgenstein sees it as logically meaningless. It only shows that Frege, or Russell, hold the propositions to be true.

So '⊢' belongs to the propositions as little as does the number of the propositions.

This would now be expressed, perhaps, by saying that the assertion sign was part of the metalanguage. It is important to say this because, from time to time, it is mentioned in *Principia Mathematica* as if it were part of the language.

The last of Wittgenstein's arguments to which I would draw attention is the one about internal and external properties and, correspondingly, internal and external relations. An internal, property of an atomic fact, or a *feature* of a fact, is one of the properties that is shown by the notation but not stated. Such a feature is, for example, that f(a, b), g(a, c) have a common object.

The holding of such internal properties and relations cannot, however, be asserted by propositions, but it shows itself in the propositions, . . .

Correspondingly, the existence of an internal relation between different states of affairs is shown by an internal relation between the propositions presenting them.

Wittgenstein calls a series, ordered by an internal relation, a *formal series*. Such a series is, for instance, the series of natural numbers. Similarly one can have formal *concepts*, as distinct from proper concepts.

Formal concepts cannot, like proper concepts, be represented by a function.

Instead they are expressed by variables.

So the variable name 'x' is the proper sign of the pseudo-concept object.

If a proposition states that 'there are two objects which . . .' this is expressed by $(\exists x, y)$. But it is impossible to say 'There are objects'. Similar considerations apply to *number*, which is represented by variables, not by functions or classes (as Frege and Russell thought). Expressions like '1 is a number', 'there is only one zero', and all similar ones are senseless.

Here Wittgenstein seems to be inclining more towards Frege's insight that numbers are connected with quantifiers.

To sum up, the aspects of the *Tractatus* which are of direct concern to *Principia Mathematica* are as follows.

(i) A clear metaphysical foundation is provided for the existence of atomic facts, and it is also made clear that a right understanding of atomic propositions automatically prevents vicious circle fallacies.

(ii) It is held that quantified formulae can be regarded as infinite conjunctions and disjunctions. But this will, of course, provide a foundation for only a tiny rump of mathematics involving almost no infinite processes.

(iii) The old question of whether relations are internal or external is answered. All genuine relations are external and they can be said in the language. But there are also formal relations, which are internal, and they cannot be said, but show themselves.

Synopsis

This chapter has described Russell's major achievement, *Principia Mathematica*. This book carries out, as well as it can, the ambitious programme of establishing the truth of mathematics by constructing it from logic. The logicist programme depends, for its validity, on the existence of atomic facts, expressed by atomic propositions. This is the aspect which first influenced Wittgenstein when he came to Cambridge to work with Russell. The influence of Wittgenstein on Russell produced major changes in the second edition of *Principia Mathematica*, but the system envisaged in this second edition, though freed from certain philosophical defects of the first edition, is less adequate for the construction of mathematics.

Notes

[1] A. N. Whitehead and B. Russell, *Principia Mathematica*, Cambridge, 1913. Second edition 1927. A paperback edition of the chapters up to *56 was published 1962.

[2] B. Russell, *Amer. Jour. Math* **30**, 222–262, 1908. Also to be found as *Mathematical Logic as based on the Theory of Types* in *Logic and Knowledge*, (ed. R. C. Marsh) Allen & Unwin, London, 1956.

[3] G. Frege, *Begriffsschrift*, Nebert, Halle, 1879. Translated in J. van Heijenoort (ed.), *From Frege to Gödel* Harvard, 1967, Chapter 1 is translated in *Philosophical Writings of Gottlob Frege* (24).

[4] P. Bernays, *Math. Zeitschrift* **25**, 305–320, 1926.

[5] L. Wittgenstein, *Tractatus Logico-Philosophicus*, trans. C. K. Ogden, Routledge & Kegan Paul, London, 1922. Another translation by B. F. McGuinness and D. F. Pears, Routledge & Kegan Paul, London, 1961. I have used the Ogden translation but with one or two amendments of my own.

[6] W. V. Quine, *From a Logical Point of View*, Harvard 1953. It should be remarked that Quine's actual procedure is to define all *theorems* to be all tautologies. This is a neutral statement as regards truth. But in the text I have followed Russell's line in regarding the main interest as lying in the truth of logic, not in its consistent formalisation.

[7] A. Church, *Introduction to Mathematical Logic*, Princeton, 1956.

[8] To do this, first observe that the sequence

$$L \supset P, L \supset Q, L \supset R, \ldots, L \supset Z.$$

is not a proof, because it does not fulfil (a), (b) or (d), though if any of the steps in the original chain used (c) it is easy to arrange for them still to be valid. It is only necessary to see that no confusions have arisen by using the same letters for variables in two different formulae.

It will be possible to fill in extra steps in the chain to make the new chain fulfil (a), (b) and (d). Evidently (a), (b) can be treated on the same footing. Suppose, for example, that at any particular point of the chain, R say, there was a quotation of A. The new chain now has $L \supset A$, and this could be justified if we had an earlier step which stated $A . \supset . L \supset A$.

This in turn could be got by substitution from an axiom if, amongst the axioms, were

$$p. \supset . q \supset p.$$

This could be put up as an axiom only if it is a tautology, but in fact, this is the case. For if we ask how $|p. \supset . q \supset p| = 0$ could arise, it would be possible only if $|p| = 1$, but then $|q \supset p| = 1$, so that the value 0 cannot arise after all.

For the sake of completeness, it should be mentioned that there is a special case as well, for the assumption quoted might have been L itself, in which case the new chain has $L \supset L$ to be justified. This could be got by substitution from the tautology

$$p \supset p.$$

Consider next the case when the step to R was by *modus ponens* so that something like this occurs:

$$Q \text{ is } P \supset R,$$

so that the sequence

$$P, Q, R$$

is

$$P, P \supset R, R.$$

In the new chain, then we have

$$L \supset P, L \supset . P \supset R, L \supset R$$

An assumption that would succeed in justifying the inference $L \supset R$ would be

$$L \supset . P \supset R : \supset : L \supset P . \supset . L \supset R$$

and this could be got by substitution from

$$p \supset . q \supset r : \supset : p \supset q . \supset . p \supset r$$

if this is an axiom. It can be taken as an axiom since, if it had the value 0, it would be the case that

$$|p \supset . q \supset r| = 1,$$

and

$$|p \supset q . \supset . p \supset r| = 0.$$

This would make

$$|p \supset q| = 1, |p \supset r| = 0 \text{ and so } |p| = 1, |r| = 0, |q| = 1.$$

But then $|q \supset r| = 0$, so $|p \supset . q \supset r| = 0$, and this would be a contradiction.

[9] B. Russell, *Logic of Relations*, in *Logic and Knowledge*[2]

[10] N. Wiener, *Proc. Camb. Phil. Soc.* **17**, 387–390, 1914. Reprinted in *From Frege to Gödel*[(3)]

[11] P. Benacerraf and H. Putnam (ed.), *Philosophy of Mathematics* Blackwell, Oxford, 1964.

[12] H. M. Sheffer was at Harvard. In *The Autobiography of Bertrand Russell*[20] are letters from Harold Laski seeking Russell's support for Sheffer against the prejudice of the Harvard faculty.

[13] Jean Nicod in 1916 is described by Russell in *The Autobiography of Bertrand Russell*[20] as 'a young French philosopher, also a pupil of mine,

who had escaped the War through being consumptive. (He died of phthisis in 1924.) He was one of the most delightful people that I have even known, at once very gentle and immensely clever.'

[14] K. Gödel 'Uber formal unentscheidbäre Sätze . . .', *Monatshefte für Math. und Phys. 38*, 173–198, 1931, trans. in *From Frege to Gödel*[3] Gödel's paper showed that, in almost any formal system which was sufficiently complicated to be able to cope with elementary arithmetic, either the system was inconsistent or it was incomplete in the sense that one could construct a statement of the system which was evidently true but was not provable in the system. A few more details are to be found in Chapter 5 of the present book, §5.5.

[15] E. D. Klemke (ed.), *Essays on Bertrand Russell*, Illinois, 1970.

[16] G. E. Moore, *Mind* (N.S.) **164**, 1–4, 1955.

[17] H. Weyl, *Das Kontinuum*, Zürich, 1917.

[18] K. Gödel in P. Schilpp (ed.), *The Philosophy of Bertrand Russell*, Library of Living Philosophers, Cambridge, 1946.

[19] I. Grattan-Guinness, *Dear Russell . . . Dear Jourdain*, Duckworth, London, 1977.

[20] B. Russell, *The Autobiography of Bertrand Russell*, Vol. 2 Allen & Unwin, London, 1968.

[21] The first three chapters are available under the title *On the nature of acquaintance* in *Logic and Knowledge.*[2]

[22] Reprinted as *The Philosophy of Logical Atomism* in *Logic and Knowledge.*[2]

[23] Hao Wang, *From Mathematics to Philosophy*, Routledge & Kegan Paul, London, 1974.

[24] P. Geach and M. Black (eds.), *Philosophical Writings of Gottlob Frege*, Blackwell, Oxford, third edition, 1980.

[25] D. F. Pears, *Bertrand Russell and the British Tradition in Philosophy* Fontana/Collins London, 1967.

[26] R. Suszko, *Notre Dame J. of Formal Logic* **9**, 7–33, 1968.

[27] G. Kreisel, *Math. Reviews* **39**, 49, 1968.

[28] L. Wittgenstein, *Philosophical Investigations*, §39. Blackwell, Oxford, 1953.

CHAPTER V

1914–1970 Contemporaries

Section 1: Russell's Later Work

5.1 I have now dealt in detail with the most important part of Russell's work up to 1911, when the first edition of *Principia Mathematica* was ready, and I have looked forward to the second edition and also to his preparation of Wittgenstein's *Tractatus*. I believe that, having done this, I have given the reader all the help that I can to put Russell in his correct intellectual context as a philosopher. His later work is lucid, readable and easily available and can be readily understood when the foundations are clearly formulated.

In this short final chapter I have three subsidiary intentions. In the first section I shall deal briefly with Russell's philosophical life after 1911, with a glance at the rest of his activity as well. In the second section I shall consider the influence that Russell's work has had in the philosophy of mathematics. I shall interpret that subject rather more widely than usual, so as to take up the effect of *On Denoting* as well. Finally, in the third section, I shall try to answer the question of why Russell has not had a wider philosophical influence.

I have already mentioned Russell's political interests after the completion of *Principia Mathematica*. These interests were strengthened by the need for a pacifist policy in the War, which had the unfortunate consequence in his working life to which I have referred. The criticism of Wittgenstein was another influence that had come near to persuading Russell to give up philosophy, but when he was imprisoned in 1918 he returned to writing, with *Introduction to Mathematical Philosophy*.[1] This was a semi-popular account of how Russell saw the ideas of *Principia Mathematica*. While in prison, he also began work on the *Analysis of Mind*.[2] To understand his thinking in this book, I must go back a little, to 1914, when Russell was lecturing at Harvard. His lectures appeared in *Our Knowledge of the External World*[3] but some of the these are also in three papers in *The Monist*[4] In these papers, which were suggested to Russell by the discussions he had with the American philosophers, he argues against what he calls *neutral monism*. This view, held particularly by Mach, and by William James, in America, is that there is no specific kind of phenomena to be called *mental*. The term *neutral monist* arises because

> while rejecting the division of the world into mind and matter, they do not say 'all reality is mind', nor yet 'all reality is matter'.

Russell gives a very clear and fair account of neutral monism in these papers. He finds, however, one difficulty 'which seems to me the main objection to neutral monism'. This concerns such a situation as when a subject opens his eyes and sees a patch of colour. Russell and James would agree that it is at any rate *possible* to suppose that the patch of colour continues to exist while the eyes are shut. So then there is a difference between the situations of the patch being and not-being one of the contents of the subject's experience. James would analyse the not-being as consisting in

> experienced relations, chiefly causal, to other contents of my experience.

Russell, on the other hand,

> cannot think that the difference . . . consists in the presence or absence of relations between the patch of red and other objects of the same kind.

Russell also raises other objections. One such objection is to the neutral monist's analysis of errors. For the neutral monist, the typical error is the illusion of perception. In order to see all errors in this way, the neutral monist is forced to analyse the mistaken view that America was discovered in 1066 in terms of an 'illusion of sense' in a world containing such non-existent entities as

'the discovery of America in 1066'.

Such a multiplication of non-existent entities recalls the devices attributed by Russell to Frege and Meinong, for dealing with empty reference. Another objection raised by Russell is to the analogous unnatural analysis of memory.

In the third of these papers Russell enters into an analysis of experience in terms of facts and relations, and in terms of a distinction between the knowledge got by acquaintance and that got by a description. This is really the clue to placing these papers in Russell's *corpus*. For they are one attempt to carry further the distinction which proved essential at the beginning of *On Denoting* between knowledge by description and knowledge by acquaintance. And they do this using, as a necessary tool, the analysis of reality into facts and relations.

To return to 1918–21, Russell became persuaded of the rightness of the neutral monist's case, so fairly had he presented it. *The Analysis of Mind* presents this case and so pushed his empiricism to an extreme. Later Russell gradually came to see that his arguments against the case were stronger than those for it, and he abandoned the position.

5.2   After the War Russell turned much more to politics and social questions. He visited the Soviet Union in 1920. It is interesting to note how, unlike very many of left-wing views who made the same journey at the same time, Russell came back utterly dispirited at the tyrannical bureaucracy. The books he wrote at the time described the factual situation but

I have not expressed the sense of utter horror which overwhelmed me while I was there.[5]

In the following year he visited China, and after a serious illness, he stood for Parliament in 1922 and 1923.

The Tarner lectures, which he gave at Trinity in 1925, formed *The Analysis of Matter*,[6] and this marked an end to the neutral monism and a movement towards what Ayer[7] calls 'physical realism'. It is rather easier to see how this position develops by looking at Russell's paper of 1924, called *Logical Atomism*.[8]

Here he begins by stressing the fundamental character of logic rather than metaphysics in philosophy. He also includes a personal aside:

> I came to philosophy through mathematics, or rather through the wish to find some reason to believe in the truth of mathematics. From early youth, I had an ardent desire to believe that there can be such a thing as knowledge, combined with a great difficulty in accepting much that passes for knowledge.

Shortly afterwards he argues that 'many of the stock philosophical arguments about mathematics' had become irrelevant because of the progress of mathematics itself. He cites non-Euclidean geometry, Weierstrass's analysis, Cantor's theory of classes and Frege's foundations of arithmetic as technical developments that have served to show that certain philosophical 'problems' are not problems at all

> As all these results were obtained, not by any heroic method, but patient detailed reasoning, I began to think it probable that philosophy had erred in adopting heroic remedies for intellectual difficulties, and that solutions were to be found merely by greater care and accuracy.

This is surely the clearest statement possible about the spirit behind *Principia Mathematica*.

A more cautious, not to say pessimistic, mood is also present. Russell has come to accept that any axiomatic system has the property that, although the truth of the conclusion follows from the truth of the premises, the reason why we believe in the truth of the conclusion is not solely because we believe in the truth of the premises. Indeed, the reasons for believing in the truth of the premises are the inductive and probable ones arising from the agreement of the conclusions with experience. Thus the logical and epistemological orders of things are reversals of each other. The result of this is that the only way in which logic throws light on mathematics is by dispelling contradictions.

> This shows that mathematics *may* be true. But to show that mathematics *is* true would require other methods and other considerations.

Russell goes on to summarise the successes of the logical approach. These are the replacement of principles of abstraction in defining cardinal numbers, the elimination of classes by reinterpreting phrases containing them, and the theory of descriptions. He then proceeds to other examples in physics, beginning with the construction of points of space and instants of time. Indeed he goes further and believes that we cannot know about any intrinsic qualities of physical objects, and that physical space is an inference, which has merely a structural correspondence with the space of perception. Matter is seen as particularly appropriate for logical treatment, since it has two properties whose neatness suggests a logical construct. These are, that two pieces of matter cannot be at the same place at the same time, and that one piece cannot be in two places at the same time. It is also the case that matter is impenetrable and Russell argues that this must be a logical fact too. The bits of reality from which the world is constructed are not bits of matter but events. An event is the combination of a point of space and an instant of time. The emphasis on events is the fruit of Russell's study and assimilation of Einstein's Special Theory of Relativity.

5.3 Russell veers between three different views about matter. His intention here is to exhibit physical objects as logical constructions from sense data. Another view is simply to define matter as the bundle of perceptions, somewhat like Leibniz's view of a bundle of predicates. He also reverts sometimes to an earlier view in which physical objects are neither logical constructions nor bundles of sense data but are postulated as external causes of the groups of perceptions. At this point I move forward in time to 1948 to take in Russell's much later work *Human Knowledge: Its Scope and Limits*.[9] Here he moves more definitely into this position of physical objects as inferred rather than as logical constructions. The difficulty is, of course, how to substantiate the inference of such external objects, and this is one which Russell never really overcomes.

The other problem with which Russell deal fully in 1948 is that of induction. This is substantially the only place in which he does so. He begins by taking a Bayesian view, contending that, if an association of events of two kinds has been invariably observed, then the probability of another such occurrence will increase with the number of observations that have been made. Now induction is important to Russell both because his theory of perception depends on it, and because he believes that it is crucial in science. It is arguable, however, that induction plays only a very minor part, if any, in science. For science *can* certainly be seen as not requiring induction at all, but in proceeding from bold hypotheses put forward as laws.

Russell perceived that his very simple view of induction would not serve for the 'grue and bleen' reason. That arises when one considers two types of entity, one of which is, in fact, always blue, and one always green. One decides, at a certain time T, to define two new colour concepts. These are *grue*, which means green before time T, and blue after T; and *bleen* which means blue before T and green after. The inductive evidence at any time before T is equally in favour of two hypotheses:

(i) that all entities of type 1 are blue.
(ii) that all entities of type 1 are bleen.

But induction does not apply to (ii). Evidently only certain special properties and classes are amenable to induction.

Russell tries to answer this difficulty[9] by distinguishing mathematical probability, understood on a frequency basis, from something else called *credibility*. But, in fact, the use he makes of this distinction may be summed up in the following way. He appeals to a result of Keynes, which states that a sufficient number of successes and no failures gives a hypothesis a probability approaching certainty, so long as the hypothesis started with some initial probability. Such a result is indeed a theorem in mathematical probability, but both Russell and Keynes confuse this with credibility and this leaves the problem of induction as far from solved as ever.

I return to 1927, the year of publication of *The Analysis of Matter*.[6] For the next few years Russell worked on various political and social books, on popular science and on education. Finding existing schools unsuitable for his children he began one of his own, though he left it in 1932. It was run on lines consistent with his views and it cannot be said to have been such a disaster as when another great philosopher, Plato, was put into the position of putting his *Republic* into action. Russell's political writing turned increasingly to the problems of power and war, but in 1938 he was invited to Harvard to give the William James lectures. These were published as *An Enquiry into Meaning and Truth*[10] in 1940, and it is the ideas in these lectures that Russell expanded in 1948.[9]

After the war Russell became increasingly concerned over the question of nuclear weapons. His writing and his political activity with the Campaign for Nuclear Disarmament precluded philosophical activity, had he been inclined to it. His death came on February 2, 1970.

Section 2: The Philosophy of Mathematics

5.4   In this section I shall take up the effect that Russell's writings, up to *Principia Mathematica*, has had on the philosophy of mathematics. I begin by considering very briefly the two early works on the *Foundations of Geometry*[11] and *Leibniz*.[12] With hindsight the *Geometry* can be seen as a dead-end. It was the conclusion of a tradition, which was specifically an English, and largely a Cambridge tradition. This tradition owes much to Kant's view of the synthetic character of Euclidean geometry. It accepts that Kant cannot be right because of the existence of non-Euclidean as special cases of the projective geometry, and then it seeks to reinstate Kant's claim, but for projective geometry. So Russell's essay in this tradition had little influence outside himself. Internally there was an important influence. The useful ontological dodge of defining points as the terms of relations, so as to establish the existence of points in terms of reality of relations was to reappear repeatedly in other contexts. Moreover the, admittedly slight, measure of success in clarifying the foundations confirmed Russell in his implicit project of establishing the correctness, that is to say, the truth of mathematics.

Russell's *Leibniz* is a very different matter. Written when much of the manuscript material was difficult of access, it nevertheless provided a good conjectural summary of Leibniz's unpublished doctrines. Moreover it chose to do this from the point of view of relations, and of regarding objects as bundles of predicates. It failed to take seriously enough Leibniz's view of logic as a universal means of argument, but it did draw attention to this aspect of logic. Despite Russell's view, expressed in his *Leibniz*, that this approach of Leibniz was mistaken, the general idea of logic as a powerful instrument of investigation stayed with him.

The other work of Russell's pre-*Principia* days to which I draw particular attention is *On Denoting*.[11] This has had little direct influence in the philosophy of mathematics, but it has been extremely influential in philosophy as a whole. One of the direct influences is the distinction which Russell draws early in the paper between knowledge by acquaintance and knowledge by description. This distinction is still important in one form or another for many philosophers. It is, for instance, arguably Strawson's distinction[14] between demonstrative identification and descriptive identification. Another related influence comes from Russell's belief that, in order to think about an object it is necessary to know the object, that is, to know which is the object of thought.

Arguments against Russell's theory of names, which is also Frege's, form an important part of Kripke's *Naming and Necessity*.[15] Kripke begins by welcoming the advance that Frege and Russell made over Mill. Mill argues that singular names have denotation but, usually, no connotation, though he does allow certain special cases where they connote. Frege disagrees, because he believes that a name is a definite description, and the description gives the sense. And Mill's *connotation* is close to, if not the same as, Frege's sense. Russell's view is a little more subtle; he believes that things that look like names, but are really definite descriptions, are not truly names, but he agrees that they have sense. Kripke gives a convincing argument for Frege and Russell's views, before concluding

> Nevertheless, I think it's pretty certain that the view of Frege and Russell is false.

In more detail, Kripke argues that, whereas Frege and Russell disagreed with Mill over singular names like 'Scott', they agreed with him over general names like 'gold' or 'human being'. Kripke reverses this: he wants to endorse Mill on singular names but not on general ones.

There is another feature of Kripke's argument which plays only a subsidiary role, but which has had an influence out of all proportion to its place in Kripke's thought. He points to the way that someone may know of someone indirectly '. . . the name is spread from link to link as if by a chain'. Then someone may be referred to without being uniquely known:

> He knows that Feynman is a famous physicist. A certain passage of communication reaching ultimately to the man himself does reach the speaker. He then is referring to Feynman even though he can't identify him uniquely.

This seems at first sight to be quite opposed to Russell's belief.

This point is discussed at length by Gareth Evans in *The Varieties of Reference*.[16] Evans points out how Kripke himself remarks on the special situations which are needed to allow such apparent conflicts with what Evans calls *Russell's principle*. None the less, Evans argues, many philosophers seem to have assumed, without evidence, that Kripke really had simply shown Russell's principle to be false. Evans discusses many other aspects of Frege and Russell's views in *The Varities of Reference* and this remarkable book serves to encapsulate the continuing importance of Russell's influence. *On Denoting* brought out into the main stream of discussion questions on reference that have continued to puzzle and perplex.

5.5   I turn now to work in the philosophy of mathematics, more narrowly interpreted, and to Russell's influence there. The situation here has been admirably summed up by Hao Wang:[17]

> He is probably the most widely read and cited philosopher of this century. Basic works such as Skolem's paper on free variable number theory, Herbrand's and Gödel's theses, Gödel's paper on the incompleteability of arithmetic all took *Principia* as their point of departure.

First, however, I ask the question of what has become of the logicist programme. The important question here relates to the elementary arithmetic of natural numbers, for it is common ground, to the logicist programme and to Hilbert's formalism, that from the natural numbers the rest of mathematics is a straightforward construction. This view is not common also to Brouwer and the intuitionists, about which I shall have something to say later.

Natural numbers are seen in *Principia Mathematica* as classes. The numeral 3 is seen as a name of the class of all triads. Frege and Russell have a difference of emphasis, it is true. For Frege, numbers are logical objects, for Russell logical fictions that vanish on analysis. But for both, they are classes. Now Frege's original programme for exhibiting numbers as classes failed for want of a cure for the contradictions. *Principia Mathematica* was intended to show that Frege's programme could be caried out in a modified form which avoided the contradictions. Its failure, if that is not too strong a word, was more subtle. It failed because it proved necessary to introduce the theory of types, and to alleviate the effect of this theory by means of the Axiom of Reducibility. The consistency of the resultant system is then in doubt. Moreover both Frege's and Russell's systems suffer from another complaint: that it just does not seem to be the case that numbers are classes. At first sight this sounds a quibble, but it has been persuasively argued by Benacerraf[18] that, if numbers were classes, one should be able to say which classes they were. Yet one cannot do this. Any collection of classes which fulfils Peano's postulates will serve equally as a model of the natural numbers.

There have been more recent attempts to salvage the logicist position. One such is that of Bostock[19] who proposes to complete logicism by abandoning the presupposition that numbers are objects, and by introducing numerical quantifiers of the form 'There are exactly n x such that Fx'. Such an introduction *tout court* would be begging the question but Bostock provides a separate argument to justify it. The resultant system, starting admittedly from a different logical basis from Frege and Russell, provides a foundation for Peano's axioms and avoids, in so doing, Frege's disastrous assumption that led to Russell's paradox. Whether or not this is indeed carrying out the logicist programme is less clear, because of doubts that I will mention below about the construction of arithmetic from Peano's axioms. Another possibility has been raised by Michael Moss.[20] This is to strengthen the logical system by introducing the quantifier 'There are an infinite number of x such that Fx'. This avoids any suggestion of question-begging. But again the whole construction remains to be carried out.

The influence of Russell on Hilbert and the formalists is more tenuous but, I believe considerable. Hilbert, beginning in 1899 with his formulation of a fully adequate system of axioms for Euclidean geometry, found himself gradually pushed, between 1904 and 1918, to the development of his *Beweistheorie*.[21] This was a response partly to the contradictions, but also partly, to the criticism of classical analysis raised in 1907 by Brouwer.[22] The result was a definite philosophical position about mathematics, which is fairly strongly opposed to logicism. But it is a view that was open to confutation and in 1931 it was confuted.

It is possible to take two different views of Hilbert's position, and he varied between them. One is to take it to be a mere methodological view, which proposes to put on one side for the present the question of the truth of systems of axioms. Instead of such a philosophically difficult question as truth, the *Beweistheorie* proposes to formulate adequate axiom-systems for branches of mathematics and then, from outside the system, to use a metalanguage to prove that the system was complete and consistent. Since the systems in question were to be logical ones, of a similar kind to that of *Principia Mathematica*, the influence of Russell need not be emphasised.

The difference was that, instead of searching for truth at this stage, completeness and consistency were to suffice. The meaning of *consistent* is clear. It is not to be the case that the system should ever allow the proof of both A and ~A. It is necessary to be a little more careful about completeness. Here the general idea is that the axiom-system is adequate to prove 'all the known results', semantic completeness. For the investigation envisaged by Hilbert, it is necessary to replace this by syntactic completeness, which is defined in this way: if A cannot be proved from the axioms and one adjoins A as an extra axiom, then the system is inconsistent.

The second view of Hilbert's position is a stronger form of formalism, which holds that such an approach is not only methodologically advantageous but that it is all that is in principle possible. In this view mathematics is a meaningless game played with symbols on paper and the question of truth is irrelevant. That this second view is totally untenable is one of the results of Gödel's 1931 paper.[23] It is interesting that the title of Gödel's paper is 'On formally undecideable propositions of *Principia Mathematica* and related systems', for this again shows the great influence that Russell had exerted. Despite the title, there is little of danger for logicism in Gödel's conclusions. For logicism, at least in Russell's hands, was concerned with the truth of what had been proposed. Gödel's paper showed the following two results, which at the time and for a number of years afterwards seemed very surprising. The first result was that, for (virtually) any consistent formal system of complexity sufficient to be able to discuss elementary arithmetic, there would always be statements which were 'evidently' true in the system but which were not provable from the axioms of the system. This shows the formalists' ideal of completeness to be unattainable. The second result was that one such statement was one, in the system, whose interpretation is that the system is consistent. This shows, in turn, that the formalists' hope of showing the consistency of their axiom-systems is doomed to disappointment. In fact such consistency can only be proved in a *more* complex system, whose own consistency is in greater doubt.

It may help to explain very briefly the role played by

elementary arithmetic in Gödel's results. This is really two-fold, a fact which has not been sufficiently emphasised. One aspect is the part played by arithmetic in the actual proof, which is simply this. The formal system involves a finite alphabet from which its symbols are drawn. It is a straight-forward but complicated matter to encode the expressions of such a system into a numerical code, so that to talk about the expressions of the system is to talk about numerical expressions, that is, to engage in arithmetical talk. But if the system is indeed adequate for arithmetic, this talk can be translated into, that is, expressed in the system, so that the system can be used to talk about its own expressions. These expressions can be numbered off and Gödel is then able to consider statements like 'The sentence whose number is n is unprovable'. The number of this sentence will depend on the natural number n; I call it f(n). The essence of Gödel's proof is to show that there is one particular value of n, call it k, such that f(k) = k. The technical argument for showing this is, in fact, one very analogous to that used by Cantor for showing the non-enumerability of the real numbers (see §3.11). The sentence whose number is k then states its own unprovability. At this stage in the proof nothing has been assumed about the truth or falsehood of the sentence. If it is true, then it exhibits the truth of Gödel's first result. If it is false, then it implies that it is false that it is unprovable, that is, that it is provable. A system in which a false result is provable might well be considered to be inconsistent, although that is not exactly the definition of inconsistency mentioned above.

This explanation of Gödel's proof is inevitably inadequate, but it is intended only to remove the mystery which might otherwise surround the entry of elementary arithmetic into the discussion. It also has the advantage of tracing the influence of Russell once more. For Gödel's sentence is the result of a natural alteration, suggested by the use of a formal system, to 'The sentence whose number is n is false'. A similar proof to Gödel's would make this sentence state its own falsehood, and this is the paradox of the Cretan again. By replacing *false* by *unprovable* the paradox vanishes and Gödel's incompleteness theorem appears instead.

So much for the first aspect of the role of arithmetic. But this aspect refers only to the use in Gödel's proof; there is another way of looking at the appearance of arithmetic which gives, I believe, a deeper understanding of its importance in Gödel's result, and so exhibits the use of arithmetic in the proof as a mathematical trick, as it were, used to mirror there the essential arithmetical feature of the result. This other way of looking at it is as follows: arithmetic is the subject that discusses the properties of the natural numbers. Consider, then, any such property, as for example that of being prime. If the natural numbers are written out in their usual order, the possession or non-possession of any property may be indicated by writing a 1 or a 0 respectively below the corresponding natural number. In the example of primeness this looks like this:

$$1 \; 2 \; 3 \; 4 \; 5 \; 6 \; 7 \; 8 \; 9 \; 10 \; 11 \; 12 \; 13 \; 14 \; 15 \ldots$$
$$1 \; 1 \; 1 \; 0 \; 1 \; 0 \; 1 \; 0 \; 0 \; \; 0 \; \; 1 \; \; 0 \; \; 1 \; \; 0 \; \; 0 \ldots$$

Any arithmetical property therefore corresponds to an infinite string of 0's and 1's and conversely. But if we then go on to regard this infinite string as an infinite decimal (but expressed in the scale of two), by putting a decimal point at the beginning of it, it becomes clear that there is a one-one relation between the properties of the natural numbers and the real numbers between 0 and 1. Now, as I explained in §3.11, Cantor showed that the real numbers were non-enumerable and this implies the same for the real numbers between 0 and 1. So there is, unsurprisingly perhaps, a non-enumerably infinite number of properties of the natural numbers.

On the other hand, any formal system with a finite alphabet can evidently make only an enumerable number of different statements and correspondingly can generate from a finite set of axioms only an enumerable number of proofs. It is therefore clear that there will not be enough proofs to go round and so incompleteness is inevitable and Gödel's proof is completely destructive to formalism as a coherent philosophy of mathematics. It is also rather damaging to the weaker form of formalism, as a methodology, since even this depends on a reasonable assurance that there is a hope of clearing away problems of completeness and consistency. Only so would the method be of help in tackling the more profound problem of truth.

5.6   There is a curious symmetry between the views of Hilbert and the formalists about logicism and the views of Brouwer and the intuitionists. For Hilbert accepts the fundamental importance of logic and of constructing a formal system, but he does not accept the importance of truth. Brouwer fully accepts the idea of truth, though with some qualifications about how the notion should be construed, but he rejects the importance of logic and even the possibility of constructing any formal system which could represent mathematics. The influence of Russell here is certainly not direct but it is none the less pervasive. For one thing, Brouwer was building on Poincaré's trenchant criticisms of logicism. In his early work[24] Brouwer was inspired by disgust at the *uses* of human language and of mathematics. He saw society as using language as a means of enslaving the individual, and he saw logicism and formalism as partaking of this. Instead of their approaches he proclaimed mathematics as a 'language-less activity of human mind', and 'synonymous with the exact part of our thinking'.

As intuitionism developed Brouwer came to a less opaque characterisation of it. He held that the foundations of mathematics could be investigated only by considering the conditions under which the mental activity giving rise to it took place. Without this, only the external appearance is studied. This view is in direct opposition to Frege, who contended that there was no hope of understanding the nature of mathematics except by avoiding speculations about mathematical thinking. And, in opposition to Russell, Brouwer held that mathematics is independent of logic, that logic is dependent on mathematical thinking and that the principles of logic are less reliable than is supposed.

Allied to these ideas was an acceptance of a different approach to the whole problem of foundations. Russell and Hilbert were at one in trying to underpin, by foundational investigations, an impressive edifice which both considered as substantially correct. The utmost effect of such a foundational investigation might be to show that one or two particular advanced topics would need amendment. For Brouwer the foundations were to be laid down first. If they were inadequate for existing mathematics, then mathematics had to be reconstructed. This programme was carried out by the Amsterdam school with remarkable, though partial, success. Many proofs in classical mathematics turned out to be invalid. In some cases the results were still true, but needed a more complicated proof than in the classical case. In others the result had to be rejected as false.

It would take me too far from my theme to give any more detailed account of intuitionism. What I have said will serve to show how Russell was useful, with Hilbert, as a force against which Brouwer could react. The subject which Brouwer and his followers produced was technically much more difficult than classical mathematics. For this reason it has not appealed to practising mathematicians. None the less, intuitionism remains a contender for a 'correct' philosophy of mathematics for one specific reason. Alone of the three views I have discussed, it is immune to the criticism implied by Gödel's theorem. Gödel showed the unprovability of an evidently true result in a fixed formal system, in which both axioms and rules of inference are prescribed. Such a system is itself in conflict with the intuitionist approach. For Brouwer there cannot be fixed rules of inference. Mathematics is seen as a continually developing activity. A new means of inference may be discovered tomorrow, so no result can be shown to be permanently unprovable.

Section 3:   Russell's Influence

5.7   I have now come to the end of my description of the context of Russell's philosophy. What I have tried to do is, not so much to explain what Russell's views were, or why they were good views, but how he came to be able to think them. In this section I turn to the puzzling question of why Russell's influence has not been greater. It is true that *On Denoting* is part of the standard philosophical literature, and has led to a large amount of work about reference. It is also true that *Principia Mathematica* has established a position of importance for mathematical logic which it would not otherwise have had, and it has also opened up ways of looking at the philosophy of mathematics. But both of these, significant though they are, are in rather specialised fields. I have argued in this book that Russell transferred the insights that he gained in these areas to general philosophy. His writing here has had less lasting success, and the reason for this is the question I now propose to consider.

I consider first some questions of Russell's personality. He makes it very clear in his *Autobiography* that he was very much a person who needed a secure base and stability, and this was what he lacked from an early age. The death of his parents left a worried and sensitive person who was not to flower until he found a second secure home in Trinity. Here he produced his greatest work but, for reasons entirely outside philosophy, his continuing association with Trinity became impossible after the Great War. His later philosophy took place, to a much greater extent than desirable, on paper. His writings benefited, it is true, from discussions on his lecturing visits to North America, but he had no students to provide a continuing give and take of ideas. The effect of this on his writing is difficult to judge but one might conjecture that its lucidity is hard to maintain in expounding a theory which recieves continual criticism during its gestation. But such continual criticism could have led to more profound if less readable books. There is another aspect of Russell as a person that, while it had no effect on the work which he produced, may have affected assessment of it. His political and social milieu, and his behaviour, disposed people to regard him as a member of the hereditary aristocracy, whose philosophising was combined with other dilettante activities. Such ideas, even if not stated publicly, could influence people's thought unconsciously.

A second circle of explanations of Russell's diminished influence contains a nice irony. As I said above, Wittgenstein's *Tractatus* grew very directly out of providing a philosophical justification for *Principia Mathematica*. The emphasis on syntax which the *Tractatus* contained helped the foundation of the Vienna Circle and the construction of logical positivism. This doctrine was imported to England where it became a dominant influence, for a time, in the most active centre of philosophy, Oxford. It was a doctrine which became quite uncongenial to Russell as it developed. He was unable to accept its rejection of metaphysics and its verificationism, and it had no use for his willingness, or indeed desire, to relate logical, ontological and metaphysical ideas. In 1950 Russell wrote[25]

> There is, I think, a danger that logical positivism may develop a new kind of scholasticism, and may, by being unduly linguistic, forget the relation to fact that makes a statement true.

Such a development was already under way and the extreme form of ordinary language philosophy which developed from it had no room for Russell's more traditional argumentation. This extreme form has now waned and the appearance of such a discussion as Gareth Evans's[16] heralds perhaps, the building of a bridge between the comprehensive humanity of Russell and the rigour of linguistic philosophy.

I believe that there is a third related aspect of Russell's thought which has proved unpopular in the last half-century, and it is one I have repeatedly stressed in this book. All his work is motivated by his quest for certainty and truth. The axioms of logic and mathematics have to be true, and since logic will serve only to show that they imply the conclusions, certainty is to be gained only by metaphysics, not by logic. The whole climate of opinion in this century has developed a profound scepticism about such an attainment of certainty. The later thought of Wittgenstein is about, amongst other things, the extreme difficulty of penetrating beyond the façade of language towards certainty. Indeed it may be contending that there is no such thing. In such a climate there is room for the common-sense approach of Moore and there is room for the aphoristic doubting of the later Wittgenstein. But scepticism of that kind has no place for the gentler scepticism of Russell, which consists only of believing that we should retain only those beliefs which we can justify. The difference lies in the means that can be employed for the justification. However, the climate does seem to be changing towards one more sympathetic to the insights provided by

Russell in his earlier work and on which he based his later philosophical books.

Notes

[1] B. Russell, *Introduction to Mathematical Philosophy*, Allen & Unwin, London, 1919.

[2] B. Russell, *The Analysis of Mind*, Allen & Unwin, London, 1921.

[3] B. Russell, *Our Knowledge of the External World as a field for scientific method in philosophy*, Allen & Unwin, London, 1914.

[4] Reprinted under the title *On the Nature of Acquaintance* in *Logic and Knowledge*, (ed. R. C. Marsh), Allen & Unwin, London, 1956.

[5] B. Russell, *The Autobiography of Bertrand Russell*, Vol. 2 Allen & Unwin, London, 1968.

[6] B. Russell, *The Analysis of Matter*, Allen & Unwin, London, 1927.

[7] A. J. Ayer, *Russell*, Collins/Fontana, London, 1972.

[8] Reprinted under the title *Logical Atomism* in *Logic and Knowledge*.([4]) It was originally contributed to J. H. Muirhead's two-volume *Contemporary British Philosophy*, 1924–5.

[9] B. Russell, *Human Knowledge, its scope and limits*, Allen & Unwin, London, 1948.

[10] B. Russell, *An Enquiry into Meaning & Truth*, Allen & Unwin, London, 1940.

[11] B. Russell, *An Essay on the Foundations of Geometry*, Cambridge, 1897.

[12] B. Russell, *A critical exposition of the philosophy of Leibniz*, Cambridge, 1900.

[13] B. Russell, *On Denoting, Mind* (n.s.) *14*, 479–493, 1905 *reprinted in Logic and Knowledge*.([4])

[14] P. F. Strawson, *Individuals*, Methuen, London, 1959.

[15] S. Kripke, *Naming and Necessity*, Blackwell, Oxford, 1980. This is a revised and enlarged edition of his paper in G. Harman and D. Davidson (ed.), *Semantics of Natural Languages* Reidel, Drodrecht, and Boston USA, 1972.

[16] G. Evans, *The Varieties of Reference*, (ed. J. McDowell) Oxford, 1982.

[17] Hao Wang, *From Mathematics to Philosophy*, Routledge & Kegan Paul, London, 1974.

[18] P. Benacerraf 'What Numbers Could Not Be' *Philos. Review*, 1965.

[19] D. Bostock, *Logic and Arithmetic: Natural Numbers*, Oxford, 1974.

[20] M. Moss, personal communication.

[21] The most complete reference is the synoptic D. Hilbert and P. Bernays, *Grundlagen der Mathematik*, I, II, Springer, Berlin, 1934, 1938.

[22] L. E. J. Brouwer, Thesis: *Over de Grondslagen der Wiskunde*, Maas and van Suchtelen, Amsterdam, 1907.

[23] K. Gödel *Über formal entscheidbäre Sätze* . . . Monatshefte für Math. und Phys. *38*, 173–198, 1931, trans, in J. van Heijenoort (ed.), *From Frege to Gödel*, Harvard, 1967.

24 A good, short introduction to the early thought of Brouwer is contained in W.P. van Stigt *L. E. J. Brouwer, the Signific interlude* in *The L. E. J. Brouwer Centenary Symposium* (ed. A. S. Troelstra and D. van Dalen), North-Holland, 1982. I have used this in the text. A reliable account of intuitionism as a whole is in E. W. Beth *The Foundations of Mathematics*, North-Holland, 1959.

25 B. Russell, in an essay 'Logical Positivism' in *Revue des Mathematiques* reprinted in *Logic and Knowledge*.(⁴)

Glossary of Symbols

Index

249